HUNGER

HUNGER

HOW FOOD SHAPED THE COURSE OF THE FIRST WORLD WAR

RICK BLOM

TRANSLATED FROM THE DUTCH BY
SUZANNE HEUKENSFELDT JANSEN

UNIFORM

WLU PRESS

WILFRID LAURIER
UNIVERSITY PRESS

Wilfrid Laurier University Press acknowledges the support of the Canada Council for the Arts for our publishing program. We acknowledge the financial support of the Government of Canada. This work was supported by the Research Support Fund.

Published and distributed in the United States of America and Canada by
Wilfrid Laurier University Press, 75 University Avenue West, Waterloo, ON N2L 3C5, Canada
www.wlupress.wlu.ca

Published and distributed in the United Kingdom by Uniform
An imprint of Unicorn Publishing Group, Newburgh Street, London W1F 7RG

www.unicornpublishing.org

This edition of *Hunger* is published by arrangement with Unicorn Publishing Group LLP and Wilfrid Laurier University Press. The images in this publication are reproduced with permission or are in the public domain.

Nederlands letterenfonds dutch foundation for literature This publication has been made possible with financial support from the Dutch Foundation for Literature.

British Library Cataloguing in Publication Data
A catalogue record for this book is available from the British Library

Library and Archives Canada Cataloguing in Publication

Title: Hunger : how food shaped the course of the First World War / Rick Blom ; translated from the Dutch by Suzanne Heukensfeldt Jansen.
Other titles: Honger. English
Names: Blom, Rick, author. | Translation of: Blom, Rick. Honger.
Description: Includes bibliographical references.
Identifiers: Canadiana (print) 20190141417 | Canadiana (ebook) 20190141433 | ISBN 9781771124171 (softcover) | ISBN 9781771124188 (PDF) | ISBN 9781771124195 (EPUB)
Subjects: LCSH: Operational rations (Military supplies)—Europe—History—20th century. | LCSH: World War, 1914–1918—Food supply—Europe. | LCSH: Rationing—Europe—History—20th century.
Classification: LCC D639.S9 B5613 2019 | DDC 940.4/83—dc23

5 4 3 2 1

ISBN (UK): 978-1-912690-19-0
ISBN (CANADA): 978-1-771124-17-1

Cover by Battlefield Design. Front cover image *Lunch time in the trenches*, CWM 19920044-058 (George Metcalf archival collection, Canadian War Museum)
Typeset by Vivian@Bookscribe

Printed in Poland on behalf of Latitude Press

For Lóa and Moos

CONTENTS

Introduction   ix

'Paris for lunch, dinner in Saint Petersburg'   1
The beginning of the war, 1914

Bully beef pie   20
The final battle, 1918

Captain Armstrong   38
Logistics and distribution

Goulash cannons and Soyer cookers   54
The cooks and the kitchen

Over the Roly-Poly   77
Life behind the front

Eat less meat   104
Food shortages in Britain

'We do not ask you to die…'   120
Food supplies in France

The wedding cake   137
Generous gifts from the home front

Bayernwald   156
Life in the trenches

Dante's Inferno   176
> Famine in Germany

Kartoffelsuppe, Kartoffelsuppe… und kein Fleisch   197
> The final battle, 1918

Bibliography   225

Acknowledgements   235

'C'est la soupe qui fait le soldat'
('An army marches on its stomach')
Napoleon Bonaparte

'The health and morale of the troops are largely dependent upon the manner in which they are fed, and it is most essential that Officers Commanding Units and Company and Platoon Commanders should pay particular attention to this important subject.'

R.C. Maxwell, Lieutenant General, Quartermaster General, British Armies in France, 6 November 1917

INTRODUCTION

Leafing through the image collection at the archive of the Flanders Fields Museum in Ypres, one photograph immediately struck me. It is an original print in approximately A3 format, taken by an unknown photographer. The photo shows seventeen men in stained uniforms, all but two of them wearing caps. Some have their legs covered in puttees. The ground in front of them is muddy, the sky leaden. This must be somewhere in the Flemish hinterland: that quagmire of misery during the First World War. The men are triumphantly clutching loaves of bread, as if they were the last thing for them to hold on to. The odd individual grins. Those loaves a bounty that has been secured and deserves to be embraced.

Wading hip-high through water in the trenches. Men who literally drowned in the mud. Screeching bombs and shells striking the positions. Attacks with chlorine and mustard gas, burning the men's lungs and leading to a slow, painful death. Fat rats that gnawed on dead bodies and bread bags. Lice and fleas in every fibre of the soldiers' attire. The unimaginable numbers of casualties who fell in a short time for a territorial gain extending to no more than a few hundred metres: as people saw it in those days, the Great War that was meant to put to an end to all wars was horrendous in every respect. Including food.

The one thing that the troops looked forward to every day – a hot, nourishing and tasty meal – was either a desperation-triggering monotony, of deplorable quality or simply not available. They were rarely granted that moment of humanity, of the hope that they might forget all their misery for a brief instant and that they might survive.

Letters, diaries, novels and memoirs are brimming with it: complaints about the food the men were served. Quite rightly so: it makes you sick to the stomach to read how, slowly but surely, with all the hardships they already had to endure, they were also wronged, neglected and forgotten over the supply of food.

'We get nothing to eat and drink,' British Intelligence Officer John Buchan wrote. 'Yesterday each man drew two bottles of water and three iron rations, and these must last till we are relieved.' That relief did not materialise until he had been on the front line for several days.

'At first hint of dawn, we were handed a mug full of iced coffee, a piece of meat, and bread splattered with mud. That made up our entire menu for the day,' French Corporal Louis Barthas noted, and this was not the first time that he was given such a meal.

German Lieutenant Ernst Jünger wrote in August 1918 about a few weeks full of misery when food left a lot to be desired: 'For a while we were given nothing to eat in the evenings apart from cucumbers, which men called "vegetarian sausages".'

During the First World War, soldiers' lives were dominated by even the smallest disarray in food supplies. British serviceman Frederick Voigt noted in his book *Combed Out*: 'A slight deficiency in the rations would arouse fierce indignation and mutinous utterances. An extra pot of jam in the tent ration bag would fill us with the spirit of loyalty and patriotism.'

Could anyone live like that? Let alone wage war? No, German NCO Carl Heller concluded in his diary: 'To live, day in day out, in the same freezing cold and soaking wet clothes, to be fed badly because there were constant hold-ups in the food supply, and without sufficient rest; not a soul could take that.'

Food, or rather the lack of it, was one of the things that decided the war's defining moments. Take those first weeks in 1914, for instance, when the German armies cut through the enemy lines with lightning speed, like a knife through butter. Provisions were not able to keep up with the men, which meant that, at the beginning of September, they reached the River Marne hungry and worn out: the cue for the French and British finally to hit back.

Or consider the last brave attempt by the Germans in March 1918, the final year of the war, to force a decision. With all available means at their disposal, the armies once again advanced with brio, but now they too were forced to break off their advance. This time because the hungry troops were laying into the plentiful food and quantities of drink they found in Allied hideouts.

Afterwards, Field Marshal Von Hindenburg observed: 'Our

advance became slower and slower. We ought to have shouted into the ear of every man: "Press on to Amiens. Put in your last ounce. Perhaps Amiens means decisive victory." It was in vain; our strengths exhausted.'

Consider also poor Germany, where the inhabitants of the big cities in particular suffered increasingly under the hunger blockades by the British ships off the German coast, which meant that hardly any food was imported. People starved, lost all hope, and rose up in armed revolt.

As early as April 1916, the German poet Richard Dehmel lamented in his war diary: 'Surely it can't be so pointless that the battle between cultural nations is decided on who has the fullest stomach?'

Despite all the problems surrounding food supplies, the troops allowed themselves to be led like lambs to the slaughter during the war. Broken and tired on account of the war's violence, but also as a result of having been looked after so poorly, rendering them defenceless. A sense of resignation that resounds in the song 'We're here because…,' which the British sang to the tune of 'Auld Lang Syne.' A song that sounds like a mantra without answer, without reward and with no end to it:

We're here because
We're here because
We're here because we're here.
We're here because
We're here because
We're here because we're here.
We're here because
We're here because
We're here because we're here.
We're here because
We're here because
We're here because we're here.

Daily bread. (In Flanders Fields Museum)

'PARIS FOR LUNCH, DINNER IN SAINT PETERSBURG'

THE BEGINNING OF THE WAR, 1914

There it is, in a glass case at the Heeresgeschichtliches Museum (Museum of Military History) in Vienna: the suit worn by the Austro-Hungarian Crown Prince Franz Ferdinand when he was shot dead during his visit to the Bosnian city of Sarajevo in 1914. A short blue coat with a red collar and cuffs, trimmed with gold embroidery. I count twenty-eight gold buttons, fourteen on each side. Black trousers with red piping and a plumed helmet with green feathers.

I'm seeing this uniform for the first time, decades after that bloody day in 1914. I only know it from black-and-white photos. Curiously, it is not particularly impressive. Apart from the blood. Large clotted stains more than a hundred years old. I see a dark spot near the heart region surrounded by rust-coloured splodges. Splashes of blood run down to the coat's red seam. In the tunic's blue fabric, a frayed cut has been made with a knife or a pair of scissors from the left elbow up to the heart region, no doubt to check the wounds and to find out if the stricken Franz Ferdinand could be saved.

During the weeks leading up to his premature death at the age of fifty, Franz Ferdinand had not really felt like visiting Bosnia and Herzegovina, a province in the vast Austro-Hungarian Empire. The Crown Prince was a family man; he adored his children and his wife Sophie. He preferred to stay with them on his country estate. What's more, as the highest representative of the Empire in Bosnia, he expected his presence to stir up ill will amongst Slavic nationalists. His visit might have political consequences. Yet, as Inspector General of the Habsburg Imperial Army, he was not able to refuse an official invitation to observe the troops there. Besides, Sophie was allowed to join him on this state visit. It was the first time that she would appear in public as the wife of the heir presumptive.

During the journey there, at the end of June 1914, Franz Ferdinand's hesitation to travel already seemed to be justified. Having broken down en route from his castle in Chlumetz to Vienna, his personal train had to be replaced by a 'simpler' first-class carriage. 'A promising start,' the Archduke grimaced and continued on his way.

From Vienna, the journey proceeded to Trieste, and from there to Mostar by boat and on to Sarajevo. There was also a problem with the carriage that transported Franz Ferdinand from Vienna. The electrical lights were not working, so the party continued on its way in a train carriage lit by candles. 'Another omen,' the Crown Prince said, and prophetically to his private secretary: 'How do you like us sitting here? Just like a tomb, isn't it?'

Once in Bosnia, things improved. The royal couple were given a festive reception, and the military manoeuvres Franz Ferdinand attended as an observer went smoothly. Sophie was treated with the necessary respect. That's how the Crown Prince liked it. Franz Ferdinand could only be content.

In Sarajevo, Hotel Bosna, where the royal couple were staying, was buzzing during the evening of Saturday 27 June 1914. All the local dignitaries – Bosnian government officials, representatives of the Habsburg Imperial Army and other distinguished guests – had been invited by the Crown Prince to a dinner. The evening had been planned as a merry *intermezzo* to the visit, and no expense was spared. The best table silver and the finest linen had been amassed from the entire city and taken to the hotel. The *diner dansant* was a festive occasion. The guests danced to the sounds of light music, to 'The Blue Danube,' and there was plenty to eat. The menu that evening read:

Cream soup

༺ॐ༻

Soufflé

༺ॐ༻

Trout
Beef and lamb, fowl

෫෯ඌ

Asparagus, salad and sorbet

෫෯ඌ

Cheese, desserts, ice cream and sweets

෫෯ඌ

Wines

Champagne
White: Rhenish and Zilavka from the Mostar region
Red: Bordeaux, Madeira, Hungarian Tokaj
Cognac

The following day, Sunday 28 June, further festivities were in store for Franz Ferdinand and his wife to celebrate their wedding anniversary. These never took place. The following morning, around half past ten, the Crown Prince and Sophie became the victims of an ambush, set up by Serbian nationalists. One of them was the student Gavrilo Prinčip. He shot the couple with two bullets from his FN Browning pistol. 'It's nothing, it's nothing,' the bleeding Franz Ferdinand gasped shortly after he was hit. But he and his wife died within thirty minutes.

September 1914. Hundreds of thousands of German soldiers had marched into northern France. The advance, via Belgium, had gone smoothly apart from the food logistics. These men could only dream of the menu Franz Ferdinand had eaten as his last supper. They had nothing. No cream soup, no beef, no fowl, no asparagus, no sorbet. The speed with which the troops marched was so fast that the field kitchens had not been able to keep up. This had been the case in August, at the beginning of the war. But August was also harvest month. En route, the German soldiers had been able to live of what the land had to offer, like potatoes or apples. They would cook these to a pulp in a small pan for spreading on bread.

The conditions were miserable in September 1914. All that was left for the troops was heat, dust and poor accommodation. Occasionally, they were able to lay their hands on a chunk of bread. Every small pause was used to lie down on the ground, their feet worn out; in the dust, in the mud, by the roadside or on rocks, whatever was available. After every bend, the soldiers hoped to be able to see their quarters for the night, but they had to keep going. Everyone was exhausted. Man after man collapsed in the street. Legs snapped, knees went, shoes dragged. Numbed, they went on. Everyone was thirsty. What was the goal? When would it be reached? No one knew.

The assassination of Franz Ferdinand was the first in a sequence of events that led to the eventual campaign. Few people mourned his death. The self-willed and intractable Crown Prince was not particularly popular. 'For me it's one less thing to worry about,' thought Austro-Hungarian Emperor Franz Joseph. He appointed Karl, Franz Ferdinand's brother, as the heir presumptive. The German Kaiser, Wilhelm II, Austria's principal ally, did not even care to attend the funeral. Instead, he went on a cruise in the waters off Norway.

In fact, Franz Ferdinand's death was not unwelcome: it gave Austria-Hungary the opportunity to curb all kinds of rights in Serbia. The intention was to incorporate the neighbouring country into the empire and subordinate it to Habsburg authority.

Supported by the Germans, Austria-Hungary issued a list of demands to Serbia on 23 July 1914, almost a month after the assassination. It was given forty-eight hours to reply.

'Grave rumours of a possible conflict of Nations are on everybody's lips,' Georgina Lee, a British woman, wrote in the opening of her diary, which she kept for her son Harry, then nine months old:

> If indeed the dread that is in all our hearts is justified by future events, my little boy will have some idea of what War means to our Country. […] The murder of the Crown Prince (and his Consort) of Austria by Serbians is the excuse for provoking war. If Austria declares war on Serbia, Russia must help Serbia as they are all brother Slavs together. Germany is Austria's ally, and France must help Russia if attacked – we are France's friends, and cannot allow her to be crushed. Therefore, my baby, whose dimpled hands, however eager, cannot grasp a weapon for the honour of your country, we must wait and see what the next fateful days bring forth.

Events progressed very rapidly. Serbia buckled, and consented to virtually all of the Austrian demands on 26 July 1914. The government in Vienna was still not satisfied, because not all their demands had been acceded to. That's why the country declared war with Serbia on 28 July. A day later, Habsburg troops attacked Belgrade. That same day, Russia, a Serbian ally, concentrated forces on the Austrian border. Like Austria-Hungary, Russia mobilised.

The German Empire had to act. It demanded the demobilisation of Russia and issued an ultimatum in eighteen hours. Standing on the balcony of his royal castle in Berlin at half past three in the afternoon on 30 July 1914, Kaiser Wilhelm II announced that there was a threat of war. A day later, on 1 August, when the Russians did not respond, the German Empire was officially at war with Russia.

The following day, the Germans occupied the Duchy of Luxemburg. They also warned Belgium that Imperial troops should be allowed to pass without hindrance across Belgian territory.

The Germans had activated the Schlieffen Plan without hesitation. Within six weeks, the German Army commanders wanted to have the necessary divisions on French soil so that they would be able to deal France, an ally of Russia, a decisive blow. Then, according to the plan, it would be Russia's turn.

On 3 August, Germany declared war on France and Belgium. The next day, the United Kingdom followed, France and Belgium's ally. As a first British act of war, agitated English youths threw stones through the window of the delicatessen owned by the German Appenrodt family. Britons with German-sounding names were attacked. Others were discharged from office or interned in camps. In Germany, British people below the age of sixty-five living there were even held as prisoners of war.

'We are in for it at last,' Georgina Lee wrote in her diary on a beautiful summer's day:

> But there is not one of us in the country who is not thankful at heart that the great fight is to take place at last. The strain has been too great for many years. We all marvel at the reckless audacity of the Kaiser who, with Austria, has Russia, France, England and Belgium to fight [...]. This has been a

day of emotion and new experiences [...]. I started off in a taxi at Paddington [...]. Numbers of weeping women began to file down the exits, accompanied by a small son or an old man trying to console them. For the first time I realise what these scenes mean that are going on round London in every station and all day. All reservists are being called up.

Germany already had a large conscript army. Yet entire classes of schoolboys were exhorted by their teachers to sign up for the front. Many of them went. For glory, romance, adventure or patriotism. Everyone thought that the war would be brief. What's more, most people thought it would be over by Christmas. Or as Kaiser Wilhelm II promised the German troops: 'Paris for lunch, dinner in Saint Petersburg.' Even more explicitly, later on: 'You will be home in the dear German fatherland before the leaves have fallen from the trees.'

When the 51-year-old poet Richard Dehmel signed up for the German Army, his general even laughed at him. Dehmel would never make it to the front. Before the elderly poet was trained sufficiently, the war would be over. Six months at most, the general thought.

The same view prevailed in Britain. Students volunteered for service at the front with the idea that they would be home again in time for the start of the new academic year. In the words of British soldier Godfrey Buxton: 'I had been up at Cambridge for a year and enlisted in the army. We were convinced that Germany would be beaten before the 7th of October and we would be able to go back to Cambridge.' The French General Joffre issued a general decree in which he predicted that the Germans would be quickly starved. They would surrender for a single bread roll.

Yet not everyone shared this view. As early as 1898, in a book titled *Is War Now Impossible?*, the Polish industrialist and banker Jan Bloch foresaw that a new war might last a long time. Bloch wrote: 'A war which, instead of hand-to-hand contest, will become a kind of stalemate. Everybody will be entrenched in the next war. It will be a great war of entrenchments. The spade will be as indispensable to a soldier as his rifle. The soldiers may fight as they please; the ultimate decision is in the hands of famine.'

France, August 1914. There was no famine yet, but there was

enthusiasm. In Paris, thousands of people sang 'La Marseillaise' when the news of the first mobilisations was announced on posters and hit the streets in big groups. Placards were held up with notices such as 'Alsatian volunteers, Jewish volunteers, Polish volunteers.' They cheered each other amongst loud applause from the crowds. The fresh soldiers were thrown flowers and kisses by women lining the street. Train carriages ready to leave for strategic locations were pelted with flowers.

Some Parisians smashed the windows of houses and shops owned by Germans; others looted them. The famous French chef Auguste Escoffier, working in London at the time, formed a committee tasked with supporting the families of mobilised French cooks. He did not know that a few months later his son Daniël, who was also called up, would be killed at the front.

In Germany, too, everyone was elated. The trains moving towards the front bore slogans such as 'Zum frühstuck' ('Towards breakfast'); 'Auf nach Paris!' ('On to Paris!'); 'Jeder Stoss ein Franzos, jeder Schuss ein Russ' ('Everyone must stab a Frenchman, everyone must shoot a Russian'); 'Franzosen, Russen, Serben, sie allen müssen sterben' ('Frenchmen, Russians and Serbs, you must all die'); and 'Soldatenmenu: Kosakensell, Französisches Piou-Piou mit Poincarésalat, Zarenbombe mit Englischem Beefsteak' ('Soldier's menu: Cossack celery, French soldiers with Poincaré salad, Tsar's bomb with English beefsteak'). Sometimes, when the trains stopped at stations on their way to the front, there were women and girls offering the soldiers bread, fruit, pretzels, chocolate and cigars.

Not everyone volunteered to go to the front for romance, adventure or out of idealistic conviction. For some men, enlisting was an opportunity to escape poverty. Many Britons who applied, for example, were not able to earn enough money in their civilian jobs to buy bacon, cheese or eggs. These men were physically in a bad way. Almost half of them did not pass the medical test they had to undergo as part of their application.

Once in the army, a British shop assistant, clerk or labourer could often earn more money than by doing his usual work and thus obtain a decent meal. The British volunteers who were enlisted in 1914 were sometimes so undernourished that their average weight increased during training thanks to army food. This was not the case for everyone, however. George Coppard wrote after the war about his time at the Aldershot training camp:

> [A] lack of money was depriving me of canteen suppers. I could get sausages and mash or liver and bacon for fivepence, and a chunk of bread for a halfpenny. Eating was my biggest worry at Aldershot for supper was not supplied as part of our rations. Occasionally word would drift round that there was soup in the cook-house. Only those with no cash took advantage of the offer, and I was generally among the poor and needy. The word calories as we know it today never existed in Aldershot. The Quartermaster-General never considered the needs of a growing body engaged in hard training, trench digging or route marching.

The Minister of War, Lord Kitchener, had warned in August 1914: 'This war is not going to be a picnic.'

The German advance through Belgium was successful. The Belgian Army hardly made a stand against the enemy troops, with their huge numbers, their artillery and more modern weaponry. It soon became clear that this would be a different war to any war previously. The Germans deployed their heavy artillery to obliterate the opposition from a safe distance and to remove their fortifications. The simple weapons with which the Allies were equipped offered little resistance to the barrages of the machine guns.

The city of Liège was taken relatively quickly, despite heavy resistance. Other cities followed: Brussels, Namur, Antwerp, Ghent. The British had managed to hold out at Mons briefly, but there, too, they had to capitulate and retreat.

Major Wilfred Dugmore, one of the many on the run, wrote of his exhaustion. He had not eaten a thing in twenty-four hours, had nothing to drink and had less than two hours' sleep. He and his company marched as if in a trance, whereby order would follow upon order. Dugmore recalled that he would quite like to have had a bullet through a vital part of his body, just to end the hardships.

During those first weeks it did look as if the war would soon be over, as had been predicted beforehand. As early as 24 August, the German troops marched into France, an invasion army extending to 1 million men. Despite having a numerical superiority, the French armies had to take defensive action and retreated in massive numbers. They tried to use forts and geographical obstacles to concede as little ground as possible. The aim was to hold out for as long as they could, exhaust the enemy and restart the offensive once the time was ripe.

The Germans marched long distances, approximately 30 kilometres a day, further into France, without encountering much resistance. There were skirmishes, small bitter fights and casualties, but because the French and British soon retreated, huge field battles did not take place during those initial days.

Unlike their advance, the provisioning of the German troops was less successful. The supply of food was rendered more difficult because the French and British had put bridges and railway lines out of commission. Besides, entire companies disappeared precisely because the advance was so quick. The field kitchens loaded with food were unable to locate these soldiers. There were times when the mobile field kitchens had to spend so much time looking for the troops that by the time they had arrived to feed them, the food was inedible: potatoes were ice-cold, soup tasted brackish and rice would be fermenting.

At other times, it might take longer than twenty-four hours before new food arrived. There was no longer any mail either. No letters with an encouraging word, no message from home, no food parcels. There was a shortage of soap and water. Only the troops moving through the Champagne region had found something to help get them through their daily trek: drink. The men boozed, litres a day. The bottles were found in wine cellars and shops' stores. In some ways it made them indefatigable. The army command took no action. It knew that this was keeping the troops' morale intact.

Sometimes the men were lucky and food would reach them in time. On the menu in the morning was flour soup and coffee. At lunchtime the men ate meat and in the evening flour soup again.

The German lines of communication began to stretch even further. German divisions penetrated into France ever more deeply. Communication lines directing the armies and logistics to the right positions became unusable. The soldiers found themselves increasingly further removed from the railway stations, where food trains and field bakery wagons transferred their food supplies on to carts and field kitchens. This meant that the troops often marched for the entire day on no more than raw carrots and cabbages picked straight from the field.

The 'iron ration,' which every man carried with him and was only allowed to use in an emergency, had long been finished. Very occasionally the soldiers came across a deserted bakery with a few loaves of bread on its shelves. Cattle in the fields were requisitioned by the army commanders. In exchange, the local owners received some form of voucher which they could hand in to the local Belgian or French authorities. These, the Germans believed, would make good the loss of their cattle.

When there was no bakery or cattle to be found, the men would beg for a piece of bread, a sausage, water. The August days when the harvest was ripe, and oats and other cereals were in the fields in sheaves, were past history. Not only for the men who proceeded on foot, but also for the horses that fell over as a result of lack of oats and died of starvation along the roadside. Not in their hundreds, but in their thousands.

It was not only the German troops who were having a difficult time: the French and British did also. Moreover, the French population pushed south in massive numbers, just like the armies. Old people in wheelbarrows, women on foot with bundles of household goods on their backs, babies in prams, children clutching dolls or other toys, entire families with hastily gathered pieces of furniture on wagons or handcarts. In and amongst the masses of people fleeing were the animals: cows, sheep, goats, donkeys, urged on in unimaginable chaos by their owners. More than once, the frightened refugees saw their road blocked by French Army barricades. They were forced to take detours over country lanes, resulting in their getting lost or stranded at isolated farms where there was not enough room for such large numbers of people. So they were sent on their way, to keep on going, ever further south.

It was a march of the defeated. For the civilians and for the soldiers: the red trousers and blue tunics of the French soldiers had become unrecognisable underneath the dirt and dust. They shuffled on with hollow eyes and days-old beards. Without much hope. Hungry and weakened. Sweating in the fierce, warm sun of late summer. Where the villages had been deserted, there was still some food to be had: in cornfields, thanks to the cattle in the meadows and in the houses left behind by their owners. There was hardly any time to take advantage of this, though, because the French were being pushed along by the Germans; slaughtered cattle were left where they were, prey to rotting.

The British, too, withdrew post-haste, afraid they would be cornered by the Germans. They wanted to regroup behind the front to engage in combat with the enemy. Just like the French, they were also weakened by lack of food. Some left parts of their equipment behind and cut off the cuffs and trouser legs from their uniforms to cope better with the Indian summer heat.

Dozens of foot soldiers fell behind. With just a few crackers and a tin of corned beef for food. Sometimes entire British units were without food. Men collapsed on the side of the road without getting up again.

'The pained look in the troubled eyes of those who fell by the way will not be easily forgotten by those who saw it,' wrote John Lucy, an Irishman who served as a corporal with the Royal Irish Rifles:

That look imposed by circumstances on spent men seemed to demand all forgiveness from officers and comrades alike, as it conveyed a helpless and dumb farewell to arms. This hopeless resignation to utter fatigue was a thing to wonder at. The pride of the fighting man was forgotten, and even the threat of immediate capture or death at the hands of the enemy had no power to change or influence it. Some who collapsed were rescued by ambulances. Others were left unconscious in deep sleep by the roadsides and in the fields, and they passed out of our ken for years. The dreadful phenomenon came on us like a creeping disease. It develops slowly. I think it was about the tenth day when the frightful agony of sleeplessness began to smite us. Men slept while they marched, and they dreamed as they walked. They talked of their homes, of their wives and mothers, of their simple ambitions, of beer in cosy pubs, and they talked of fantasies. Commonplace sensible remarks turned to inane jibberings [sic].

Pushed on by the Germans, the British were forced to retreat via a different route from the one they had been ordered to follow. Because no account had been taken of this in provisioning, they could not be supplied with any food. In an attempt to get some food to the men, British Army Command left food supplies at random junctions under the orders of their Quartermaster General, Wully Robertson. The army staff hoped that the majority of the troops would pass by these places and thus be able to help themselves. This was far from always the case: sometimes the food stayed where it was; at other times the Germans, fortunately for them, found the stacked food supplies.

According to the Schlieffen Plan, France was supposed to have been brought to its knees after thirty-nine days. Order from the Kaiser: the German troops should not give the French a break, not even for a second. And thus it continued, day after day. Until their soles had worn paper-thin, and everyone was walking around on big blisters and with their skin grazed down to raw flesh. There were day-long marches, in full kit, stretching some 60 kilometres. Columns of soldiers overran northern France. The German troops, dressed in *feldgrau* (field grey), blocked the streets and roads so comprehensively that field kitchens or wagons with provisions could no longer get through.

But the advance was successful. Within ten days, by 5 September 1914, the Germans had taken the cities of Lille, Valenciennes, Cambrai, Arras, Maubeuge, Mezières, Saint-Quentin, Laon, Soissons and Rheims. And not only the cities, but also the coal and iron mines, and the regions where wheat and sugar beet were grown. During these battles in September, more than 200,000 French soldiers died, got wounded or went missing, as well as almost half of all officers. Amongst the British, too, there were many fatalities, sometimes entire units. Nor was their ordnance spared: within a few weeks, more cannons were lost than during the entire American War of Independence in 1775, which lasted eight years.

The German Army Command was firmly convinced that the French, entirely according to plan, could quickly be brought to its knees, so they transferred two army corps to the Eastern Front. At the beginning of December, a German plane flew over Paris dropping leaflets announcing that German troops would be entering the city within a few days. Upon hearing this, 1 million Parisians fled south. The French government had even moved its seat to Bordeaux. It provoked the grudging French who were left behind to come up with an amended version of the 'La Marseillaise': 'Aux gares, citoyens, Montez dans les wagons…' ('To the stations, citizens, board the carriages…').

For the Germans, it was a question of counting: 60 kilometres to go, then 50. The soldiers had got so close to the French capital that they attacked the Parisians who had taken the train to Château-Thierry. Only another 40 kilometres before they reached the city. At their marching pace, this meant two days.

None of the army units that transported food supplies for the soldiers reached the troops at the front. These included field butchers and bakeries. The German divisions were worn out when they arrived at the River Marne. The men fell into roadside ditches gasping with exhaustion.

The French, meanwhile, had withdrawn to the other side of the river, where the British were also stationed. At the Marne, the Allies had found a natural border behind which they could regroup. Here, too, they had taken out the bridges to prevent German reconnaissance units reaching the opposite side. The British had had a few days of rest there. Arms and equipment had been partly repaired, partly replaced. Finally, they had been given enough to eat. In fact, the men were ready for a counter-attack.

While the troops were waiting for the moment to strike back, French General Joffre was comfortably ensconced behind his dinner table. In front of him was his favourite dish: roast leg of lamb with white beans. There, he received the message that the British were ready to resume the offensive. Joffre, who normally did not allow himself to be disturbed during his meals, which could last over two hours, raised his arms and called out: 'Let's advance then!' After which he resumed eating.

During the late evening of 4 September 1914, the order to commence the offensive was issued. Approximately 600,000 French and British troops were facing some 500,000 Germans. On the first day alone, the Allies achieved success. They managed to cut off German communication lines, especially those between Compiegne and Amiens. This was the road the German troops had arrived on, and along which the convoys of food supplies and ammunition had to follow. Some of these transports were seized. Food and ammunition ended up in French hands. The result was that the German troops had to suffer even more.

The Allied armies went on the move and threatened the German flanks. Extra French units were dispatched by train from Paris. Others were transported by the thousands to the front in requisitioned taxis. Every taxi conveyed five soldiers: one next to the driver and four in the back. Ten thousand men drove through the Porte de Pantin north of Paris towards the city of Meaux on the banks of the Marne.

Consequently, the Germans faced the French dog-tired and starving, instead of attacking them in the rear as planned. Their front line fell apart, connections were cut off and the different army units became separated. After three days, the German General Von Gronau reported that since the afternoon of 5 September, the infantry and the field artillery of the IV Reserve Corps had had to hold off heavy opposition in scorching heat, without food and water, waiting in vain for relief and reinforcement.

A reversal was nigh. 'From the village of Pécy which was on a hill, we were able to see their infantry halted on the road,' Major Tom Bridges wrote on 6 September. 'An Uhlan patrol which reconnoitred us was hotly dealt with. I sent back a frantic appeal for guns. A German battery barked at us and set fire to a house. Then the phenomenon occurred. Under our eyes the enemy column began to wheel round in the road and retire to the north.'

The French and British troops set off in pursuit. In the places which shortly before had been occupied by the Germans, they sometimes found traces of drinking sprees. Occasionally, there was food, which the Allied men had been warned might have been poisoned by the Germans. Yet some risked it. A British soldier's ration consisted of four army biscuits, a pound of bully beef and some tea and sugar. Every bit of food was a bonus.

John Lucy:

My section had the job of leading in the clearing of one village, and we found it in a strange condition. Tables loaded with wine bottles were set up in the open street. All the shops were looted, and all kinds of merchandise were scattered about outside them.

Overturned chairs showed that the enemy had retired in haste. We worked slowly through the ravaged village, cat-walking in single file, as we hugged the houses on either side, and, finally making clear, came on the German bivouac in the fields on the northern side. This deserted bivouac was the strangest I have ever seen. The German soldiers had taken the mattresses from the houses of the villagers and made their beds on them. Those who could not get mattresses had looted clothing of all sorts, men's, women's and children's, and had made piles of these to sleep on. On and about this conglomeration of bedding were heaps of stolen foodstuffs, preserves, and bottles of wine, and in the narrow spaces between some of the beds there was fresh human excreta and newly opened tins of peas and other eatables.

A further retreat of German troops was ordered, up to the far side of the River Aisne. Men, equipment, horses, wagons, supplies, trains, ammunition, artillery: everything had to go back under enemy fire. It was a sad procession of outcasts without preparation, route or plan. During this retreat, German officer Walter Bloem took the opportunity to have a quick wash in the town of Noroy-le-Bourg. He was flabbergasted when he stood, undressed, in front of the mirror. 'I was nearly bowled over. Skinny like a skeleton, my skin covered in a layer of dust and dirt, my cheeks hollow, my hair longer and much greyer and my chin and jaws hidden behind a grubby beard.'

The German hope to force a decision on the Western Front within thirty-nine days had evaporated. No one had taken into account a retreat. But already then, less than three months after the murder of Austro-Hungarian Crown Prince Franz Ferdinand, German Kaiser Wilhelm II observed: 'The war has been lost. It will continue for a long time, but we have already lost.'

The Great War had only just begun, but nobody was thinking about the death of Franz Ferdinand. In the museum in Vienna, the Crown Prince also seems to have disappeared into complete anonymity. The bloodstained uniform is displayed in a glass case.

It is on the ground floor, immediately to the right of the entrance, near a greenish chaise longue on which he was stretched out after the attack and later died, and near the open-topped Austrian Gräf & Stift Phaeton car in which Franz Ferdinand was driven through Sarajevo. The bonnet sports a gold-coloured pennant with the Crown Prince's coat of arms. There is a bullet hole just forward of the right-hand door.

No one is visiting this wing dedicated to the First World War. The display case with the uniform looks like a coffin, but without a body. It feels as if, decades after the assassination, I am the only person to say goodbye to the Crown Prince of the past. Here lies history, stone-dead and forgotten.

POTATO SALAD

Ingredients
potatoes
citric acid (or vinegar)
salt
if desired, pepper and mushrooms
water
oil

Preparation
Peel the cold or warm potatoes which have been boiled in their skins and cut into slices. Make a dressing with citric acid (vinegar), salt (if desired, pepper and mushrooms), a little water and oil if possible and mix this into the potatoes.

Die Gulaschkanone (The Goulash Cannon)

CARROT SOUP (for one hundred and twenty)

Ingredients
meat
1.5 kg lard
20 kg carrots
pepper
salt
bay leaf
thyme
2 kg rice

Preparation
Place half of the meat and the bones in a pot filled with cold water. Boil for one hour. Skim carefully. In a second pot, melt 1.5 kg of lard; add 20 kg of sliced carrots, with pepper, salt, 2 bay leaves and a little thyme. Leave to simmer for an hour. Take the pot off the heat and put the carrots in the soup. After two hours of boiling, add 2 kg of rice. Leave to boil for another hour and pour everything through a sieve. Cut the meat into portions and add to the soup.

Handboek voor den kok te Velde (*Handbook for the Field Cook*)

DUCK

Ingredients
duck
apples
flour or bread

Preparation
Clean the duck, rub salt into the skin, stuff with apples and pot-roast for two hours in a pan with water. Duck roasts in its own fat and the sauce is also ready after roasting. Just stir in flour or crumbled bread.

Kochbuch für den Schutzengraben (Cookbook for the Trenches)

BOILED FISH

Ingredients
fish
vinegar

Preparation
Fish is boiled in salt water with a little vinegar (or citric acid, if possible mushrooms, also julienned vegetables). Cooking time approximately 10 minutes. The fish is ready when you can easily remove the fins.

Die Gulaschkanone (The Goulash Cannon)

APPLE SLICES

More than once we have served our men apple slices. Preparing them costs very little. We have as much fat as we want; flour is not especially expensive and, in the right season, apples can be bought at a reasonable price. The apple slices are served as a side dish, or a dessert if preferred.

Ingredients
beef fat
5 kg flour
8 l milk or beer
apples
sugar

Preparation
Dissolve 5 kg flour in 8 l of milk or beer, if necessary in water, until you have a thick liquid batter. Melt part of the beef fat in your cooking pot. Dip your peeled and sliced apples in the batter and throw these in the fat. Remove the slices from the fat as soon as they are golden. Make sure you take some sugar from the rations of each man, which, after having been stamped to powder, will be sprinkled over the slices.

When it's not possible to obtain apples, *croustillons* [doughnut balls] will have to do. These are made by dropping a spoonful of batter per *croustillon* into the fat and this creates doughnuts without apples (fried batter, very tasty). Sprinkle with sugar like the apple slices.

Handboek van den kok te Velde (*Handbook for the Field Cook*)

BULLY BEEF PIE
THE FINAL BATTLE, 1918

No 26 Ieperstraat, diagonally across the road from the Memorial Museum Passchendaele in the village of Zonnebeke, is home to Brasserie-Restaurant-Party Venue De Volksbond, also called Chez Ingrid Demuy, according to its business card. De Volksbond is a large village hostelry, erected in brick and topped with a step-gable that is supposed to give the building some authenticity, even though it cannot date back much further than the 1920s. Everything was destroyed here during the war, after all.

The sun is shining. A red awning bearing the name of the establishment has been unfurled outside, and the terrace has been set out with white seats and tables with white tablecloths. On the roadside stands an advertising board with the slogan 'Taste the food of the front soldier' chalked on it. And next to it 'Tommy Tucker Menu,' followed by a huge exclamation mark.

Inside, lunch has started. Two elderly couples are sitting in the restaurant section which has been separated from the bar by flowerpots and are prodding listlessly at some potatoes. Young lads from the local football club are lounging at the bar. They are drinking a glass of Coke and discussing that morning's game in the dialect of western Flanders. At the entrance, trophies of the local Royal Cycling Club (motto: 'Strength through Unity') are displayed, and the columns supporting the ceiling are adorned with yellow enamel tiles bearing Lions of Flanders, the region's coat of arms.

I sit down at a table at the window with a view of the advertising board outside. Flemish and German *schlagers* sound from the speakers: 'Du siehst so glücklich aus' ('You Look So Happy'), I hear, and 'Love Will Never Pass.' On a typed insert, at the back of the menu, the Tommy Tucker menu is listed as a new speciality at eleven euros.

Soup
Passchendaele Pie (Bully Beef Pie)
Coffee or tea and cake

The landlady who runs the establishment makes her way over to my table. Ingrid Demuy, for it is she, is a cheerful lady of around sixty, stout and short. On her head rest two pairs of glasses: reading glasses in her permed hair, and glasses for normal vision on her nose. A wet tea towel is draped over her left shoulder. What would I like? I order the Tommy Tucker menu and ask her if it's a popular choice. 'Well,' Demuy says, her eyes aglow, 'today is the first day it's on the menu. Let's see if it will work.'

A great deal of preparation has gone into its introduction, Demuy tells me. They sought cooperation with Memorial Museum Passchendaele 1917, the village's cultural council had a say and Zonnebeke's entire parish council has been to De Volksbond to sample the bully beef pie. 'Absolutely!' Demuy beamed. 'And they were very happy, sir.' And although it seems a joke today, Sunday 1 April, I am the first person to have the honour of ordering the Tommy Tucker menu.

September 1914. The Battle of the Marne led to the Race to the Sea and eventually to a front of trenches stretching from the Swiss border to the Belgian coast. A defence system spanning almost 800 miserable kilometres. Here the men were positioned, behind a bank of sand and stones, standing on duckboards or in the squelchy earth. Some days up to their knees in the water, at others baking in the gleaming sun. Four days at the front, four days in reserve, four days at 'semi-rest,' with the French being relieved after three days at the front. In theory at least; in practice, the men might bivouac at the front line far longer. The troops lived like labourers in a crazy shift pattern. 'Dig or die' was the motto. Dig or die. For four years.

They were years of continuous repairs to the trenches, comprising a front line, support line and reserve line, constructed in a zigzag shape to reduce as much as possible the effect of grenade shelling. The men moved towards the front line like heavily loaded pedlars. The British hauled a day or two's rations, 150 cartridges, extra socks, a raincoat, water bottle, cooking tin, mug and cutlery, a blanket and groundsheet, sometimes a pocket-sized Primus stove, paraffin, a few tins of beans, Vaseline, a Tommy cooker, a can of extra fuel and a rifle.

They carried the prescribed and mandatory kit: two tins of corned beef, twelve biscuits, two coffee tablets and two packets of condensed soup, a sachet of sugar, regulation underwear and a second pair of high boots. But experienced soldiers always managed to find room for a few more tins, some extra tobacco, chocolate, methylated spirits and woollen clothes. Every German soldier carried a rifle, ammunition, a rucksack, mess kit, extra boots, trench tools, a knife and a host of other pieces of equipment.

Perpendicular to the trenches were the communication trenches. Cramped and fitted out with earthen sides which collapsed time and again. Food, water, ammunition and troops had to be transported along these trenches to the front line. At the front were the shelters, the dug-outs. These could be a simple hole dug into the trench wall, big enough for one man to take shelter. Elsewhere there were ingenious constructions able to accommodate dozens or even hundreds of men. A few dug-outs, those for officers, were wallpapered and sometimes even housed a gramophone for playing records. Men would sleep during the day in their dug-out and await what might happen outside. Letters were written, coffee was made; bacon fried, and beans heated up in a small pan on a stove or *au bain-marie* on a spirit stove.

They were years of utmost boredom, but also of man-to-man combat with rifle and bayonet, of filling sandbags and digging latrine ditches. There were small posses that went 'over the top' at night to conduct raids, to repair barbed wire in no man's land or to reinforce the collapsed defences with sandbags.

They were also years of standing in the freezing cold, with men groaning with pain, flat on the ground in no man's land, the area between the two enemy lines that was often no wider than a few dozen metres, sometimes a kilometre. The men at the front had to withstand waves of shelling that hit with deafening noise. At the same time, there was the fear of snipers who were always lying in wait. There were casualties and fatalities. Attacks with chlorine mustard gas. Tanks thundering through the positions.

They were years of madness and decay, of hopeless strategies and pointless massacres, of territorial gains extending to a few dozen metres, if that. It was unimaginable bedlam. And if that wasn't enough, food supplies tended to be terrible.

'The work of the army in the field depended to a high degree on their rations.' This is what the German General Ludendorff wrote in his war memoirs. His British equivalent, Field Marshal Haig, noted in his memoirs of the First World War that this was absolutely key to the end result. Because without food there would be no morale. Without morale, no victory.

The famous Prussian General Von Clausewitz likewise emphasised this in his standard work about warfare, *Vom Kriege* (*On War*). He added something else: food supply is even more important when there is a standstill; when the troops no longer have the urge and strength to advance and entrench; when the soldiers and officers fight from defensive positions, such as in a trench war.

The different army rations varied somewhat. The Americans were best off with 4,714 allocated calories a day. Next came the French with 4,466 calories. The British were given 4,193 calories a day in food, and the Germans were least well off, with less than 4,000 calories. In the German Reich, scientists had calculated what a soldier needed in order to be able physically to withstand a campaign. The daily ration that they came up with was along these lines:

7oz bread
500g biscuits or 400g egg biscuits
375g fresh or frozen meat, or 200g preserved meat
1.5kg potatoes, or 130g fresh vegetables, or 50g dried vegetables
20g coffee or 2.5g tea
18g sugar
20g salt
2 cigars and 2 cigarettes, or 1.25g pipe tobacco, or 20g rolling tobacco, or 15g snuff

The British, too, went into the war with rations that had been set by scientists and defined in the *Field Service Pocket Book*, which was reissued in a revised edition in 1914. According to the field rations, each day the men were entitled to a catalogue of foodstuffs:

1¼ lb fresh or frozen meat, or 1lb (nominal) preserved meat, or 1 lb salt meat
1¼ lb bread, or 1lb biscuit, or 1lb flour
½ lb bacon
3 oz cheese
⁵/₈ oz tea
¼ lb jam
3 oz sugar
½ oz salt
¹/₃₆ oz pepper
¹/₂₀ oz mustard
½ lb fresh vegetables, or 2oz dried vegetables

Apart from this normal ration, the men also had a reserve or iron ration for when daily food supplies were not available or did not reach the troops. The 'Last Hope,' as the British called it, was put together in such a way that one man could survive on it for a day. It comprised some meat, biscuits, sugar, coffee and salt. The emergency ration for the French included a salted soup cube, a cube of coffee, a bag of sugar and a tin of corned beef. In their bag with their 'iron supplies' the Germans carried two tins of meat, two tins of vegetables, two packets of hard biscuits and a packet of instant coffee.

The number of calories that every man was calculated to have daily was high. If you compare this with today, an adult male should be on 2,500 calories a day. But during the First World War, physical labour had to be carried out continuously, under great stress and under difficult circumstances. It is for this reason that generous rations were prescribed.

Just as depressed people tend to eat to lessen their feelings of pain and misery, so too did the food at the front bring a moment of contentment, warmth or at times even happiness. No food (or bad food) could lead to illness, exhaustion and stress. The will to wage the war would ebb away. Moreover, food supplies often went awry, especially in winter. Snow and ice could be a source of drinking water, but the frozen and extremely slippery mud by contrast made the roads and trenches impassable. At these times, the supply of food was an outright nightmare. Food would arrive tepid, ice-cold or frozen.

A field kitchen in a provisional camp. (In Flanders Fields Museum)

Canadian soldiers sort rations, including crates of mixed pickles and bacon. (George Metcalf Archival Collection, Canadian War Museum)

There were meals including dried vegetables that were so poor that they were called 'barbed wire' or 'field wreckage.' There was food that resembled cattle feed. In the lines, food arrived soaked with rain, covered in mud or hours late. The food carriers had been held up by enemy fire or had got lost in the depth of night in the twisting, confusing entrenchment and run into the enemy. And when they stumbled in the dark with their vats of soup, old milk churns or jam kettles, more than half of their contents would be lost. At times nothing would arrive: not a shred of meat, no potatoes or soup.

For the dispatch of cold food to the front line, donkeys, horses and even occasionally dogs would be deployed. Mules with their small hooves were best able to deal with the mire or the mud and were not as jittery as horses. Sandbags with sugar, tea, bread and canned food were taken as closely to the first support line trench as possible. There the animals' load was picked up by a section of soldiers who transported the rations onwards on foot, because in many places motorised transport could not get to the front line.

Everything was strapped on to the backs of men who lugged this towards the front line like pack mules. The troops were handed their food through the lines, which had been dug in a zigzag pattern.

Cuistots (cooks) the French called them, or *ravitailleurs* (supply vessels), or, very prosaically: *hommes-soupe* (soup men). These men hauled twelve heavy bottles of wine tied together on a strap, and loaves of bread held together by rope.

At around 4 a.m. the food carriers brought coffee. The British were often given a ration of rum as well, usually a free swig. The alcohol was kept in a stoneware jar, with the letters SRD: Service Rations Department. The soldiers soon dubbed this 'Seldom Reaches Destination,' 'Service Rum Diluted' or 'Soon Runs Dry.' Whereas the rum was still 94 per cent proof in 1914, some veterans claimed it was only served diluted.

The British supplied rum under strict rules: after the morning roll call and not late in the evening, for fear that the men would become sleepy during their watch. While the alcohol was dispensed, an officer had to be present at all times to check how much each man was getting. The men were not allowed to keep the rum but had to drink it immediately; teetotallers would share out their portion. The exact amount of rum doled out differed from company to company.

The French were given a quarter-litre of wine every day. Initially, the French Army Command only dispensed the drink in exceptional circumstances. But because these became more and more frequent, it was included in the rations. In 1917, the amount was even increased from a quarter-litre to half a litre a day. The army bought the wine in France itself but also in Algeria. In 1914 this amounted to more than 225,000 litres. After wine rations were increased, it ran to just under 1 million litres. Because of this increase, and as a result of poor grape harvests, the army was forced to obtain the wine from Spain and Portugal.

Lunch would follow at around 11 a.m., and at 6 p.m. the food carriers would bring the evening meal. Dry rations were kept in used sandbags. British food carriers also used their sandbags to take extra chocolate or biscuits to the front line. Bags of sugar were tucked into the sack's corners and carefully bundled up in small parcels. Packed on top of that were tins of jam, meat, bread and the post. The wet rations, stew and porridge, were strapped on to the men's backs in containers. Very occasionally the carriers would take parcels and newspapers.

It was dangerous work carrying the supplies to the front. For a start, the food tins could glint in the sun and thus become an ideal target for the enemy. The enemy knew exactly how the food carriers moved from the rear to the front line and deliberately aimed their shellfire at these lines. Officers who gave orders to polish the kettles with sword polish to give them a good shine were wholeheartedly cursed. The men would rather drag the pots through smoking straw or they used charred wood to blacken the iron.

French Sub-Lieutenant Campana recalled after the war how much danger the food carriers had been exposed to. On a cold night in March, he sent out a unit of eight *ravitailleurs*. They returned the following morning without the rations, having lost them en route to the front. The next night a new group of eight men set off, none of whom returned. The night after that, Campana sent a hundred men. These were all killed by enemy fire, he recounted after the war. After three nights without food, the soldiers in the front line were forced to search the clothes of the dead men for food; many of the bodies were in an advanced state of decay.

In some areas, Army Command, both amongst the Allies and the Germans, spared the food carriers as much as possible. There, rations were pushed in trolleys along a timber railway line to the front lines. Other concepts had been devised to make the despatch of food quicker and faster. The British soldier James Munson suggested in a letter to then Minister of War Lord Kitchener that reels of fishing rod should be used together with extra strong wire to cast the rations into the trenches. His idea was never put into practice.

At the beginning of the war, no arrangements had been made for the supply of food; the battle would soon be over, after all. During that time, all that the men expected was some bread and biscuits. No one had taken into consideration that the conflict might be lengthy, let alone become a war of stagnation with an enemy line close at hand. This meant it was difficult to reach the front, and not without danger.

As the war progressed, food supplies became better organised. Yet fresh meat was hardly ever available in the trenches. Instead, the British were given bully beef (corned beef), pork and beans, or Maconochie's stew (containing beef, carrot, onion, beans and potatoes). It might have been nutritious, like the bully beef I am being served up at Brasserie-Restaurant-Party Venue De Volksbond in Zonnebeke, but tasty the British tinned food was not. Especially if you had to eat it every day.

At the front, Maconochie's stew was eaten cold or heated up in its tin. 'If we wanted to heat up a tin of Maconochie,' Arthur Halestrap, a British soldier, told the author Richard van Emden after the war, 'we would make a stand of half a dozen candles and put the Maconochie on empty cans or anything we could find, put the tin bridging the gap, and those candles would soon heat up the food.'

Not only the British troops, but the soldiers from the colonies, such as India, had to be fed as well. A difficult task, because these men tended to have special dietary requirements; from religious convictions, they regarded much food as unclean.

An Indian soldier with the 18th Lancers, Jemadar Abdul Khan wrote on 20 February 1917:

I have scrupulously performed all the necessary rites, prayer, charity and abstention from what is unlawful; but, through weakness, the flesh is now beginning to assert itself. I have used nothing of this country up to date, except water and fruit, and have not touched even any tea, coffee, biscuits or jam, but now my inner man begins to prompt me and I am afraid of falling.

The extra treats the troops received were equally monotonous. Tinned jam formed an important part of the British rations. But there was no other kind of fruit, only tins of plum and apple jam were handed out, manufactured by Tickler. And if that wasn't bad enough, already at the end of 1914 the conserve arrived mouldy at times. 'Even at this early period the jam was rotten and one firm that supplied it must have made hundreds of thousands of pounds profit out of it,' British soldier Frank Richards noted after the war. 'The stuff they put in instead of fruit and sugar! One man swore that if ever he got back to England he would make it his first duty to shoot up the managing director and all the other heads of that particular firm.'

Apart from tinned jam, occasionally there would be tinned fruit and milk, and the odd handful of raisins. The Germans were given Dutch cheese now and then, distributed in large chunks.

But as the war dragged on longer and longer, their rations became increasingly monotonous and frugal. 'When we were at rest, our daily ration consisted of 300 grams of bread and a litre of thin soup, usually made with turnips, cabbage or dried vegetables,' German Carl Heller recorded in 1917 when he was stationed in Flanders:

The officers had a separate kitchen and many a piece of meat or potato that was actually meant for the men would find its way there. This constant hunger would make us embittered and despondent. For a civilian who did his daily work and was able to rest at night, this ration was preciously meagre. For a soldier at the front who, when lying in position, did not have any rest day or night, it was far too little. We constantly thought of nothing else but food and waited impatiently for the hour that the kitchen arrived. Then we'd eat the bread and soup immediately and we'd have to wait another 24 hours, sometimes even 48 hours, for new supplies.

The British gunner Leonard Ounsworth complained for his part:

Mostly the cooks got frozen meat, cut it up and made a stew, and you went along with your dixie [camp kettle] and got so much stew ladled out. Breakfast was two slices of bread with bacon between them, and if you were lucky the cook would dip it in the grease for you. For tea you might get corned beef or sardines, but it was mostly bread and jam for tea. There wasn't any supper unless you'd managed to save any of your own rations.

The Americans, too, had reason to be dissatisfied. They were often given food that they called 'slum' or 'goldfish.' This was foul-tasting stew or tinned salmon, respectively. Another type of meal was called 'monkey meat,' which was usually Argentinian horse meat or corned beef. This was something the men were even less happy with. Shortly after his arrival in France, the American soldier Benjamin Dexter heard a rumour. A company was passing, led by men carrying a stretcher with an imitation of a monkey. They also had a banner with the text: 'Be it resolved. When we get home again we will petition Congress to enact laws to the effect that in future wars troops won't have to eat his ancestors.'

The longer the war lasted, the more troops that were needed. These took up the space in ships previously used for stowing fruit and vegetables. This resulted in even less food reaching the front. The food that did arrive had deteriorated because of the long interval between its production and its arrival at the front.

The careful scientific calculations had stopped applying for some time. Fresh bread was now defined as no older than eight days. 'I got up. It was still night. I was very hungry. The field kitchens were outside,' Ludwig Renn wrote, the pseudonym of German ex-officer Arnold Friedrich Vieth von Golßenau, in his book *Krieg* (*War*). 'Was there still any food?' he asked the cooks. They replied that there was no longer anything. Even though that night a lorry loaded with bread had arrived. 'I'll have that,' Renn said, pointing at the bread. He took a bite. Renn: 'It tasted bitter and was soft inside like runny cheese. I held it up to a lantern. On the outside it was green and on the inside white. It was totally mouldy. I threw it away.'

Lack of water was another problem troops had to contend with. Bully beef and biscuits made them so thirsty that the small amount of tea that everyone was entitled to was too little to quench their thirst. The men filled their water bottles before they went to the front line. However, they were only allowed to drink this water in emergencies and when an officer gave them permission to do so.

Drinking water had to be brought in from behind the front, because the groundwater at the front line could be contaminated due to the many dead bodies present there. The Germans had factories where green bottles were filled with mineral water. These were transported in crates to the front.

The British pumped their water from underground sources or rivers; they then purified it and transported it in pipes to water stations at the front. These were large canvas tanks holding 9,000 litres. The water from these tanks was carried to the front lines in iron kettles or Price's Motor Spirit, British Petroleum or Shell jerry cans in the middle of the night. To try and get the cans as clean as possible, the men would throw a lit match into them to burn off the last bit of fuel.

Because of the decline in the quality of food and drink, many men suffered from chronic heartburn, troublesome digestion and diarrhoea. Another familiar disease was trench teeth or trench mouth, a condition that tended to begin with painful gums, an uncomfortable feeling and tiredness. The gums were eroded, covered in a grey layer of dead tissue, and bled easily. Eating and swallowing was painful. Often the lymph glands under the jaw would swell up and the men would have a mild temperature.

'Those boys at the front, sir, had a tough time of it,' says Ingrid Demuy in Brasserie-Restaurant-Party Venue De Volksbond, after I've finished my tomato soup with bread and while she puts the bully beef pie on the table.

In front of me is a pie on a thin aluminium dish measuring around 15cm in diameter and 3cm in height. The pie is covered in a layer of puff pastry. 'That's what it was like in the war as well,' Demuy says. 'That would keep the food would warm to some extent.' She can't help me with the recipe. 'The chef has thrown it away,' she says. Then I'll have to try and track it down myself. When I put my fork in the puff pastry topping, I hit a piping hot mass of potato, carrot, peas, mince, green cabbage and wafer-thin pieces of gherkin. A delicacy it is not. What is poignant is that it won't taste all that different than it did to the men at the front.

When I pay up, the two pints I've drunk with the meal are on the house. 'Because you were the first person to try the menu,' beams Demuy.

British soldiers cooking dinner in the trenches on a commandeered stove. (US National Archives)

MEAT SOUP

Ingredients
beef or veal meat, cut into 2 or 3 kg pieces
water
salt
pepper
mushrooms or garlic
vegetables or dried soup greens

Preparation
The meat is not boned. Fat, tendons and skin are not removed. Wash the meat. If a particularly nourishing soup is wanted, put the meat into a pan with cold water. If the meat is intended to become soft, boiling water is used. Veal is always used with boiling water. Add seasoning, mushrooms or garlic, vegetables (or dried soup greens) and bring the meat on medium heat to the boil till done. The readiness can be tested by prodding with a sabre or by cutting. Soup with beef should be cooked for approximately three hours, veal around an hour and a half. If the soup is too rich, skim off the excess of grease, collect it and use it for the preparation of vegetables, roasts, etc.

Die Gulaschkanone (The Goulash Cannon)

HERRING SALAD

Ingredients
herring
potatoes, cut into small cubes
pickled gherkins
oil
vinegar
white wine
seasoning

Preparation
Clean the herrings and cut them into pieces. Mix in potatoes, pickled gherkins and whatever is in stock. Add the dressing: mix oil, vinegar, gravy, white wine, herbs, all to taste and with whatever is available.

Kochbuch für den Schutzengraben (*Cookbook for the Trenches*)

BRAISED BEEF SCHNITZELS

Ingredients
1 pound of beef
salt
peppercorns, crushed
1 bay leaf
onions, cut into cubes
250 ml water or broth
1 tbsp flour
1 tbsp tomato purée (optional)
1 cup of red wine (optional)

Preparation
Cut beef into 1 cm thick, hand palm-size schnitzels and beat them until flat. Add seasoning. Put butter into a pan and slowly fry meat on both sides. Add onion, peppercorns and bay leaf. After frying put the beef into a casserole and sprinkle flour over the onions while continuously stirring. Bake al dente. Add water or broth and bring to the boil. Pour the sauce over the schnitzels and let them slowly cook till done with the lid on. For an even tastier dish add tomato purée and red wine.

Ragout can be made in the same way, but then cut the meat into small cubes.

Brattische Kochvorschriften für Feldküchen (Brattische Cooking Instructions for Field Kitchens)

FRIED LIVER WITH ONIONS (for one hundred men)

Ingredients
3 lbs dripping
flour 1½ lbs
salt as required
butter, 4¾ lbs
liver, 25 lbs
onions, 25 lbs
pepper as required
stock

Method of Preparation and Cooking
Wash and cut up the liver into slices ¼ inch thick. Mix 1½ lbs flour with 1½ ozs of pepper and 3 oz salt in a mixing bowl. Dredge the liver in the mixture. Well grease the dishes with some dripping. Place in one layer of liver only and fry on hot plate or in oven. Keep from burning by constantly moving. ONIONS – clean and cut the onions into rings and steam or fry till tender. Cover the liver with stock, add all the onions and serve hot. Time for liver: 40 minutes.

Manual of Military Cooking and Dietary

M. & V. CROQUETTES (for one hundred men)

Ingredients
18 tins M. & V.
9 tins P. & B.
4 lbs flour (or 5 lbs biscuits)
seasoning

Method
Having removed the fat from the M. & V. and P. & B. tins, pass contents through mincer; add pepper, salt, flour (or biscuit dust with a little flour to bind). Mix well together, shape in 2 oz croquettes, roll them in biscuit dust, and fry in hot fat until brown. Serve 2 per man.

Cooking in the Field

CAPTAIN ARMSTRONG
LOGISTICS AND DISTRIBUTION

The Liddle Collection at the University of Leeds has in its possession hundreds of maps, boxes and envelopes full of recollections of the First World War. There are handwritten letters, diaries and typed-up memoirs. But also postcards, cigar boxes containing medals, photos, recorded interviews with veterans, drawings, diplomas, dried flowers and menus of festive meals at the front. One box left to the collection by an ex-soldier contains a harness and a pipe. More than ninety years on, I can still smell the pungent odour of the tobacco.

The collection was set up in the 1970s by the British historian Peter Liddle, who wanted to ensure that experiences acquired during the First World War would be preserved. His collection forms part of the university's immense library.

It is warm in Leeds, and in the reading room dozens of students clad in shorts and flip-flops are bent over reference works. At the Special Collections Department, archivist Richard Davies places an initial box from the collection in front of me with an encouraging nod. Elsewhere in the archive are other collection documents I would like to peruse. The box in front of me contains an article from the British newspaper the *Daily Chronicle* dated 26 August 1915. Its author is journalist Philip Gibbs, a war correspondent officially accredited by the army. It is a mood story about the work of the logistics units at the front. The title: 'Staff of Life of the army. A drive with the commissariat, adventures in the van of a supply column.'

'Pious men in the trenches, who are also very hungry men, utter their little morning prayer of "Give us this day our daily bread," and after sniping a German or two, wait impatiently for breakfast,' Gibbs noted in the newspaper. 'Their prayer is not unanswered, and already at the break of dawn, along many highways of war in Flanders, the Divisional Supply Columns are coming up from railheads to refilling stations with the Army's food. They are the life preservers of the fighting-men who take their grub for granted.'

Good logistics, even before the food carriers could set out, were vital in order to guarantee the supply of food. During the war, the British alone supplied more than 3 million tonnes of it to, what eventually turned out to be, 2.7 million men. Each British division needed 200 tonnes of supplies per day. More and more personnel had to be deployed to be able to keep up with logistics and distribution, and before long the Allies recruited workers from other countries, such as China, to carry out that work.

The number of horses and mules deployed grew to more than 400,000. Almost 7,000 kilometres in roads had to be maintained, and supplies were transported in hundreds of ships via canals and rivers, from loading docks to points where lorries and horses and carts were available.

A system of railways with train stations developed in order to transport reserves, ammunition and victual to the troops as quickly as possible.

The Germans, for instance, laid almost 8,000 kilometres of railway track on the Western Front, along which some 4,000 locomotives supplied equipment and food to the troops. More than 100,000 men were set to work on the construction of this railway line and the distribution of goods.

In the relatively short period that the Americans were quartered at the Western Front, they laid 1,000 kilometres of narrow-gauge railway. On this travelled 347 locomotives and more than 3,000 carriages, loaded to the brim, between the hinterland and the front lines.

The British, too, had at their disposal thousands of railway carriages and hundreds of locomotives. At the end of war, they employed 41,000 road workers, 29,000 men laying railways, 11,000 to unload the ships and a further 8,000 in other transport units.

The French executed their tour de force during the Battle of Verdun in 1916 with the construction of what may well be the most famous stretch of railway and road from the war years: the Voie Sacrée. This lifeline was used to provision daily the hundreds of thousands of men who were at the tiny front at Verdun. A lane measuring barely 7 metres wide was all it was, but along this Voie Sacrée every fourteen seconds a lorry loaded with ammunition, troops or food would shuttle back and forth to the front line.

'The other morning, sitting by the side of a young captain of one of those columns, whose motor-car led the way for all his lorries, I realised the romance of our progress in the light of dawn,' journalist Philip Gibbs recorded about the British transport division which he joined for a few days as a guest:

> Outwardly there was nothing romantic or adventurous about us. An artist would not have found a picturesque subject, perhaps in this long line of heavy motor-wagons, painted a dark green, spaced out along the road like a fleet in line of battle, and loaded with bread and meat and groceries. Fowls cluttered away from our wheels, frowsy Flemish girls came yawning to the doors of squalid cottages and flung out dirty water on the side-walks; only the boom of guns, rumbling intermittently, came as a reminder that we were in the war-zone and not much beyond range of the enemy's great guns.

While I am reading Gibbs' article, archivist Richard Davies places a few new boxes with material from the war on the table in front of me. He taps his finger on one of them and says: 'This might be of interest to you.' The box file contains hundreds of handwritten letters home. The author is one J.C. Armstrong. In his letters I read that he commanded the British 1st Divisional Supply Column. He turns out to be the young captain in Gibbs' report.

Armstrong wrote in a letter on 5 October 1914:

> The life we are leading is just a pure picnic. Refilling point is only about ½ hours away from here; so we are always home by 2 o'clock, and, as everybody knows the road, exactly where to go and what to do, the whole show goes with extraordinary smoothness […]. When we get in the lorries pass the petrol lorry and are filled up by a hand pump, and are then ready to run to the station yard the next morning, when the railway train arrives. Our days are by no means

idle as there are many letters to censor and there is always a lorry under repair which we are supposed to keep an eye on. We also have very often to run over to G.H.Q. [general headquarters] and do some job or other. In the afternoon one of us is left here, and the rest are free to go for a walk or a run in the car. We went for a long run the other day to see the cathedral of Rheims.

A few months later he noted:

We are living on the fat of the land here in an unoccupied chateau. The men are in a large empty granary at a mill, and with lots of straw are very comfortable. The lorries are parked down the main road of the village and make a fine show, 59 all told. I have established the workshop party in the garage of the chateau; they have their homes in the loft and work in the garage; the great catch of this is that there is a pit for the men to work in under the lorry they are repairing. My workshop staff consists of 1 warrant officer, 2 staff sergeants, 14 fillers, 2 blacksmiths, 2 carpenters and 1 electrician, and they are a jolly good crew […]. There is also a crew of 8 cooks under a sergeant, and […] before he went bought his boilers for cooking tea in and we have lots of dixies […]. There is also a lorry for petrol under a corporal, who has two assistants to help him; they are responsible that every lorry is filled up every day […]. The post lorry also belongs to us, and, in addition to the corporal who looks after our own letters, has 3 men of the R.E. [Royal Engineer] postal section to look after the mails of the division. The first aid lorry carries two drivers and two fillers and is always in rear of the column; it carries […] spare parts to do simple repairs […] the rest [of the lorries] are available for carrying supplies […]. I would not swap my column for any other I've seen so far, vehicles or men […]. I confine myself to running the column, looking after the men and vehicles, discipline, company money and books and general supervision of the whole show.

Armstrong described his life behind the front in a plain style, like a bookkeeper whose most important task it was to make sure that the books balanced at the end of the day and that no item was outstanding below the line that might cause problems. It has to be said, Armstrong did a good job. Later in the war he would write that the operation led by him went so smoothly that he was almost sick with boredom and that he couldn't wait to be back in the United Kingdom.

During the time that he spent with the column, reporter Philip Gibbs could see the romantic side to the enterprise.

> [H]earing all its story since those days in August a year and more ago, when it came up the Seine to Rouen with 38 lorries in an eight knot tramp, and then plunged straight away into the bloody tumult of Armageddon. As the captain led the way to the refilling station there was more behind him than bully beef and biscuits, or pickles and marmalade. There was history behind him, of wild days and nights with an army in retreat, of a column of supplies searching for brigades which had gone astray down the roads, of narrow escapes from bursting shells and hostile cavalry, and of winter months when mud ditches on the slope of a steeply-cambered pavé had had an irresistible attraction for all his lorries.

'The division had always been fed,' stated Gibbs in his article. 'That was the main result of all his struggles and the chief credit of the column. Good enough, it seems to me.'

Yet the men in field did not think much of the work of the Army Service Corps (ASC). This included the transport divisions, such as the ones commanded by officers like Armstrong. The ASC men were not involved in combat did not take part in exhausting day's marches and did not stand in the trenches with water up to their hips. The soldiers in the trenches carried out the dirty work; that's what it felt like to them. So the British sang sarcastically:

> We are King George's army
> We are the ASC
> We cannot fight, we cannot march
> What fucking good are we?

But when we get to Berlin
The Kaiser, he will say
Hoch, Hoch, Mein Gott
What a bloody fine lot
Are the boys or the ASC!

Things were pretty good for Armstrong. The one time that he looked like a front soldier was when he tripped and fell into a muddy puddle, he laughed in one of his letters.

In another letter he wrote:

I expect you picture me in worn khaki, with a beard, and drinking dirty water out of a ditch. Well I can tell you I'm not living that way; not much, not in a long way. We've got our little [store] in the village shop, surrounded by bales of stuff, frying pans, mouse trap, boots, shoes and heaven knows what. We've got a fellow who can cook top hole and a fellow to wait on us […]. As for grub we draw rations like the men and we buy butter and eggs from the local farmers, and sometimes run over to the local town and buy 'extras' […]. Of course it was not like this on the retreat [from Mons]; it was push on all night and day and sleep anywhere, and we all ate bully beef with a pocket knife and rations biscuits and drank vin-ordinaire or tea, or anything, and grew beards and did not wash. Of course we have to do our daily round and common task but we are always working by day and not by night. When we get close to the troops, as close as they will let us take the lorries, we chuck out the grub and forage and stuff […]. I could do with a glass of beer; French beer is poor stuff and the wine is worse, and the water not fit to drink till its boiled; so we drink tea or cocoa at all our meals […]. Well I hear some meat frying, so I must dry up and not bore you anymore.

At that time, Armstrong was in charge of 240 men and fifty-two Leyland trucks, but these numbers would rise to more than 300 men and seventy-eight trucks. With these he had to transport 117 tonnes of food per day in order to feed 25,000 men.

Logistics gradually assumed huge proportions on all fronts. The unloading capacity in the French ports such as Bordeaux, Saint-Nazaire, Nantes, Le Havre and Brest were enlarged, and there, too, Chinese men and workers from other countries, primarily colonies, were deployed. All the same, dockers could not be prevented from taking their chances. They stole food before it went inland to the troops.

Hundreds of supply depots and field bakeries were constructed. American bakers produced more than 3 million pounds of bread for their armies, which were stationed in France from 1917 with a growing number of soldiers and officers. British slaughterhouses supplied more than 10,000 kilos of meat to the troops daily, enough for 40,000 men. Each day around one hundred cows and almost 300 pigs were slaughtered for this.

In order to provide the troops with more fresh vegetables, farmland was cultivated immediately behind the battle zones. The men themselves sewed, planted and harvested rapeseed, potatoes or hay for the horses and donkeys. On a plot to the south-east of Amiens, the British set up a central farm measuring almost 20,000 hectares. They brought dozens of tractors and ploughs over from England to break the ground, and men were specially trained to operate the machinery.

In addition, at the beginning of 1917, the British experimented with keeping pigs near Étaples: a simple pen with wooden sties and enclosed with a wooden fence and barbed wire. The animals were not only good for meat production; the pigs also polished off large quantities of organic waste from a neighbouring army camp. The British Army also introduced goat farms near Rouen and Marseilles in order to be able to provide the Indian troops with enough meat.

The pig farm was such a success that the British Army Command ordered pigs to be kept near all large army camps. A small slaughterhouse with a capacity of a hundred pigs a day had to supply the troops with fresh meat. In 1918, pig farms were set up in many places in France. Later that year, an outbreak of swine fever put an end to this keeping of livestock.

The Germans had also established a kind of food industry behind the front. German officer Ernst Jünger wrote:

In the middle of April 1916 I was detailed to attend an officer-training course [...] at Croiselles, a little town behind the divisional lines. A number of excursions and inspection visits to the units in the hinterland (which were very often improvised) gave us, who were in the habit of viewing everything that happened there, an insight into the massive work that goes on behind a line of fighting men. And so we visited the slaughterhouse, the commissariat and artillery repair workshop in Boyelles, [...] the dairy, the pig farm, and rendering plant in Inchy [...] the bakery in Quéant.

Despite these efforts, the Germans had a hard time. They did not have as large a fleet as the Allies. Besides, the distance between their front line and their homeland stretched hundreds of kilometres. Especially now that railways and roads had been destroyed in the parts of France and Belgium that had been captured, it was difficult to devise alternatives for getting goods to the front. What's more, the Germans had no access to the sea, unlike the British and the French, who could use it to ship in their new supplies.

Armstrong explained the process amongst the British:

Supplies of food and forage reach the base from oversea and are forwarded thence by rail to railhead. This is some station sufficiently advanced for motor transport to keep up communication between it and the troops, and at the same time not so far advanced as to be nominally exposed to attack from the enemy. Railhead must be connected to the Army by good and suitable roads. At railhead supplies are transferred from the train to motor lorries. As soon as the supply column is loaded it makes its daily trip from railhead to rendezvous. This spot is fixed by corps or divisional headquarters the previous night, and is some central position well in rear of the troops it is supplying. As soon as the tactical situation admits, a refilling point is decided upon to which the supply column advances from rendezvous, here meeting the horse-drawn vehicles of the supply section of the train. Supplies are then transferred and the supply column returns to railhead while the supply section of the train proceeds to the troops.

Fusiliers at a campfire. (In Flanders Fields Museum)

Open air cookery near Miraumont-le-Grand. Officers using a brodie helmet to knock up some additional nourishment in the field. (National Library of Scotland)

The supply train wagons on arrival in the area where troops are billeted proceed direct to their own regiments or batteries and hand over their supplies. They then return empty to some central position in the billeting area and are parked for the remainder of the night. Next morning they proceed to the refilling point and repeat the programme of the previous day.

Of the thirty-eight lorries that set off under command of the Captain in 1914, twenty-three were still in perfect order a year later. Armstrong was proud of the fact that his mechanics kept everything on the road, just as the drivers were proud of their vehicles and the speed at which they worked. Vehicles that looked identical but had been ascribed personal characteristics. Gibbs wrote in his article:

There was 'good old Hartley' – always cheered along the road by the boys who were at Mons and Le Cateau. I travelled on it myself, back from the refilling point, and sure enough as we passed a battalion on the road, the men grinned, and shouted out, 'Good Old Hartley! Still running?' For months she has never failed to bring up the supplies to the ammunition train, dodging shells on her morning trips.

Then there was 'Old Lazenby,' sometimes called 'Pickles.' She had been through many a narrow shave, and had hogged scores of times, and had almost been scrapped until the master-mechanic who loved all the column this side idolatry, had put in some new spare parts, and tightened things up a bit, and kept her on the road. It was the same with 'Hovis' and 'Jacobs' and 'Old Carter Paterson' – their medical history is so full of details that there are not many of their original parts left, and only the outer body and the inner soul of the lorry remains unchanged after all this patching up and refitting of fans, radiators, cylinders, magnetos, cardan shafts, axles, valves, pistons and die cases.

Gibbs understood Armstrong's pride:

[T]his young officer – carefully concealed behind a slight air of boredom and the upward twist of a fair moustache – when at the cleaning parade in the afternoon he went along the line of lorries and pointed out their various characteristics. The drives and loaders were greasy men just then squatting beneath the chassis with oil rags, or polishing up the engines until they shone like silver and gold, but as the captain passed telling the tale of each lorry, as though of an heroic chariot of war, the men listened and their eyes brightened with the pride of engineers who have taken a tramp steamer, and urged on its boilers to rough many an ugly sea. 'Ah!' said one of them. 'That was a great day at Meaux, when we nearly got cut off by the Germans. Do you remember, sir? We'd hardly time to cross the bridge before it was blown up.'

During times of standstill, which was the case during the major part of the war, it became increasingly complicated to reach the troops. The terrain became heavy going; because of the rain, because of the thousands of vehicles that had to drive along the narrow roads and because of the endless files of troops that had to march along the road to and from the front, thus making quick transit impossible. In addition, the countless bombs and shells that landed almost continuously destroyed large parts of the roads.

Delays in the transfer of food occurred ever more frequently and became inevitable. Supplies dwindled. Transit to the front was frequently closed. Trains or lorries with food might take a wrong turn or be hit by shells, which meant that the food arrived late or not at all. If the lines were reached, the officers allowed themselves first choice and took the best they could lay their hands on. Only then did the men get something to eat.

As the British sang in 'Oh! It's a Lovely War!':

Come to the cookhouse door, boys, sniff the lovely stew
Who is it says the colonel gets better grub than you?
Any complaints this morning? Do we complain? Not we
What's the matter with lumps or onion floating around
        the tea?

MULLIGATAWNY SOUP (for fifty men)

Ingredients
6 gallons stock
5 tins bully beef (put through mincer)
2 lbs onions
2 lbs carrots and turnips (or soaked dried veg.)
2 lbs apples and 3 lemons (if obtainable)
2 lbs crushed biscuit
A few mixed herbs
Curry powder and salt

Preparation
Cut up the vegetables and apples in small pieces and fry in
a little fat till brown, add the biscuit flour and curry powder
to taste. Fry for a few minutes with sufficient fat to soak up
the biscuit; then add all to stock with minced bully beef,
and stir all the time until it boils and is fairly thick. Then
allow to simmer for two hours.

Cooking in the Field

BEAN SALAD

Ingredients
green or white beans
citric acid (or vinegar)
salt
pepper and mushrooms to taste
water
oil

Preparation
Cut and string the green beans, and boil in salted water. Then prepare like a potato salad.

Soak white beans overnight, boil in water without salt until soft, add salt once they've been cooked, drain and finish like a potato salad.

Die Gulaschkanone (The Goulash Cannon)

MINCED MEAT

Ingredients
raw meat
tinned meat
water

Preparation
Mince the raw meat in a mincer, as well as the tinned meat of which the fat has been removed. Fry the meat with water (about 250 ml per kg of meat) and mix in the flour. Add the tinned meat. Mix everything, season and bake in greased baking tins or trays.

Anweisungen für Truppenküchen (Instructions for Soldiers' Kitchens)

PIGEON

Ingredients
pigeon
butter
smoked bacon
salt
sour cream
flour or bread

Preparation
Put some butter and finely cut smoked bacon in a pan or pot. Once this has browned, add the pigeon which has been rubbed with salt in the pan. If available, wrap the breast in slices of bacon. The roast should be liberally doused in butter sauce. If this turns brown then gradually add a little water. Allow for an hour of roasting for this kind of fowl. Once it is almost cooked, add some sour cream mixed in with flour or crumbled bread stirred in a little butter sauce. Heat thoroughly and add salt to taste.

Kochbuch für den Schutzengraben (*Cookbook for the Trenches*)

WELSH RAREBIT (for one hundred men)

Ingredients
8 lbs cheese
4 lbs biscuits or bread crumbs
3 ozs dry mustard
2 ozs salt
1 oz pepper
1 tin milk

Method
Grate the cheese and crush the biscuits. Place all the dry ingredients into a mixing bowl and mix well together. Place the mixture in a baking dish, barely cover with milk and bake for 45 minutes.

Cooking in the Field

GOULASH CANNONS AND SOYER COOKERS

THE COOKS AND THE KITCHEN

On a Saturday morning at the end of April, a year after my visit to Brasserie-Restaurant-Party Venue De Volksbond, it seems as though war has broken out in the village of Zonnebeke. The entrance to the local chateau grounds has been blocked off by barbed wire. To the right of that are a few tents and a group of men dressed in Belgian First World War uniforms. Passing a provisional barrier, I see a group of British soldiers led by a sergeant marching – *left, right, left, right* – towards the chateau. To my right, German men are digging a trench. A little further along are two encampments with French, Russian and Australian troops wandering around. Two mounted officers make their way slowly along the shingle path meandering through the chateau grounds.

More than a hundred men and women are spending the weekend re-enacting the First World War. 'Re-enacting' sounds a little unfortunate, considering the seriousness with which it is being carried out. To some visitors it may seem like a First World War version of *Dad's Army*. But these men and women are more than hobbyists; they are experts who know from memory entire detailed histories about the regiments whose members they are imitating.

Amongst them is Kristof Blieck, Education Officer of the Memorial Museum Passchendaele 1917 and organiser of the museum's weekend with its 'big historic evocation,' as it is called in the promotion leaflet. He is wearing the uniform of a Belgian soldier from the war era. Blieck is a large figure clad in khaki, with a brown belt tied around his corpulent stomach and a copper helmet on his head. He has arranged for me to assist the three cooks in their preparation of the food for the re-enactors. 'The forgotten heroes,' Blieck suggests, referring to the cooks in the war. He points at three men in greasy aprons standing in the field kitchen they have set up in the museum grounds. The cooks have started making breakfast: baked beans, white bread, vegetarian sausages for the devotees and Lorne sausage, a kind of mince that has been pressed into slices and is fried in large frying pans.

The field kitchen consists of two rusty Soyer cookers and a blackened oven, attached to which is a baking tin measuring a metre in length. On these, four cauldrons are bubbling. Delicate wisps of smoke spiral out of the cookers' chimneys. Behind the cooking units stands a white marquee stocked with further cauldrons, tins of baked beans, and bags of potatoes and frozen meat. Kitchen equipment is spread out on to a table, and there are crates with pots of salt, pepper, parsley, packets of tea, matches, metal plates, mugs, soup spoons, whisks and other small items.

The inventory resembles the list of kitchen utensils described in the *Handboek van den kok te Velde* (*Handbook for the Field Cook*), written by 'a commander of a unit' within the Belgian Army. It is a catalogue of the bare minimum a soldiers' kitchen should have in wartime in order to prepare a nutritious meal. It includes a decent butcher's knife (with a 26cm blade), a steel, a tin opener, a butcher's saw, a skimmer for fried dishes, a nutmeg grater, two meat boards, a coffee filter and a wooden masher.

A special mention on the list – because it was the most important tool for a cook according to the guide – was a mincer. This could be used for all kinds of tasks: grinding coffee, mincing meat 'for the meatballs and pies,' chopping vegetables and grating cheese for macaroni.

According to the British regulations, the mincers were especially useful for grinding bones into small pieces. These pieces of bone had to be kept in nets marked 1, 2 and 3, so that the cooks could differentiate between the bones from the first, second and third day. All nets had to be stored in a stock pot, and each day the contents of this pot had to simmer for six to eight hours. The dirt that rose to the surface had to be skimmed off as often as possible. The stock pots were indispensable for supplies of stock, soups, stews, meat pies and gravy.

In Zonnebeke, I am measured for a uniform from a Tasmanian unit that served in the war; green trousers and a jacket with a white and red emblem on its sleeves. Above the jacket's epaulettes is spelled out in metal letters the word 'Australia.' It is not exactly a suitable outfit for a kitchen auxiliary, but that doesn't matter, Blieck thinks: 'In civilian clothes you'd stand out too much. Now you're part of the set-up.'

The cook with a Royal Scots Regiment cap on his head wipes his hands on his apron, shakes my hand and introduces himself as Pete Scally. 'You're late,' he barks. He runs his eyes down me and growls: 'Do you know Gordon Ramsay, that grumpy chef from Scotland?' I nod. 'I'm also from Scotland,' replies Scally. 'And I'm even more grumpy than him. Take those hands out of your pockets and get to work, or bugger off.'

Cooks worked hard during the war. They were the first to get up to prepare breakfast and went to bed last. Between these times they were constantly busy keeping the fires burning in their kitchens, cooking and making sure their working environment was clean.

Even though a cook by no means always worked in the front line, neither could he be sure of whether he would live or die. Like high church steeples and the chimney stacks of factories, the plumes of smoke rising from the field kitchens were an ideal target for enemy fire. Those field kitchens were sometimes reduced to rubble as a result of shelling, and the cooks themselves would not be spared. But there were definite advantages: a cook was not, or rarely, involved in exhausting exercises, was not part of the working parties that had to dig out the collapsed trenches, and hardly ever took part in man-to-man combat. An exception was during the Second Battle of Ypres in 1915, when the British cooks saw off a German attack. One of the cooks was armed with no more than a spoon. In Zonnebeke, John Stelling, one of Scally's colleagues, demonstratively waves a large ladle in the air and laughs: 'Can you imagine what it must feel like to be hit by one of these?'

'Start dishing out the sausages,' Scally orders when breakfast in Zonnebeke is ready and I have meanwhile tied a white apron around my waist. A long queue of waiting soldiers, officers, machine gunners, cavalrymen and Red Cross nurses gather with their mess tins, plates and cutlery to be served their food. I see

Germans with handlebar moustaches and steel helmets, British men who have carefully smeared mud on their faces because they were supposed to have been lying face down in a trench. In the queue are Australians with their plumed hats and French re-enactors wearing long blue coats. As if there isn't war on, but world peace has broken out instead.

Scally is up for it today. He is a decent guy whose nose is put out of joint sometimes, or rather, pretends it has been. 'Smile boy, smile, or aren't you happy you're getting some food?' he says to a lad in the queue. 'Smile! Like that! Here, your plate. And now bugger off.' His eyes peer from below his bushy eyebrows at the queue slowly filing past. He stands with a stoop, as though he is preparing for a rugby scrum. When Scally was serving with the Royal Military Police in Northern Ireland he was injured in his spine after a bomb attack. 'That back is getting worse and worse,' Scally says. 'In ten years' time I'll be completely bent double, my head resting on my chest. It could've been worse. There was nothing left of one my colleagues to find after the attack.'

Scally was not only a member of the Royal Military Police; for twenty-five years he was also a Cook Sergeant in the British Army, and during that time prepared food for a company of one hundred men. Now he is retired, partly because of his back trouble, but he still misses army life. That's why, in 1996, he set up the 29th Field Kitchen with a group of military history buffs who arrange authentic catering for First World War and Second World War re-enactments. The division of roles is clear: Scally is the boss; John Stelling from Newcastle works as a kind of sous-chef and stirs the pot containing the baked beans; Andrew Harris, from a village near Belfast, is responsible for making tea and stoking the cookers and the oven. I haul in wood, occasionally stir in one of the cauldrons with a wooden spoon, fry sausages and do the washing-up.

The field kitchen was the highlight in the daily gloom of the war. It had to try and keep the men on their feet during long marches. When marching at normal pace, the troops usually got a ten-minute break every hour. During the marches, the cook drove the horses that pulled the wagons carrying the cooking pots. Together with his assistant cooks, he was responsible for keeping the field kitchen's fire burning. After fifty minutes of marching, the men lay down on the ground, massaged their stiff muscles and smoked a cigarette. There was no rest for the cook. The break was used to allow the food in the pots to cook until done. The coal had to be poked; cauldrons had to be stirred. He was not allowed to be distracted by anything. Only after a long day's marching, when the last food had been served to the waiting soldiers and officers and the cauldrons had been scrubbed clean, was the cook able to think about himself.

'I was up all night making tea for the lads as they come out of the line,' British soldier William Bink wrote on 26 July 1915 in his diary. Bink was working in France with the transport division of the 1/8th Leeds Rifles Battalion (West Yorkshire Regiment):

> We moved again on the 27th and it is no fun cooking for your own men and then making tea for 1,000 men and officers and having to drive your own cookhouse about. We stopped two days and moved again at night and it rained again in torrents. I am about half dead with cooking all day and then at night in the saddle 6 and 7 hours at a stretch with two spirited horses that it takes you all your time to hold and wet to the skin.

After the Race to the Sea, the kitchens had to be better equipped and made more mobile. It was absolutely vital that the wagons, sometimes pulled by mules, could come close to the front line. If the lines between the kitchen units and the men in the front line were too long, then this would render the supply of food more difficult.

The mobile field kitchen tended to comprise a front and rear wagon, the latter intended as a cooking island on wheels. The front wagon consisted of four asbestos sections to keep food warm. The rear of the front wagon contained the knives, a hatchet and other kitchen utensils. The rearmost wagon was made of steel with five to eight cauldrons to cook in. In drawers at the back, the cooks kept their supplies of sugar, tea, salt and herbs, but also candles, cleaning brushes and canvas buckets. The cooks were only able to prepare the simplest of meals in a field kitchen; little more than stews, beans, carrots and potatoes were served up as hot food.

On the Western Front stood hundreds of cooking installations. The British *Manual of Military Cooking and Dietary* from 1917 describes the use of all kinds of ovens and other appliances with curious names such as the Richmond Cooking Apparatus, Warren's Improved Appliance, Dean's Iron Ovens, Dean's Steel Boilers and Dean's Combined Cooking Apparatus. Most of these pots or ovens were big enough to prepare coffee or boil vegetables for fifty men.

The Germans used two types of field kitchens during the war, pulled by two horses: the large field kitchen (the *Heeresfeldküche Modell 1911*) and the small field kitchen (the *Heeresfeldküche Modell 1912*). These were called *Gulaschkanonen* (goulash cannons) by the Germans. The large field kitchen was meant for companies of 125–250 men. The most important part consisted of a round, double-walled, 200-litre cauldron. The inner wall was made of nickel, the outer of copper. The space between the walls was filled with glycerine to stop the food from burning. The large field kitchen also included a single-walled, square coffee kettle that could hold 90 litres. In a later version, which was produced from 1913 onwards, the cooks also had a 30-litre roasting and warming oven at their disposal.

Thousands of cooks were needed to prepare the food and to gather wood for the field cooker fires. It was a quite a job getting these going if the wood had been rained on and was wet. The cook had to lay small criss-crossed bundles of dry wood on top of the coal and cover this with more coal. Then he could light the fire. If no suitable fuel was to hand, the British cooks would sometimes use the hard (in actual fact inedible) biscuits from the men's ration to light a fire.

Thriftiness was the order of the day when it came to using fuel. The fires were not allowed to burn any longer than was necessary. Once the soup had reached boiling point, some of the coal and wood had to be removed from the fire. This could be re-used later on. Only strict, specific rations of coal and wood were allowed to be used per type of oven or cooker. Warren's Improved Appliance was clearly economical, as it roared on 2 kilograms of coal, whereas a brick kiln needed more than 7 kilograms.

Where there were no field kitchens, alternatives had to be devised. The British guidelines for these, in the *Manual of Military Cooking and Dietary*, read like an SAS survival guide. Beer barrels could be used as cooking pots by cutting off one end and covering the sides and top with clay. Dug-out sections of trenches or hollowed-out ants' nests were suitable substitute ovens. Shepherd's pie could easily be made in washing bowls, and empty Maconochie tins were perfect for cooking pastry-based pies. Puddings could be prepared in ration sacks, and there was no better makeshift oven than a biscuit tin.

Only after all the re-enactors in Zonnebeke have been given their meal are the cooks allowed to eat. This can involve some waiting, as the odd person doesn't say no to a second helping. We have a thirty-minute break. Perched on folding chairs, we chew the baked beans, bread and Lorne sausage. The pressed slices were pink before they landed into the pan, now they are golden and taste unexpectedly good.

The cooks are proud of their field kitchen and of their oven, retrieved by the cooks themselves at the beginning of the 1990s from a British Army storage depot. The original appliance had been kept there for a while in case of a nuclear war, when cooking units would be needed that worked without electricity or gas. They are also proud of their Soyer cookers, with their 45-litre volume, all original as well, and invented by the Frenchman Alexis Soyer in an attempt to feed the troops during the Crimean War better than had been possible before. 'Soyer, the Gordon Ramsay of his time,' Harris tells me.

Cooks, good cooks, were highly valued in the war. If they managed to improvise in impossible situations and prepare a hot meal with precious little firewood and under enemy fire, they were worshipped. At times, there was plenty of food. The cooks would make thick soups or stews full of vegetables and meat. The men could have two helpings, two full mess tins. And when they were finally eating, entire companies would sit down in silence. In a crouched position, stooped, to prevent the soil from the top of the trench dropping into their food. Or because shells would splash the mud up so high that it ended up in their stew or scrambled eggs with fried potatoes.

At other times, the news of losses, of yet further fatalities, would take days to reach the reserve lines. Those lines would hold rations for more men than was needed. At such times, there was food aplenty.

The cooks at or behind the front not only took care of feeding the troops. The field kitchen or kitchen unit was also known as the 'village pump,' the place where people gathered for the latest news, gossip and tall stories: that a regiment had to be broken up in order to be moved to another part of the front; that the French General Joffre, the German Crown Prince or the British King – always one of them – had been killed in battle; or that peace, peace at last, would soon be declared and everyone could go home again. The 'Cookhouse Official' is what the British called these vague persistent rumours and half-truths emanating from the kitchen brigade.

Amongst the cooks who prepared the supplied provisions and stirred their big pots were experienced men. They included distinguished figures such as the French master chef Morla, who was decorated with the *Cross de Guerre* (Cross of War) for the valour he had shown wielding the ladle under enemy fire. There were cooks working at the front who had stood behind the stoves of hotels and restaurants in major cities such as Frankfurt, Wiesbaden, Sheffield, Leicester, Lyon and Bordeaux. Chefs who thought nothing of preparing roast pig with plump lentils. But more than anything these were the men who were of little use in combat and were therefore placed behind the stove, just as conscientious objectors were able to contribute to the war effort as cooks or assistant cooks. Older men too, or men who had large families at home, were sometimes spared by being allowed to work as cooks and keeping them away from the firing line as much as possible.

A few months after my visit to Zonnebeke, in the Reading Room of the Imperial War Museum in London, I have in front of me dozens of letters from British soldier Jack Sweeney, who was deployed as a cook at the front. Large yellowed sheets with scrawling handwriting, and smaller notes he penned with a small nib or blunt pencil under candlelight. There are also postcards issued by the army at the time, on which Sweeney could mark in a kind of multiple-choice menu whether he was injured, would soon be on leave or that he was doing well, by deleting what was appropriate. A single line, no more than that.

The ink in the letters has watered down and faded over the years, and this makes the handwriting difficult to read. Sweeney wrote down long confessions: about his love for home, his homesickness, his growing aversion towards the conditions in which he had to live at the front and about how pointless he thought the war was. But things didn't always turn out badly for Sweeney. In a letter dated 17 December 1915 he wrote to a friend that he had been lucky and had been deployed as an officers' cook. Earlier in the war, Sweeney had worked as a cook, when he had stood behind the pots in an area where there was little to fear. Now he wrote that, much to his regret, he nonetheless had to go to the front to cook. Anything was better than standing guard, but he found it tough going. It was hard work preparing food on an old bucket filled with coal while his officers expected a five-course dinner.

And yet the position of cook was sought after. The men who cooked for officers in particular had a relatively good existence. The men Sweeney served were not only given large portions but also the best of what was available. Food that the cooks could have themselves. Sweeney was deployed in a trench in which he had the use of a dug-out to cook in. Once the officers had eaten, they would usually leave so much that Sweeney would invite the men in from the trench and offer them a hot meal and a cup of tea. These were leftovers, but the soldiers were glad that they were able to eat something and shelter from the rain. They crawled into the dug-out like wet dogs and snuggled up against each other. The warmth inside wicked the moisture from their clothes. It cheered him up, Sweeney wrote to a friend, that he could give them something.

Like Sweeney, most cooks at the front had no practical experience whatsoever. Only later in the war were prospective cooks trained for a few weeks in especially established cookery schools before they went to work at the front. The Americans had set up a butchery school in Florida where men learnt how to cut and debone meat. The US Army also sent trained butchers to France to teach the cooks these skills. But this training was often inadequate and not completed.

Complaints about the quality of the food were plentiful. In the trenches, the men sang, to the tune of 'What a Friend We Have in Jesus,' the song 'When this Lousy War is Over':

When this lousy war is over no more soldiering for me,
When I get my civvy clothes on, oh how happy I shall be.

No more NCOs to curse me, no more rotten army stew,
You can tell the old cook-sergeant, to stick his stew right
    up his flue.

At the end of 1915, the British organised the training of cooks and catering staff in the army in earnest, with the appointment of a catering inspector and fourteen catering instructors. The Cook Sergeant, a Pete Scally type, was the boss in a battalion kitchen. He allocated the work, took orders and, most importantly, guarded the key to the pantry. Officers were responsible for ensuring that a few men in every British company focused on the instruction of field kitchen construction, cutting meat and cooking itself. This did not stop inexperienced cooks from preparing food throughout the war, such as the gunner Stuart Chapman, who occasionally was put to work in the kitchen, for example, in October 1918. The rations had just arrived, and he was tasked with cooking. He did not have much cooking experience, but he was a dab hand at improvising. He found an old bucket in which he cooked cabbage and potatoes, fried beans in four ounces of butter and added some tea. In order to peel the potatoes and cut the meat, he used an old shaving knife. In Chapman's opinion, it was the best meal he had eaten since Christmas 1916.

The *Manual of Military Cooking and Dietary* from 1917 defines a number of the cook's tasks. In this guide, cleanliness is paramount. The kitchens must be spotless and the utensils spick and span, even if you only had a handful of grass, hay or ashes from a wood fire to scrub and polish the iron pots with.

There were further guidelines cooks had to keep to, such as those outlined in the booklet titled *Things that every cook should know*. The cook and his assistants had to wear clean, washable aprons over their canvas uniforms, and they were forbidden to shave or relieve themselves in the kitchen unit and pantry. Each cook needed to have at his disposal a washing bowl, soap and a clean towel. Food had to be covered in muslin in order to protect it against dust and flies, and every pantry had to have a meat safe for storing the meat. No food residue or kitchen items should be on the floor of the pantry or kitchen unit. There, the rule applied that once a week the entire area should be cleansed by whitewashing.

German soldiers having a meal. (In Flanders Fields Museum)

German soldiers sharing a beer. (In Flanders Fields Museum)

If meals were prepared in a field kitchen then the cooks had to clean the cauldrons thoroughly every day. Without this cleaning mania, too much food would perish and be lost, while the warm summers and primitive circumstances were already responsible for food going off quickly.

Private W.D. Corney, a member of the South Lancashire Regiment, was one of the British soldiers who was taught to cook. He followed a course at the School of Cookery in Brighton. The Imperial War Museum in London has a well-thumbed green-marbled notebook that once belonged to Corney. It extends to eighteen pages. When I open it, I see that he has noted down recipes in a graceful script for, amongst other things, bread baked with baking powder, tinned-meat pie, rice with apples, and braised meat with rice for one hundred men. Apart from recipes, the notebook also contains drawings by Corney: sketches of a French kitchen and a so-called Aldershot oven with instructions for how to build it; portraits drawn with a fountain pen of, according to their captions, one Cecily Debenham and 'The Dawson Girl' also feature. The prospective army cook clearly had other things on his mind than ovens and recipes.

An Aldershot oven had to be installed if there was no regular oven or field kitchen available. According to Corney's description, its construction was a rather complicated affair. It starts with a list of what was needed to build one: two arched sections, four bars, two ends, one bottom plate, one peel and a baking tin. Then follows a set of instructions which suggest that the cooks evidently needed to have engineering skills: place the oven on a gentle slope, avoiding sandy or marshy ground. Smooth and clear the site. Place the four bars in position and attach the arches to these, the flanged back arch in such a way that it overlaps the front one. Face the mouth of the oven towards the prevailing wind. Fix the back plate firmly in the ground and attach two arches to this with wire. Lay an arch of two rows of bricks over the front of the oven. Cover the remaining part of the oven in a clay mixture of up to twelve inches thick with a backwards slope of ten inches, which needs to continue for a further twenty-three inches to carry off the rain. Built like this, the cook had a functional oven at his disposal which would cater for 200 men.

The description is almost unintelligible. It's no surprise Corney had his mind on other things and was also thinking about Cecily Debenham and 'The Dawson Girl.'

In the Liddle Collection in Leeds, I come across another notebook, by a gunner named O'Brien. He also gives a description of the Aldershot oven, with an even more lucid drawing. The notebook also contains a sketch showing the edible parts of a cow.

Zonnebeke. After breakfast I take a thirty-minute turn around the site to see what the other re-enactors are doing. There is a stall staffed by Red Cross nurses on which all kinds of medical attributes from the First World War are displayed. Elsewhere, soldiers and officers are polishing saddles and cleaning guns. Over our heads buzzes an old, small yellow plane. A model from just after the war, but okay. Even though the atmosphere is a little lethargic and sluggish, it gives an impression of what it must have been like at the front.

When I return, Scally says: 'Ah, there you are. I thought you'd deserted.' He gives me the recipe for potato soup for one hundred men which will be served for lunch: '52 pounds of potatoes, cut into slices. 22 pounds of leeks, cut into pieces. A little salt, pepper, parsley, thyme and coriander. Cook everything until the potatoes are done and falling apart. This gives the soup body.' He shoves a knife into my hands. Those potatoes and leeks are for me, I understand.

As was the case with the British, the German Army initially worked largely with inexperienced cooks. In Germany, it was not until 1916 that men were deployed for work in the kitchen who had properly learned their trade. Better organisation was also needed. Witness the booklet *Die Gulaschkanone, Soldatenkochbuch fürs Feld!* (*The Goulash Cannon: A Soldier's Cookbook for the Field*), compiled by the German cook Walter Schmidkunz. Commissioned by the army in 1915, Schmidkunz had tried to give the troops in the field some 'no experience necessary' cooking instructions for all possible circumstances. In his foreword, Schmidkunz wrote:

> My field experiences proved to me that the kitchen menu hardly, if ever, rises above soup with beef, preserved foodstuffs, rice, goulash, tinned beans, potatoes, coffee and tea. This is always due to inexpert officers or a bad cook.

It belongs to the main army responsibilities that the meals of the field kitchen should be greatly improved because of the extraordinary importance of varied, nutritious and tasty food for the troops in the field. The cause of numerous gastric and intestinal diseases which occur on a daily basis in parts of the front, yes, even an overall physical malaise amongst the soldiers lies in the frugality of what the kitchens have to offer. For this the *Gulaschkanone* offers a contribution. Moreover, this booklet will prevent harmful food preparations as well as urgently advises the use of diverse ingredients.

Ultimately, Schmidkunz wanted to see more beaming faces above the mess tins. And he never wanted to hear again: 'In God's name, food is food and an order is an order.' 'Because,' Schmidkunz wrote, 'like love, the way to victory is through the stomach!'

The growing shortage of food in Germany and, by extension, amongst the troops meant that the preparation of nutritious meals became ever more important. It required skill to be able to serve up good food with limited means. For that reason, from June 1916 onwards, a growing number of soldiers received cookery lessons. The main goal during the three-week course was to train twenty-five to thirty kitchen teams, led by an experienced professional chef, in preparation of varied meals. The men who learned a genuine trade in this way came under the responsibility of the quartermaster, the officers of a regiment, the *fourrier* (quartermaster) and *Küchenfeldwebel* (kitchen sergeant). Answerable to the cook were two assistant cooks. These had to peel potatoes, cut vegetables, chop wood, fetch water and keep everything clean. Exactly my role in Zonnebeke during the museum weekend at the end of April.

The booklet *Anweisungen für Truppenküchen* (*Instructions for Soldiers' Kitchens*), which was used in the training of German cooks and which had been drawn up by a committee of three men, contains a raft of practical suggestions:

Take advantage of the cooking skills of campers. Use a spirit burner with two pans with tightly-closing lids and a large surface area for rapid heating, for example the one offered by Natterer from Munich, a practical field kitchen called 'Sieg' [Victory], an appliance that burns on methylated spirit. Bicarbonate of soda is good for improving drinking water and helps soften dried vegetables. Potassium is important for preserving meat. If, after transport or due to warm weather, meat is in the first stage of decay, it should be soaked in potassium for a short time and rinsed in water. The meat will lose its unpleasant smell and taste. Instead of butter for roasting and sautéing, lard, grease or vegetable oil can be used just as easily. Before transit, eggs are best packed in flour, sugar or salt; butter in a loaf of bread of which the inside has been scooped out; meat in a cloth soaked in vinegar. Tough, old meat becomes tender by rubbing it with brandy, wine-spirit or stomach bitter.

There were other people who gave some thought to what soldiers were given to eat, such as one Hans Werner, who wrote a recipe booklet for the trenches: *Kochbuch für den Schutzengraben* (*Cookbook for the Trenches*). It is full of recipes for roasting meat and preparing fish, eggs, potato dishes, sauces, rice, vegetables and dishes with apples. Werner also wrote a heartening poem:

> Whoever joins the soldiers
> Likes roast in his hide-out.
> Sometimes with a piece of fish
> The lieutenant enriches his dish.
>
> Yes. In the entire trench, it's true
> One gladly wants good stuff.
> Caviar and truffles are too dear,
> Therefore, take eggs, about some four
> Make a pancake or an omelette.
> Shouldn't it come off, it's again your move.
>
> Potatoes in their jackets
> With gravy or just dry, whichever you want.
> Oatmeal, peas, bones or rice,
> Nothing healthier to feed on.

Even a genuine water hater
Cooks his veggies in some water,
So let it all be to your taste
Whenever there's a cease-fire.

This booklet of general's quality
Makes you prepared for heroic deeds.

Just as with the British regulations, the German ones emphasised the importance of hygiene in the kitchen. The clothes of the kitchen staff had to be clean at all times. Pots and kitchen utensils had to be cleaned immediately after use. Constant airing of the kitchen units behind the front was important, and smoking was not allowed. Dogs and cats were only allowed in these kitchens to catch rats and mice, and only after cooking and when there were no longer any articles of food present. NCOs and men who worked there had to make sure they were checked twice a week for infectious diseases.

It was not only rats and mice that had to be controlled, but also flies, which were especially dangerous as they would come into contact with the food and contaminate it. They could transmit diseases such as dysentery, an infection of the digestive tract, and typhoid, an illness that is characterised by high fever, drowsiness, skin rash and diarrhoea or constipation. That's why the kitchen windows had to be sealed in muslin and all articles of food had to be covered. Waste had to be removed instantly. Dung and waste heaps were not allowed to be near a kitchen, as these would attract flies.

The longer the war lasted, the scarcer food became. It became increasingly important to use it efficiently. The British document *Things that every cook should know* advised the cook to keep the meat of fat and bones and turn this into a stock. This meat could be used for pâtés, shortcrust pastries or brawn. Fat should not be thrown out, but collected and melted, and could thus serve as a base for sauces and for making sautéed potatoes, apple slices or macaroni. In order to avoid waste, cheese should not be cut into chunks, but into 1.5-inch square cubes. Any remnants of cheese could be incorporated into a cheesecake or Welsh rarebit. Food that was left on plates could be utilised as a filling for pasties. In Zonnebeke, Pete Scally used all kinds of leftovers to make his famous soup: the

'Goesinto,' thus named because 'everything goes into it.' The motto in the various manuals was clear-cut time and again: do not throw anything away, because days of plenty are rare.

The French distribution system collapsed as early as 1915. When, at the time, the army tried to hoodwink the general population into believing that the men at the front were getting two meals a day, Army Command received tens of thousands of furious letters from soldiers who knew better. The Germans had to make ever greater efforts to get sufficient food to the front line. This was not least because the country was completely cut off from the outside world as a result of the Allied blockade and virtually unable to import anything to alleviate its great need. The situation for the British was not much better: because of the submarine warfare declared by the Germans, the number of British ships transporting food across the channel diminished rapidly. The British government placed the responsibility with the men themselves. It campaigned for less baked beans with beef and less bully beef. They shamelessly called on the men to 'Eat Less and Save Shipping.' But the soldiers adopted the slogan and soon corrupted it into 'Eat Less and Save Shitting.'

Zonnebeke, late April. When, on Sunday morning at 8 a.m. I arrive on foot at the chateau grounds, I see that Scally, Stelling and Harris have already started preparing breakfast: scrambled eggs with a slice of white bread. I'm late again. The previous night we worked until 9 p.m. cleaning the pots and pans. After that we drank pint after pint on a terrace in Ypres until 3 a.m. Scally, Harris and Stelling told stories: the modern-day Cookhouse Officials. The story of Scally, for example, who, somewhat the worse for drink, was preparing a dinner for a group of officers. He made savoury biscuits with pâté as an appetiser. After the meal, officer after officer came up to Scally to heap praise on him for the quality of the food and especially the biscuits. Everyone wanted to have the recipe. The following day, sober again, Scally saw that instead of pâté he had spread cat food on to the biscuits.

Truly fit we are not this day. After a short night with much alcohol we get on with our work wearily and in silence. Harris makes tea and, standing at a burning Soyer cooker, wipes the sweat from his brow. In a temperature of 23 degrees, and with the field kitchen positioned in full sun, it is hot in front of the fires. Stelling breaks the eggs in some pans and Scally lays out slices of white bread. I kneel with difficulty in front of a tin of warm water and begin to do the washing-up. From the chateau domain, gunshots ring out from the trenches dug yesterday: Germans firing at the British. Dozens of Belgians who have come to the museum weekend watch the battle from the tops of the trenches.

It's all about routine in the kitchen, I realise: starting the fire in the morning, hauling wood all day long to keep the fire burning, maintaining the water in the Soyer cookers at the right temperature so that men and women can have tea at any time of the day, and constantly getting yet another meal ready.

Routine or not, cooks take pride in their work, in Zonnebeke as well. Four factors are key here, Scally, Stelling and Harris teach me later that day. The food should not only be nutritious, but tasty. The meals should look appetising and should be served on time. This last aspect is something we are not managing particularly well today. Because the shops did not open until 8 a.m., and we were only able to buy our ingredients then, all the meals are served later than planned. Scally isn't happy with that. 'Fucking shops,' he complains. After having made me clean the cookers and cauldrons, he tasks me with peeling dozens of kilograms of potatoes at speed for mashed potatoes, which will be served that afternoon alongside Scottish stew. Once again, those potatoes. 'Faster lad, faster!' Scally urges me. 'People are hungry!'

With a knife in my hand, my fingers dirty from the soot of the cooking pots, I dispatch bag after bag of potatoes. I ask Scally where the satisfaction lies for him, with all that routine of preparation, cooking and cleaning, followed by more preparation, cooking and cleaning. He rubs his chin and ponders this. 'Satisfaction, eh?' he asks, pausing to think. 'I think it has to do with a kind of family feeling,' he finally says. 'Everyone here does his or her best. Everyone in their own way and as best as they can.'

He places his hands on his stomach and muses: 'It makes you feel good, doing something for the men and women who also work hard here. We are all like coals in a fire. If the little coals don't burn, the big ones won't either.'

BROWN FLOUR SAUCE

Ingredients
lard
flour
water

Preparation
Heat the lard or butter. Add the flour, stirring constantly until the sauce turns brown (for each spoon of flour use a nut-sized piece of butter or lard). Slowly add some cold water. Boil this down until it is done and, while stirring constantly, little by little add small amounts of water until the sauce has the desired richness. If it suits the dish, mushrooms and herbs can be fried in the lard at the same time.

Die Gulaschkanone (*The Goulash Cannon*)

CABBAGE SOUP

Ingredients
one small Savoy or white cabbage
2 tablespoons of lard
4 tablespoons of flour
1.5 litre of water
pinch of pepper
salt

Preparation
Clean the cabbage, cut into slices and wash. Heat up the lard and braise the cabbage in this. Sprinkle flour over the cabbage and stir well. Add 1.5 litre of water and simmer for one and a half to two hours. Season with salt and pepper.

Kriegskochbuch, Anweisungen zur einfachen und billigen Ernährung (War Cookery Book: Instructions for Simple and Cheap Nourishment)

CHILI CON CARNE (for one hundred men)

Ingredients
25 pound meat scraps
6 ounces chili peppers, ground
6 quarts beans, chili
lard
meat stock

Preparation
Trim all the fat from the meat and chop into half-inch cubes approximately. Place in a bake pan and fry in the same manner as beefsteak but using a smaller amount of fat; cover with about 1 inch of beef stock; add the ground chili pepper and salt to taste. Run two thirds of boiled chili beans through a meat chopper and mix all together and then add the remaining third of the beans whole. While cooking it may be necessary to add more beef stock to replace that lost by evaporation. When ready to serve there should be sufficient beef stock to cover the preparation.

Extracts from Manual for Army Cooks

SAUSAGES (for one hundred men)

Ingredients
20 lbs meat without bone
8 lbs bread
4 ozs salt
2 ozs pepper
1 lbs sausage skin
seasoning

Preparation
Cut the bread into slices and soak in cold water, cut the meat into small pieces and pass through a mincer. Once the bread is soaked, squeeze out all the moisture. Place the minced meat, bread and seasoning into a mixing bowl and mix well together and again pass through the mincer. Stuff the mixture in the casing and tie with a string to make sausages. Prick the skin with a fork, put them in a greased tray and cook for 30 to 40 minutes.

Gunner O'Brien's notebook

RISSOLES (for one hundred men)

Ingredients
18 lbs meat
10 lbs bread
3 lbs onions
4 ozs salt
2 ozs pepper
seasoning
enough flour for binding, 3 lbs is allowed

Preparation
Cut the bread into slices and soak in cold water, cut the meat into small pieces and pass through a mincer. Peal, clean and cut the onions. When the bread is sufficiently soaked, squeeze out all the moisture, place the minced meat, bread and onions and seasoning into a mixing bowl, mix well together and again pass through the mincer. Spread out on the table and sprinkle well with enough flour to bind. Roll out into sausages of about 5 inches long. Place in well-greased baking dishes and cook for 40 minutes.

Gunner O'Brien's notebook

OVER THE ROLY-POLY

LIFE BEHIND THE FRONT

If you ask Henry Allingham about the secret of his old age, he invariably exclaims: 'Cigarettes, whisky and wild, wild women!' I read this online and it rendered him sympathetic even before I had met him. And then there was the photo with Allingham in his wheelchair and a WRAC-type blonde woman next to him. On Allingham's face, three, four lipstick marks. He beams at the camera lens as if he has been caught out in the middle of an intense kissing spree. Dennis Goodwin, chairman of the First World War Veterans Association, had told me over the phone 'Henry is in excellent shape. Tip-top!'

Speaking to Allingham is no problem, knows Goodwin. Allingham is healthy, energetic and completely with it. The only issue is his diary. Goodwin: 'Next week will be difficult. He'll be in Bristol, a five-hour journey from here. He'll be visiting secondary schools for three days to tell his story. The week after that would be preferable, he has some time then, would that suit?'

Henry Allingham was born in 1896 and at the time of writing was the oldest man in Europe. For me, the first veteran of the First World War encounter in person. As early as in 1916, Allingham was involved in the Battle of Jutland. In September 1917 he was transferred to the Western Front; or rather, just behind the Western Front. Allingham was an Air Mechanic First Class, and for the majority of the remainder of the war was stationed in a depot at Dunkirk to repair aircraft and recover planes that had been shot down over enemy territory.

The meeting is at Dennis Goodwin's home in Goring-by-Sea, on the Sussex coast. I arrive forty-five minutes early for my meeting and am a little nervous. Shortly I will be shaking the hand of a man who has been through all this. A veteran who was in France in 1917, who experienced the life I only know from reading diaries, letters and other notes from First World War veterans. This man is a hero. *My* hero; at least that's how it feels to me.

Dennis Goodwin and his wife Brenda's house is full of photos. Dennis and Brenda together with Allingham at a remembrance event in France. Allingham next to His Royal Highness Prince Charles. Allingham with Queen Elizabeth II. With German veterans. With French soldiers. With everyone, it seems. The Goodwin's' home is like a scrapbook full of memories.

At a quarter to eleven that morning, Dennis Goodwin's light blue Ford Escort pulls up on the drive in front of his house. Behind the wheel, Goodwin himself. Next to him in the passenger's seat, the old veteran: beige corduroy coat, plaid cap, greyish-blue flannel trousers, blue-checked shirt, and a brown and white chequered travelling rug over his knees.

Goodwin gets out of the car and opens the boot to retrieve a wheelchair. Allingham remains seated in the passenger's seat and is greeted exuberantly by Brenda, who removes the rug from his knees, folds it and places it in the back of the car. I take my chance, make my way towards the vehicle and shake Allingham's hand. His fingers are weather-beaten and gnarled; his nails yellowish-brown. The back of his hand reveals a network of small, deep-purple veins.

Allingham looks at me, but I doubt if he can see me. His pale-blue eyes lie behind a kind of dull haze: the man is almost blind.

The wheelchair Dennis Goodwin manoeuvres towards me appears to be surplus to requirements; I am there to help out, after all. Together with Brenda, I lift Allingham from the car seat. With him in our arms, we shuffle to the front door, step by step. With a one-two-three-in the name of God we clear the obstacle of a 10cm doorstep. 'Shall I sit here?' Allingham asks hopefully when we have got as far as the living room. But we have to move on. In the side room stands a large pink armchair with an equally pink footstool. This is the final destination. We have a last wobble, but then Allingham flops down. He heaves a sigh of relief.

Once Allingham is sitting, he is smartened up. His cap and corduroy coat are taken off. Brenda arrives with a blue blazer with all his medals pinned to it. 'We can't have you looking like a tramp,' she encourages him while Allingham struggles wheezily as he is fitted into the blazer. As soon as he has placed his legs on the footstool in front of him, a midnight blue slipper drops from his left foot on to the carpet.

I have brought some Dutch chocolate and a bottle of Bordeaux for Allingham, because I know he liked to join the French for a glass of wine during the war. My bottle causes some confusion. 'Gin?' he beams, giving me a quizzical look. 'No, wine, Henry!' bellows Dennis Goodwin in the veteran's ear. Allingham is not only almost blind, his hearing is no longer functioning all that well either. 'Wine?' he asks. 'Wine? But that's for starters!' And he roars with laughter.

Fair's fair, Allingham did not have too bad a time of it during the war. At least, not like the men who were active at the front. They fought that war and they suffered, he thinks. These men would go without food for three or four days and be hungry all the time. Allingham had enough to eat in his position behind the front. There was plenty of bread, fresh from the oven, he recalls. For breakfast, he and his mates were given bacon and eggs. Biscuits were served with their cups of tea; for lunch, a decent portion of meat, sometimes potatoes with some vegetables and always more than enough rice, sugar and raisins.

Allingham was stationed in the hinterland: the sector men dreamed about throughout the entire war. A return to civilisation from the mud and misery. Preferably back home, but leave was more of an exception than a rule. A week a year, occasionally a little longer; more time was not feasible. That's why the men spent their days off primarily just behind the front.

Quartermasters went ahead to try and find as much accommodation as they could with private families. The farmers and civilians were paid for lodging troops: five francs per officer, one franc per soldier. But these rates were subject to negotiation. The sum that was eventually paid per head tended to be lower. If there was too little or no straw in the barn, or if the men had to sleep on a stone or earthen floor, then the rate was no more than ten centimes per person.

Once the price had been agreed, an officer would chalk on the wall the number of men who would sleep in that particular location. Unlike the French and the Germans, the British did not pay in cash. Three certificates were drawn up. One for the village's mayor, one for the quartermaster and one for headquarters, which settled the payment.

Civilians who took in lodgers did good business, especially when they had a garden and grew their own vegetables. This was also the case for mainstream hospitality establishments. These were able to push through price rise upon price rise thanks to the enormous demand and scarce supply. Clever marketing tricks were used as well. British officers were given a card which allowed them to have a meal in a French hotel or café within thirty minutes of leaving the front line. Charley's Bar in Amiens was one of their favourite locations. Here they bought Old Orkney whisky in bottles which they took back to their dug-outs at the front at the end of their leave.

Needless to say, the officers behind the front claimed the best facilities: rooms with real beds and lavish meals. They had more money to spend than the soldiers; enough to buy the best wares in the French or Belgian shops, such as sardines, ham, cheese, olives and wine. Mostly, they took the food to their billets, where the landlady would cook it for them for payment. Private soldiers were less well catered for; they had to use the back entrance of the shops where the officers picked up their delicacies, in order to get their chocolate milk and biscuits.

During times of rest, food quality improved momentarily. Rations were generally supplied on time as well. The men behind the lines might still be eating the same bully beef and plum and apple jam, but also on the menu was fresh fruit, a few potatoes and a small helping of cabbage that had been taken from a field, often to the considerable annoyance of the local population. Farmers complained that cows were being milked and that chickens and fruit were being stolen. Yet the farmers earned a decent sum from the sale of coffee, fried eggs and potatoes to the men, and of chicken, eggs and cream to the officers.

Sometimes a village had been abandoned by its inhabitants who had fled the misery of war. 'The food was still on the table,' Henry Allingham recalls. 'As if the people were still there. You could fill your water bottle with water from the tap.'

There were special billets, for example in Poperinge, or 'Pop' as it was called by the British. At the time, it was one of the Belgian towns behind the front not occupied by the Germans. A garrison town with various divisions passing through on their way to the front. It was also a place where troops could spend their time off. Officers used the Skindles Hotel, the Savoy restaurant, Cyril's Dining Rooms and all kinds of clubs. They invited nurses who worked in the field hospitals around Poperinge to have dinner with them and dance. Soldiers ate in simpler establishments.

Poperinge was a pleasant town for officers and soldiers, with restaurants where you could eat well and were served plenty of champagne, Reverend Noel Mellish recalled. He was attached to the Royal Fusiliers as a chaplain. Mellish knew many eating places where you could buy bread and, better still, Belgian chips, which you were given in exchange for bully beef from the trenches or stew from the army's kitchen.

Unique in its set-up in Poperinge was Talbot House, a British 'soldier's club' where both officers and soldiers were able to lead a social life, of a kind, away from the front.

In 1915, the premises were bought by British Chaplain Philip Clayton, nicknamed Tubby, who, together with other clergy, believed that they could be more useful behind the front than in the trenches. Talbot House was officially opened in December that year. On their way to and from the front, the troops could get a meal, and bed and breakfast, irrespective of rank or class. There were bunches of flowers in vases, pictures on the walls, there was a piano and comfortable chairs. The men played games or borrowed a book against their cap as security. The quarters became a kind of second home.

After a visit in 1917, Lieutenant Colonel F.R. Barry wrote:

> For countless men, to step inside that door has been to enter into a new world – the world of all things that are really true – and to know that all without was a long nightmare. Toil as we might, the various recreations rooms we tried to organise for the troops were still conspicuously lacking in something not easy to define. They were far too much like institutions. This was different: it was a home. [...] It recalled us to forgotten things. It brought us face to face with ourselves again, revived in us again the men we were

before our personalities were merged in the impersonal drive of the machine.

Although Talbot House was an Every Man's Club, there were small differences. According to Tubby, the men swarmed through the building between 10 a.m. and 8 p.m., and the officers from 7 a.m. until the leave trains arrived or departed. The officers were asked for a contribution of five francs towards their lodging, whereby the principle prevailed that you had to ask the rich for something in order to pass it on to the poor. For this sum, the officers were given a cup of hot chocolate and Bath Oliver biscuits when they arrived on the 1 a.m. leave train, or a cooked breakfast before their departure at 5 a.m.

Talbot House still exists. It still has its painted sign saying: 'Talbot House, Every-Man's Club.' In between, a time period is given that suggests the war is still ongoing: '1915 ---- ?.'

You can still rent a room. When I enter the building for a night at the end of April, three ladies await me at the entrance with coffee and tea. They are dressed in long black skirts, black silk blouses and black hats: the clothes women wore in Poperinge in 1917. As earlier, in Zonnebeke, a kind of re-enactment is going on here. In one of the rooms, a man is sitting at the piano. Next to him a man in a kilt is singing, to his accompaniment, popular tunes from the war: 'It's a Long Way to Tipperary,' 'Mademoiselle from Armentieres' and 'Over There.' Everywhere, seated or standing, people are singing along. The ladies in black are going back and forth with thermoses of coffee and tea. It is crowded, busy, rather like during the war years, when more than half a million soldiers and officers passed through its doors. Although there weren't any women then. 'Well, perhaps in the evening, secretly,' says one of them, giving me a wink.

The kitchen was situated where there are now toilets, on the ground floor, and was a lot smaller than the present one. However, just like today, you were expected to help yourself. It was fully equipped and was available to the visitors, who had to bring their own ingredients or could buy them in Talbot House. The articles offered for sale constitute a long list: from herring to marmalade, and from curry powder to tins of chocolate milk.

For a few days' leave, the towns behind the front were the best place to regain one's strength. German soldiers and officers sauntered through Brussels and Strasbourg as if it was peacetime. British men did likewise in Poperinge or Amiens. French soldiers preferred to go to Paris, looking at shop windows, gazing at the displayed goods and the women parading the boulevards in their summer dresses. Boulevard de la Chapelle was known as a place where you could easily pick up a sweetheart, for instance. Every soldier and every officer felt pleased as Punch after long days in a trench, which they had climbed out of tired and caked in mud and sweat. That was the place where they had to scrape the tasteless meat and vegetable mash from their mess tins, where the threat of getting injured or killed was ever present. Once behind the lines, it was different. Scrubbed clean, the men would sit around the table in a bar or café. Waitresses would arrive with drinks and plates of food. Bottle after bottle of beer or wine was placed on the table.

Officers preferred to dine in proper restaurants. Like landed gentry, they were seated at tables laid with porcelain plates and silver cutlery, such as in the Godbert restaurant in Amiens, famous at the time for its langoustines, fresh fish, soufflé and roast duck. No watery beer there, but bottles of champagne to wash away the food.

The private soldier drank a glass in a bar or *estaminet*, often a shabby hole in a small barn or in someone's living room. Its furnishings were simple: a wooden table, a few chairs and benches, a bar and a shelf with bottles of alcohol. The men would sit side by side, or stand leaning against the wall. In the British sector of the hinterland, these small establishments were only open part of the day, just like back home in Britain, although the food offered here was omelette with *patat frites* and the men drank white and red wine, a watery type of beer or *café avec*: coffee with brandy. There was sometimes a piano around which people would drink and sing until closing time.

'I called for beer, a glass cost a penny,' British Private Thomas Higgins recorded in his diary:

That was three farthing too much, it was awful. I saw soldiers drinking red wine. I found it was a franc a bottle, so I had one. To my surprise it tasted sour. I saw the others enjoying

it. Theirs was sweet, mine was sour. The secret lay in the fact
if you asked for Vin Rouge, you got it sour. For another 2d
you had some bitron, a very sweet liqueur, mixed with the
wine and it tasted like port.

Private Arthur P. Morris wrote in a letter to his elder brother Herbert
in a bit of a huff that the *estaminets* were only open between 11
a.m. and 1 p.m., and between 6 p.m. and 8 p.m. Morris found
the French beer terrible, but the *vin rouge* and *vin blanc* was to
his liking. Occasionally, he and his companions managed to buy
English beer. For this they paid one dime a glass and at one point
even one franc and 20 centimes for a bottle of Guinness.

Although the *estaminets* were not cheap, and the French
benefitted from the presence of the troops, the men often found
the temptation to spend their money there too great. This worried
Chaplain Noel Mellish, who started his work at an infantry base in
Rouen in the north of France, and saw that every night a new draft
of men had to be taken to the station. Young NCOs, boys often
who had just left school, were detailed to take them there. It was
a 5-kilometre trek straight across the city. There were *estaminets*
everywhere, and it was not unusual for men to enter these for one
last drink. They would frequently not make it to the station and
were eventually punished. Mellish thought it would be a good
idea to assist these young NCOs in accompanying the men to the
station to prevent them from entering the *estaminets*, and to guard
them from the women who feathered their nests on them and their
money and robbed them of their health and honour.

It was a well-intended act by Mellish, even though he did
understand the men. Mellish also considered the troops' rationing
deplorable. They were doled out heavy tins of meat weighing 7lb
each, and he thought it was understandable that they did not want
to lug these around, as they were already carrying an enormous load
on their back, and that most of the meat was immediately given
away to French children calling incessantly: 'Souvenir, souvenir!'

For the British, *estaminets* were under the constant surveillance
of the Royal Military Police. Drunkenness was severely punished.
Minor offences were given a maximum of twenty-eight days field
punishment no.1. This punishment was inflicted on the soldier's

German field kitchen in the reserve line. (Europeana 1914–1918)

German officers enjoying tea, cigars and beer. (Europeana 1914–1918)

entire unit and consisted of extra duties, forfeit of all pay and comforts, no access to the canteen, coupled with a prohibition on leaving the camp.

Private W.G. Bell described the discipline imposed on him for public drunkenness after the war:

> First Field Punishment was no joke. It meant you had to parade in full pack and go up and down the road at the double: *about turn, left, right, left, right, about turn, left, right, left, right.* It was all done under the military police and it was hard going, because you had a full pack, tin helmet and all your stuff, sweating up and down the road. Then you took your pack off and it was up against the wagon wheel. They marched me into a field and twice a day I was strapped up against the wagon wheel of a General Service limber for an hour in the morning and an hour at night.

It could be worse. 'Drunk on active service' or 'drunk when warned for active service' was considered an extremely serious offence, punishable by death. Generally speaking – as was the case with insubordination – offenders were given a prison sentence with forced labour of six months to two years. Often, they were released earlier.

When leave was nearly over and the men had to return to the trenches the next day, they emptied their pockets and spent their last centimes on drink and food. The next day could be their last, after all. During those final hours behind the front, jokes and tall tales were told. Dice flew across the table and games were played for money: bridge, poker, blackjack, kitty nap, pontoon and brag. Those who wanted to play for high stakes played Crown and Anchor, a game that was banned by British Army Command. Men sang songs with dirty lyrics at the top of their voices. It was about more than drinking and eating. They were joined together, freed temporarily from the fears and tensions of the front.

Henry Allingham remembers well the atmosphere in those bars. The hubbub, the singing, the glasses of alcohol that were knocked back and the swearing when a soldier had bet too much in drunken recklessness and lost his pay playing cards.

Does Allingham still know a song that people used to sing then,

I ask? One about food, maybe? Insofar as his stiff body allows, he jumps up and bursts into song:

> Over the Roly-Poly
> Mother used to make
> Roly-Poly which I love
> Roly-Poly that's the stuff
> Now that I think about it
> Makes my tummy ache!
> Oh Lord let me
> I want me mummy
> And the pudding
> She used to make!

After that last line, which he more or less belts out, he claps his hands, shrieks in a shrill voice 'Hey!' and beams at us.

There was one day Allingham did not join the others for a drink, he recalls. A supply wagon loaded with cheese, bread and other delicacies had to be guarded. Why don't you go ahead, he waved his mates towards the *estaminet* and stayed on his own with the supply of food. 'You bet I laid in,' he says. 'Until I was completely full. If they'd found out, I'd probably be facing a firing squad the next morning.'

The men desperately needed the relatively better-quality food behind the lines in order to make up for the lack of proper nourishment in decent quantities at the front.

Although towns like Dunkirk, where Allingham was billeted, were considered to be part of the French front, there were also British Royal Navy air bases. 'Ah … Dunkirk!' grins Allingham. As though life in those days was only hunky-dory, because he never ate awful meals there. If he was still hungry after a solid lunch, the flight mechanic would happily walk forty-five minutes to the French or American troops to join them for a glass of wine and a plate of food.

Allingham explains:

> I was a loner, you see. And just a boy. I was always starving.
> I didn't belong to some unit or other and so I was free to go
> where I wanted during leave. I took advantage of that, even

though I risked being court-martialled, because I sometimes left my post even on non-leave days. I would get to an American field kitchen, and they would say help yourself to as much as you like. I had to take with me what I couldn't finish. I stuffed myself there. Those Yanks were very kind and generous, that's in their nature. That's why I was given so much to eat by them. With the French it was no different. They had plenty of red wine. Delicious! I was given salmon. Three decent meals a day. Three!

While the Allies could afford to pull back each division after a few days at the front, the Germans had to stay on the front line with increasing frequency. The British and French armies had more men in active service at their disposal and were therefore able to grant more leave than the Germans.

What's more, as the war progressed, there was increasingly little doing for the Germans behind the front. Cities such as Lille, Metz, Nancy, Cambrai and Rheims were partly destroyed and had but a smidgen of the gaiety of Paris or Amiens. Besides, in these cities, the amount of available food decreased by the month.

Behind the front, in the regions of France and Belgium occupied by the Germans, every strip of soil, from road verges to city parks, was used for growing food. Flowers were no longer allowed to be grown and owners of large country estates were ordered to convert their lawns into potato fields. Parks became kitchen gardens.

'It's extraordinary how in every location around the city in between the new houses and on the landscaped ring boulevards, use is now made of the smallest strip of land or unsold building lot, where there was formerly grit or vegetable waste, shards of glass and earthenware, and amongst which the nettle flourished,' Virginie Loveling from Ghent wrote in her war diary in May 1915. 'Potatoes are coming up strong and flourishing. On request, the unemployed have each been given a plot from available land, without rent. The produce is theirs.'

At the beginning of the war in Belgium, 31,000 families together cultivated 1,700 hectares of land. At the end of the war, these numbers had increased to 180,000 families and 5,000 hectares. The German occupier stimulated cultivation of the soil with *De landbouwer* (*The Farmer*), a weekly magazine that was sold in Belgium in conjunction with the German General Government. The publication included tips for the amateur market gardener. It recommended using all 'withered leaves and all kinds of animal and plant waste' as compost. In later editions, the magazine advised, amongst other things, that ash from fires, soot from chimneys and the contents of sewers should be used for this purpose.

With the consent of the Germans, a small group of Belgians set up the *Nationaal Hulp- en Voedingskomiteit* (National Relief and Food Committee) in 1915. The NHVC, which took care of the distribution of imported food articles and other relief supplies, was actively involved in the planning and organisation of the production of food in occupied territories. It also published practical guides about how to achieve better vegetable and potato crops.

However, intensive cultivation led to soil exhaustion. Bad weather and a shortage of fertiliser meant yields fell far short of what was actually needed.

As the war progressed, despite all efforts, there was increasingly less for the German troops to look forward to when they were spending a few days behind the front to rest. In the Allied part of the front, a lively trade sprung up, but on the German side there was not all that much to buy. In the description of a German officer:

> In the afternoon I rode on horseback to Roeselare. Its inhabitants have returned in dribs and drabs although the town is within reach of enemy fire. There is a butcher, with a few sausages on offer. In another shop there are three tins of mushrooms, a few tins of sardines and some bottles of salad oil. A few hours later I managed to ride off with a basketful of shopping. I passed a farm with turkeys wandering around. I exchanged one turkey for a loaf of bread which would be delivered the following morning by a dragoon. We looked forward to the turkey, the farmer to his bread. After a lot of to-ing and fro-ing we managed to agree with another farmer that he would supply milk.

Although German soldiers were not able to get hold of very much in northern France and Flanders, the food there was better than at home and much better in terms of quantity than the food the army could supply the men. 'In the town all the shops were open. There was sewing cotton, and bread rolls were for sale. I immediately bought a few and ate a piece of real ginger cake in a bakery. We had not been able to buy these in Germany for years,' Ludwig Renn wrote in his book *Krieg* (*War*).

German NCO Carl Heller also purchased items which were either no longer available in Germany or which had been rationed for a long time. 'The soldiers bought articles such as soap, sewing thread, jam, and so on, obviously for extortionate prices, and sent these home,' he wrote in his diary. And later:

> In the French shops we were still able to buy the odd thing. In particular 'foodstuffs' were snapped up because our own food was truly awful and we were constantly starving. The only 'foodstuffs' offered for sale was a kind of biscuit made with flour which they sold to us for a 'giveaway' price of one mark a piece. And yet they were bought and many a person spent all his money on them. Our daily ration when we were stood down, usually consisted of 300g bread and a litre of thin soup, generally made with turnip, cabbage or dried vegetables. The officers had their own separate kitchen into which many a piece of meat or potato actually intended for the men disappeared. This constant hunger made us embittered and despondent at times. For a civilian who executed his daily work and had his rest at night, this ration was preciously meagre. For a soldier at the front who when lying in position had no rest, day or night, it was far too little. All the time we thought of nothing but food and impatiently awaited the hour that the kitchen would arrive. We ate the bread and soup immediately and had to wait for 24 hours, sometimes 48 hours before a new supply would arrive.

Behind the front, shopkeepers seized their chance with the lack of foodstuffs. Amongst all the misery, the craving for the best food and drink was great, and so the prices went up. On the Allied side, prices were also driven up by the arrival of the Americans and Canadians, who were paid two to three times more than the British and French, and who were also prepared to spend more money.

Of the Allied troops, the French were the worst off. Until the middle of 1917, no canteens or other reception facilities had been set up for these men. British soldiers going home on leave were fed at the large railway stations in canteens run by women. At Victoria Station, waiting crowds gave out cigarettes and chocolate to the soldiers and officers. When the French went home for a few days, they stood shivering in the cold at the railway stations, lodged for a few days in a town where they did not know a soul, to return to the front without actually having been home. Rail transport was arranged so badly that their leave was finished before they had even managed to arrive at their destination. Cafés, meanwhile, were prohibited from serving the men alcohol between 11 a.m. and 5 p.m. But there was more that led to disaffection: the unremitting losses, bad accommodation, exhaustion and the attacks felt to be pointless.

All this changed after the debacle in 1917, which had been caused by the new commander-in-chief, Robert Nivelle. Every year previously, offensive after offensive had led to hundreds of thousands of casualties. But a new disaster presented itself. On 16 April 1917, Nivelle announced an attack on the German positions on the River Aisne which, he believed, would bring the war to a glorious close within fourteen days. 'The hour has come! Confidence! Courage! Long live France!' his general orders declared.

On that same cold and rainy day, the French *poilus* (infantry soldiers), under orders from their Army Command, were meant to take the enemy positions following heavy shooting at the German lines. Unprotected, they ran up the hill and were thus easy targets for the Germans and their machine guns. The offensive ended in a bloodbath. For more than three weeks, the French tried to break through the front. In that short time, more than 140,000 were injured or killed.

The survivors were different from those in 1914, who allowed themselves to be led to the slaughter like lambs. Now, they were men who wrote anti-militaristic and pacifist pamphlets. They were soldiers who were critical of the command's incompetence and indifference. Men who criticised the clothes they were handed and the bad arrangements for leave. And men who complained about the food.

Many a time a riot would break out when soldiers were used as cannon fodder, as the men behind the front experienced the offensive. They sang inflammatory songs and waved red flags. Scattered throughout the trenches, men sat stoically with their arms crossed. They refused to take even one step towards the front line. A French soldier wrote:

> After 18 days on the front line we went into reserve at 3 a.m. on the 10th of April. That same night we had to go back to do work on the front line. We could barely stand up. We refused. They threatened to court-martial us, but that did not scare us. They could not make us more miserable than we already were. Because in the trench, we each had no more than a little bit of meat and a small tin of sardines and a cup of butter which we had to share between 14 men! On top of that, we were expected to do a full-week shift without sleep on the front line. If they want us to stay in the trench, they might as well give us poison.

French Army Command found the cause for the mutiny above all in the living conditions of the soldiers: in the poor pay, the awful lodgings during leave and the meagre rations. Commander-in-Chief Nivelle was dismissed; General Pétain was appointed in his place. The first thing he did on 19 May 1917 was to issue directive no. 1: no more unnecessary offensives. Moreover, the arrangements for leave improved under his command. The number of days' leave increased from seven to ten. Cooks stirring the pots in the field kitchens were given additional training in a genuine cookery school, and the men were entitled to more and better-quality wine: half a litre a day. *Foyers du soldats* were set up, a joint service programme between the French Army and the American Young Men's Christian Association (YMCA), where men returning home were given food and drink when there was a delay.

'It is nine o'clock and we are opening for the day. Already there waits a crowd of shivering Poilus [sic] very eager for the hot coffee which is ready in a huge "marmite",' poet Robert Laurence Binyon recalled, who worked as a volunteer under the auspices of the British Committee of the French Cross in one of the newly opened canteens. 'A bowl of coffee and a crust of bread content the abstemious Frenchman. […] As is the rule in all their canteens, nothing may be charged for.' In the evening, every table in the room would be occupied with men playing games who would be served chocolate at quarter to eight. 'Bowls were filled and emptied, washed and refilled again and again.' Closing time was 8 p.m., just like the cafés in the town.

As the war continued, the need grew to formalise supplies of extras such as chocolate, pens, writing paper, tins of fruit and other articles of food. Logistics, distribution and relief was organised. The armies became more or less self-sufficient, as if they were never going to leave.

At the beginning of 1915, the British created the Canteen and Mess Co-operative Society, and opened a branch in France. Dozens of canteens were set up behind the front in quick succession, where the men found a safe haven. In 1918, there were almost 300. There were other private institutions which assumed responsibility for some of the care of the troops. These included the Queen Mary's Army Auxiliary Corps, which sent some 6,000 women to France to cook for the men in canteens behind the front.

Religious organisations also entered the scene behind the front, the YMCA for example, which opened its first accommodation as early as November 1914 in the French port of Le Havre; this is where the British disembarked after their crossing from England. Other centres followed, such as those in Rouen, Boulogne, Calais, Paris, Abbeville and Dunkirk. Midway through 1915, the YMCA was also allowed to pitch marquees behind the front. Hot drinks, biscuits, cakes, writing paper and cigarettes were sold. Alongside the YMCA, canteen reception facilities for the British troops, managed by the Church Army Canteen and the Church of Scotland, also materialised. The Catholic Club, The Church Army, the Scottish Churches' Huts, the Christian Association, the Club Huts, the Catholic Women's League, the Soldiers' Christian Association, the Wesleyan Soldiers' Institute and the Salvation Army all set up relief facilities. In the end, you would not have been able to escape them. There was not only food; people played music and stories from the Bible were told.

In contrast to the British, the Germans were not able to offer much. Christian organisations were active, but they only operated in Germany. With the scarce resources available back home, they tried to help the men from their homeland. The few places that were set up for the soldiers and officers behind the front were nevertheless no less welcome. Ernst Jünger describes such a facility in *In Stahlgewittern* (*Storm of Steel*):

> Douchy, where the 73rd Rifles were billeted, was a medium-sized village, that had not suffered much from the war at that point. This place, nestled on the hilly ground of Artois, became, over the 18 months of stationary warfare in that region, a kind of second garrison to the regiment, a place of rest and recreation after gruelling days of fighting and working on the front line. [...] For the non-active hours, Douchy had much to offer. Many bars still had plenty of food and drink; there was a reading room, a coffee bar and, later on, a cinema was set up in a large barn. The officers enjoyed an excellently equipped mess-room and a bowling alley in the rectory garden. There were regular company parties, in which officers and men, in the timeless German fashion, competed with each other in drinking. Not to forget the killing days, for which the company pigs, kept fat on the scraps from the field kitchens, bit the dust.

During the war, the US Army Organisation officially did not provide official entertainment or religious services for its soldiers and officers. This was also covered by civilian organisations such as the American division of the YMCA, the Catholic Knights of Columbus, the Jewish Welfare Board, the National Catholic War Council, the American Salvation Army and the American Red Cross. The latter had set up 130 canteens in France over a period of twenty months, in which a total of well over 15 million men had been given food and drink: more than 6 million meals and almost 13 million mugs of coffee, hot chocolate and other drinks. In March 1918, the first month they were in France, the Knights of Columbus distributed as many as 37,719 bars of chocolate and 25,250 packets of chewing gum.

In 1917, the YMCA was authorised by American General Pershing to work for the social, psychological, intellectual and moral well-being of the troops. During the war, and during the post-war occupation of Germany, the YMCA ran forty-four workshops for the production of cakes and sweets, and some 4,000 canteens or huts, as they were called at the time. Later in the war, the Christian organisation also created almost 1,500 huts for French troops. The word 'hut' suggests a small and makeshift structure, but nothing could be further from the truth. The YMCA did it the American way: on a grand scale. Some of the huts could accommodate more than 500 men.

Together with the US Army, the YMCA also erected thirty-three leave centres, where a total of 300,000 men were able to stay during the war. The centres were located in the most diverse regions in France: the Alps, on the Mediterranean, in the Pyrenees, Nice and Monte Carlo. World-famous casinos were rented by the Christian organisation and remodelled as officers' clubs. On offer were a bed and dinner, sight-seeing tours and theatre visits.

Katharine Morse was one of the American YMCA volunteers in France. She ran several canteens, including one in Saint-Thiebault, where the regiment's headquarters were based.

Back of the wash-house lies a group of long French barracks, and here lives Company A of the – Regiment, infantry and 'regulars.' Beyond the mess-hall is the hut, a French *abri* tent with double walls. Ducking under the fly, one finds oneself in a long rectangular canvas room, lighted by a dozen little isinglass windows. The room is filled with folding wooden chairs and long ink-stained tables over which are scattered writing materials, games and well-worn magazines. Opposite the door, at the far end, is the canteen counter, a shelf of books at one side, a Victrola [a record player] and a bulletin board, to which cartoons and clippings are tacked, on the other. Back of the counter on the wall, held in place by safety pins, are the hut's only decorations, four of the gorgeous French war posters brought with me from Paris. There are two stoves resembling umbrella-stands for heating in the main part of the hut and behind the counter another, about the size and shape of a man's derby hat, on which I must make my hot chocolate [...]. For the rest, the hut is equipped with a wheezy old piano, a set of parlour billiards, and a man secretary. It is invariably dense with smoke, part wood and part tobacco, and usually crowded with boys.

The men arranged their post and banking affairs, and bought all kinds of items such as toiletries, tobacco and food. While other welfare organisations supplied free cigarettes and confectionery, these had to be paid for at the YMCA, to the men's annoyance. To them, the letters YMCA stood for 'You Must Come Across': you had to cough up. Payment was welcome in any currency; the YMCA volunteers weren't fussy. Morse wrote: 'French money, Belgian money, Swiss money, English money, Spanish money, Italian money, Greek money, Canadian money, Luxembourg money, Indo-Chinese money, money from Argentine Republic, and yesterday a German mark even, all come across the counter and go into the till without comment.'

Once a week, the YMCA showed a film, and performances were programmed jointly by American and French men: a soldier who sang 'Papa Eating Noodle Soup,' or a French *poilu* crooning the dramatic ballad 'Il y a moyen de coucher avec.' Once a week, a lady would come to Morse's hut to teach the American troops French. According to Morse:

> There were two lessons to be sure in which they took a degree of interest: the lessons about buying and counting money, and the lessons about food and drink. But when they had once learned to ask the price of things and to understand the answer, and had learned the words for eggs, bread, butter, beer, ham, beefsteak, chicken and French fried potatoes, their interest lapsed until it became positive boredom.

Above all, the men were encouraged to feel at home at the YMCA and other organisations. But, as ever, food came first. Most important to them were the three Cs: chocolate, coffee and cigarettes.

A weekly menu in Morse 's canteen looked like this:

Sunday   Hot chocolate and cookies
            Religious Service with special music
            Song Service. More chocolate.

Monday	French Classes
	Hot chocolate and jam sandwiches
Tuesday	Boxing and Wrestling Matches
	Hot chocolate and sardine sandwiches
Wednesday	Band Concert
	Hot chocolate and jam sandwiches
Thursday	Movies
	Hot chocolate and cookies
Friday	Sing Fest with Solos
	Hot chocolate and jam sandwiches
Saturday	Stunt Programme
	Canned fruit and cookies

As far as food was concerned, it was rather monotonous. As Morse lamented in one of her letters:

> If my fairy god-mother should lend me her magic wand, the very first thing I would wish for would be a dinner, a real dinner just like Mother used to cook, for Company A. It would start with turkey and cranberry sauce and end with several kinds of pie, ice-cream and chocolate layer cake [...]. Such a meal I am sure would do more to raise the morale of Company A than the news of a smashing allied victory. It is the everlasting sameness, the perpetual reiteration of a certain few articles of food, I suppose, that makes the boys 'chow' so depressing.

The men were overjoyed when they saw the kind of products William C. Levere had displayed on his table in his YMCA hut. Like Morse, Levere was one of the 13,000 volunteers who went to work in France for the YMCA during the war. His station was a hut in the Vosges. There, Levere covered a table with coloured tissue paper, which he had found in boxes as wrapping for French *petits-beurre* biscuits. On top of this coloured paper he laid out the wares he had been issued by the US Army or which he had bought himself: some chocolate bars, tins of sardines, packets of dried figs, tins of jam, packets of salted peanuts, chewing gum, two kinds of razor blades, Chesterfield cigarettes, tobacco and cigarette papers.

It wasn't much, Levere wrote in his memoirs, but it was a feast in the eyes of the American soldiers. In order not to miss out, from the first day, they crowded around the stand immediately after their mess and emptied their purses.

The best thing, according to Levere, would be to make doughnuts. A battalion cook in the area had a recipe. Only when the men stuck their teeth in the bun would they truly feel at home, Levere believed. The US Army soon supplied him with a chariot full of flour, sugar, lard and baking powder. On a cold January afternoon, the men were queuing up for their dinner.

'It swelled the heart to look at their fine New England faces,' Levere wrote in his memoirs. 'Clear, honourable and with all the eagerness of a boy knocking at the pantry door at home. If the people in America could have seen them at that moment! […] Just to think that a doughnut could create such a furore! There was no brooking their impatience. […] They demanded their right. They demanded doughnuts.'

Levere was not the first person to have brought doughnuts to the troops far from home. A few months earlier, the 'doughnut dollies' from the American Salvation Army had preceded him. In October 1917, Salvation Army volunteers Helen Purviance and Margaret Sheldon were stationed in the French town of Montiers-sur-Saulx. It had been raining non-stop for thirty-six days and everything looked grim and grey. With the prospect that the soldiers would be stuck in the damp for a while longer yet, the ladies agreed to give them some real American cooking. Supplies had run low, however, and it was difficult to buy good-quality ingredients that would serve their purpose in the local shops. The only things they could find were flour, sugar, lard, baking powder, cinnamon and tinned milk. They could make pancakes with this, but these would not taste good cold and without syrup. So they arrived at doughnuts.

'Literally on my knees I prayed in front of the small stove that somehow this home touch would do more for the men than satisfy a physical hunger,' Purviance later recalled.

Remembering the Salvation Army, Henry Allingham rubs his hands. The people who worked there had their hearts in the right place, he believes. 'I remember it well. When the boys came back from the front, exhausted and hungry, after a long march from the front line, they'd be standing there. Clutching fresh coffee and hot chocolate. Those boys came home, that's how it felt.'

In March 1918, Henry Allingham had left his post in France and had been stationed near Ypres. The Germans had just launched their spring offensives. 'That month they broke through at Ploegsteert,' the veteran recounts. 'But they had soon run out of shells, ammunition and food. We pushed them back and cut them off at Ypres.'

Allingham falls silent and rubs his hands on his flannel trousers, as if he wants to ponder for a moment and retrieve the memory of all those decades ago.

'While we chased them, further past Ypres, sometimes there was more than enough food for us, at other times very little,' he finally says. 'But we always had something. I never starved.'

When the conversation with Allingham is finished, we decide to have lunch somewhere local. Another slow shuffle through the living room follows. Coat on again, left foot in midnight blue slipper, scarf and cap on and into the car. Once inside the restaurant, few people look up when the decorated Allingham is wheeled in in his wheelchair. He is clearly a regular and knows the menu. Allingham will have his usual: a hearty portion of meat, potatoes, carrots and broccoli.

He does not have much time to talk while he is eating. His eyes focused on his plate and the glass in front of it. Every so often he folds his hands over his stomach and chews his food with his eyes closed. He has emptied his plate before the rest of the party.

Once he has finished eating, Allingham puts down his cutlery, gives his stomach a satisfied rub and says: 'The food I had in France may have been good, but oh boy, you can't beat home cooking.'

BISCUIT DONUTS (for one hundred men)

Ingredients
12 lbs biscuits
3 lbs dripping
2 lbs sugar
1 tin of milk
½ oz salt
lime juice to flavour
a little flour

Preparation
Powder the biscuits, and add salt, dripping, sugar and flour and mix well together. Make a hollow in the centre, and add milk and lime juice flavouring. Mix into a stiff dough. Roll out and cut into round cakes. Fry in hot fat until brown. Jam should be served with them for tea meal.

Cooking in the Field

MACARONI

Macaroni is not supplied by the Commissariat, but delicious cheese is. The thing that takes least time in the preparation of macaroni is cheese.

Ingredients

125 g macaroni per person (the present price is 1 franc per kilo)
cheese
1.5 kg lard
pepper
salt

Preparation

Push half of the cheese through the mincer. This will be used to make a tasty macaroni. Drop the macaroni, which has been divided into 5 to 10 cm pieces, in the pot in which plenty of salted water is boiling.

Remove the pot from the heat once it has been cooked and allow the macaroni to drain. Put 1.5 kg of lard (supplied by the state free of charge) in the empty pot. When it has melted, add the macaroni and cheese. Pepper, salt and stir continually; as soon as the macaroni has separated in threads, remove it from the heat and place it in a galvanised kettle until it is served.

Handboek van den kok te Velde (*Handbook for the Field Cook*)

MUTTON STEW

Ingredients
mutton
1.5 kg lard
turnips
potatoes
pepper
salt
thyme
bay leaf

Preparation
Should the occasion present itself, do not fail to make a fine mutton stew. Braise the supplied mutton in 1.5 kg of lard. For each person in the mess add 200 g of turnips; allow to simmer for 15 minutes, add your potatoes (400 g per head) and warm water until everything is covered. Pepper, salt, and a little thyme and 2 bay leaves. Simmer for 45 minutes.

Handboek van den kok te Velde (*Handbook for the Field Cook*)

MINCEMEAT SAUSAGES

Ingredients
raw meat
lard

Preparation
Prepare as for minced meat, shape into portions and fry in hot lard.

Anweisungen für Truppenküchen (Instructions for Soldiers' Kitchens)

HEART

Ingredients
heart
vinegar
mushrooms
soup greens
herbs
herb vinegar

Preparation
Cut the heart along its side, remove the heart chambers, blood clots and blood vessels. Place the heart in some vinegar, mushrooms and herbs, if possible. Braise everything in lard, add soup greens, herb vinegar and water, simmer until done.

Die Gulaschkanone (The Goulash Cannon)

EAT LESS MEAT
FOOD SHORTAGES IN BRITAIN

'For a hundred years we in this island have been living immune from danger, thanks to our Fleet and to the power of our nation, though this power has been dearly bought by the sacrifices of our forefathers,' Georgina Lee wrote on 26 August, at the beginning of the war, in the diary she kept for her nine-month-old son Harry. 'We believe in the ultimate result, for the nation is determined to go on fighting until victory is achieved. But what suspense there is from day to day as to the fate of and movements of our Army.'

During the war, London was only 150 kilometres away from the battle lines. And even though it was separated by a sea, the artillery was sometimes audible in the British capital, for example during the preliminary British shelling of the German positions before the Battle of the Somme in 1916.

For the first time in a hundred years, war made itself very much felt to the people of London. First, there were the boys and men who went to the front and were killed in their hundreds of thousands or who came back with injuries. At the end of August 1914, the first contingent to be sent to the front consisted of professional soldiers. An army of 100,000 men that proved to be insufficient in size after just a few weeks. This led to a country-wide recruitment appeal for more men to join the forces. Everywhere posters appeared with the picture of the Minister of War, Lord Kitchener, pointing his finger to show the nation how serious things were. The poster said: 'Britons, Your Country Needs You, Join Your Country's Army!' Placards were affixed to taxis, buses and public buildings, summoning men, in red letters, to present themselves at the front. The men who did not do this had a white flower pinned to the lapel of their jacket by women so that they could be identified as cowards. Thus, social pressure forced them to join the forces after all.

After those first weeks of the war, London was subjected to a blackout to prevent air strikes by German Zeppelins and airplanes. Lit shop windows, as well as illuminated external advertising signs, were no longer allowed. Street lanterns were turned off or dimmed. Train and bus windows were fitted with curtains.

This could not stop Zeppelins attacking London in 1917 and 1918 from bases along the Belgian coast. During these attacks, a total of 800 civilians were killed and 1,500 injured. But more than anything, the fear had taken hold that the war with all its horrors had got so close. 'I saw today the results of Sunday night's awful bomb,' Lee wrote on 19 February 1918 in her diary:

> The devastation is terrible. One of the lovely old residences in the grounds of the Royal Hospital Chelsea, to the left of the beautiful Chapel façade, was sliced in half by a bomb of terrific force, and literally crumbled to dust.
>
> Red bricks and splinters of wood littered the grounds where bits of carpet, tiny fragments of wool out of mattresses hung on the shrubs along the outside railings, over the heads of the people watching in awestruck silence as the workmen cleared the mountains of debris. Two of the five children were found impaled on the railings, dead. The bodies of the Father, Mother and lady guest were also found in the wreckage. The other three children were rescued unhurt.
>
> Every house in Leonard's Terrace and Burton Court beyond the great open military ground, had its windows blown out. All the buildings in the precincts of the Royal Hospital Grounds were coated with yellow dust. Their windows were mostly broken, the latticed panes of the Chapel included. It gave them a sinister desolate appearance.

Not only that, London was also facing a food problem during the war years. The United Kingdom did not have any economic or industrial plans ready for when a war would break out. Once the war was underway, the government did not see any need to draw these up. The thinking was that the fighting would be over by Christmas. Moreover, to reassure the population, the government stated in August 1914 that agricultural supplies from the entire

American continent were available to the nation. In so doing, the British made themselves almost completely dependent on imports.

The government announcement did not stop a pound of imported meat already costing a penny more during the first months of the war. A 4lb loaf of bread soon cost eightpence more. In order to discourage panic and stockpiling through fear of food shortages, shopkeepers and a group of advertisers came up with the slogan 'Business as usual.' But people did stock up: 'People have lost their heads, and all are seeking to hoard food!' Lee observed at the beginning of the war:

> This is a fatal mistake, as it creates a famine. Also an enormous rise in prices, which is most unfair for the rest of the community. I hear of one woman who ordered £500 worth of groceries at Harrods […]. The Bishop of London in a sermon a few days later said nobody, however rich, should have more than two courses for dinner.

Although there was virtually full employment and many people therefore had an income to support themselves, this was less and less of a consolation as the war proceeded. In February 1915, the Trades Union Congress published a pamphlet in which it argued that, relatively, the value of people's income was falling because of the rising price of food, especially staples such as wheat and meat. According to the unions, the price of wheat had gone up by 72 per cent compared to what it had cost on average in 1914. Barley and oats had also become 40 and 34 per cent more expensive, respectively. Fish had become so costly that the Archbishop of Westminster gave his parishioners permission to eat meat substitutes that were cheaper than fish.

A few months later, the government called on the population to be frugal when buying food. 'Meat only once a day should be the limit for each household,' wrote Georgina Lee. 'No lamb or veal is to be killed throughout the Country.'

That month, there was a strike in the Welsh coal mines, an important supplier of fuel to the arms industry: 300,000 men walked out. As a result, the steel works had to close temporarily, as they were not able to operate without coal. Earlier, workers in arms factories had laid down their tools for higher wages. After a few weeks, the mineworkers' demands were met and coal production could resume. During the autumn of 1915, fuel was rationed and meatless days were introduced.

At the time, a war recipe book was already available in the British shops: *The Belgian Cook Book*. It featured recipes by Belgian refugees who had sought safety in the United Kingdom in large numbers. Part of the proceeds of the book went to the Belgian Relief Fund, which had its headquarters in London. This fund dedicated itself to helping the Belgian population, which was suffering as a result of the war. The book included simple and cheap recipes for Flemish soup, Dutch herring, Belgian carrots, cheese soufflé and beef with apricots, amongst others. Recipes which, its editor claimed, could be of use in the British wartime kitchen.

In May 1915, the Germans launched submarines in the British waters in order to shell not only naval but also merchant navy ships. This too affected food supplies, because less could be landed at ports. Not a year later, the German navy sank on average more than 300,000 tonnes of ships' stores per month.

The fact that global harvests failed as well did not make the situation around food supplies any easier, especially now that the United Kingdom had made itself dependent on the United States through its food imports.

In December 1916, of necessity, a Ministry of Food had to be set up in the United Kingdom. Shortly afterwards, in February 1917, this ministry called on the British people to live voluntarily on a ration of bread, meat and sugar. The advice was to eat no more than 1,250g of meat, 1,750g of bread and 350g of sugar per person per week. In addition, the duties on tea and beer were increased sharply. Hunting protected game for consumption was allowed from that month onwards, in order to meet people part of the way as well as to prevent the animals from eating the corn in the fields.

During that time, it was also decided to cultivate vacant land in towns and cities for agricultural use, as farming yields had plummeted. One of the reasons for this was that many farm workers were at the front. A shortage of labour meant less could be produced. Besides, many horses had been requisitioned by the army and could no longer be deployed on the land. For that reason, some farmers bought a tractor in order to take over their work. Thus, a start was made with the industrialisation of agriculture: towards the end of 1917 there were 3,500 tractors in private ownership and a further 1,500 tractors worked the land in public service, according to the British government.

Steam-driven ploughs had already existed and had been used in the fields. However, only half of the 500 available ploughs in the United Kingdom were available for use during the initial stages of the war. Some were under repair, but most were stored in barns because no one knew how to operate them; the men who did know how to do this were at the front. The Food Production Department tracked down 300 of them, brought them home and made them repair the ploughs. This meant that practically all agricultural equipment was available for use again by the end of 1917. The area that was ploughed under steam extended to almost 500,000 hectares.

Women, children and prisoners of war also worked on the land. But, like the machines, they were not able to replace all the absent agricultural workers. This was sufficient reason for the Food Production Department to bring back home from the front 2,000 men skilled in using the scythe to help bring in the harvest.

When Germany announced an unrestricted submarine war on 1 February 1917, food supplies in Britain declined even further. Merchant navy or navy, Allied or neutral – all of a sudden, all ships were being attacked. That month, 230 boats were sunk by German torpedoes. A month later, more than 5 tonnes of goods were torpedoed to the bottom of the sea: a record. Fewer and fewer ships, and therefore less food, reached the island.

During that time, Georgina Lee's diary entries acquired an ever-grimmer tone. With increasing frequency she noted that there was a lack of food. Hunger became a real anxiety. On 13 February 1917 she wrote:

I have just finished my frugal tea all alone in the drawing-room. Formerly I should have felt disgracefully mean – a small rack of toast, the loaf (no cut bread and butter), a little butter and jam, no vestige of cake, scone or buns to offer the casual visitor. The meanness now lies in purchasing these luxuries. I feel dishonest at going into the cake shops, unless I am expecting someone for certain. The funny thing is that this economy is not for the sake of saving one's pocket. We have no longer to think in pennies or shillings, but in ounces and pounds. Whatever I can save in terms of bread and flour in my household, leaves the more for those who mainly live on these two essentials. Shall we ever outlive this urgency of economising the foods stuffs for the sake of everybody?

Ten days later, Lee wrote:

Today the new food restrictions have burst upon like a bombshell! As I walked into Mrs Byrne's drawing-room to tea this afternoon, I found her and three astounded ladies poring over the evening paper announcing the drastic measures which Lloyd George's Government have imposed, 'to avoid disaster,' says Lloyd George in his speech.

These measures should have been taken 2 years ago. They are now absolutely essential. We are to give up importing tea, coffee and cocoa […]. The supply of food in the country is lower than it has ever been […]. There are other restrictions, but these hit the housewife hardest. For a long time past, since the war started in fact, I have kept no stores in the house except for a week's requirements; and if everybody did the same it would be much fairer. But there is a great deal of hoarding going on.

In April 1917, German U-boats sank 373 British ships and boats from neutral countries. On 18 April, Lee wrote about the consequences of this: 'The bread question is getting more and more serious. We are all begged now to save one more pound of flour per week, making 2lbs flour our ration. We can eat one slice of bread at breakfast, but generally have a half-slice. We make up with oatcake and barley scones.'

As a result of food shortages, and rising prices that same month, 750,000 workers went on strike. The reason this time was again lack of food and high prices. In May 1917, Lee wrote:

The food question becomes daily more acute. More and more

Milking the cows. (In Flanders Fields Museum)

Indian soldiers eating Naan bread. (In Flanders Fields Museum)

shipping is being destroyed by German U Boats. It seems really to be a race now as to whether we can bring Germany to her knees before we get starved out. When one asks for any particular item in the shops, one is told 'none to be had.' Cereals of all sorts, macaroni, raisins etc. are 3 or 4 times the old price [...]. Bananas have become unprocurable, and with oranges at 3d each and small apples 4d, it is difficult to obtain fruit. The import of all these foreign items has practically ceased. We never realised now how England's market supplies were so dependent on foreign lands.

The government took new initiatives to help the population. On 21 May 1917, England's first soup kitchen opened. Queen Mary and her daughter, also named Mary, handed out portions of food. On the menu were rhubarb, sausages, mash, minced meat with mash, fruit and pudding.

A few days later, the British Food Controller wrote in a letter to the head of every household in England that they should reduce their consumption of bread. Everyone should eat less, and no food should go to waste. If the enemy were to succeed in starving the British, the Food Controller argued, the soldiers would have died in vain. He therefore asked the people to restrain themselves 'in the national interest' until the next harvest could be brought in. Every mother had to see to it that her family made sacrifices and that not a crust of bread was unused.

Increasingly often, appeals were made to eat less. There were posters everywhere saying 'The Kitchen is the key to Victory, Eat Less Bread.' And because 48 million slices of bread were said to be wasted every day, the Ministry of Food also distributed a flyer featuring a Mr Slice O'Bread: 'I am "the bit left over"; the slice eaten absent-mindedly when I really wasn't needed; I am the waste crust. If you had collected me and my companions for a whole week you would find that we amounted to 9,380 tons of good bread – WASTED. Two Shiploads of good Bread!' Similarly, it was explained that if every Briton was to save one teaspoon of breadcrumbs, this would yield a total of 40,000 tonnes of bread per year.

In the wake of *The Belgian Cook Book*, new war recipes appeared that would allow the British people to put on the table a complete and nutritious meal using limited means. Companies advised civilians through advertisements in the newspapers; Oxo printed a recipe for war pudding in the daily papers, for instance. Cookery books were published, such as *Flourless Puddings*, *The Allies' Cook Book*, *The Cow and Milk Book* and *The Eat-Less-Meat Book*, the latter written by Dorothy C. Peel.

Peel brought out her book to 'help those people who wish to do their duty to their country' and to make sure that 'every atom of food' was utilised 'as intelligently as possible': 'Only a great and united effort can ensure that the rising generation and the generation yet unborn shall receive their proper nourishment in the months ahead of us,' Peel wrote.

The supply of food had become such a huge problem in May 1917 that the House of Commons began to get increasingly worried. The shortage of food meant that people formed long queues outside the shops for white bread, meat, margarine, sugar, potatoes and tea. And it was not only ordinary people who had to queue for hours; the shopkeepers themselves did too; they waited in their hundreds outside wholesalers for their wares.

One Mrs M. Hall, a munitions worker, recalled after the war how difficult it had been to buy food:

> I remember going into a shop after not having milk for seven days and they said, 'If you can produce a baby you can have milk' – that was it! I went into a butcher's shop to get some meat because we were just beginning to be rationed and I said, 'That looks like cat.' And he said, 'It is.' I couldn't face that.

The rising prices only exacerbated the food problem. British people found it ever harder to buy their food. One of the causes was that some of the suppliers kept their prices artificially high; they released provisions in dribs and drabs, and held back entire stocks. Good reason for the Mayor of Leicester to quote from the Book of Proverbs during a protest demonstration about high prices: 'He that withholdeth corn, the people shall curse him: but blessing shall be upon the head that selleth it.'

The government introduced all kinds of measures to try and

prevent producers and retailers from selling their goods at too high a price. In September 1917, a farmer was given a fine of £5,500 for selling large quantities of potatoes above the fixed maximum price, for instance. Another was sent to prison for two months and fined £3,700 for a similar offence. Shopkeepers, too, would be penalised if they procured potatoes for a higher sum than the fixed price. If they refused to sell articles to people who were not regular customers, they would likewise be fined.

Retailers who crossed the line too often could look forward to a prison sentence. A London grocer, charged with selling margarine above the fixed price, said: 'It is my shop, my margarine and I shall do what I like with it.' He was fined £50 and imprisoned for six weeks.

Feeding animals food that was fit for human consumption also became an offence. A woman from Dover who gave her fourteen dogs bread and milk was fined £5. A lady from Wales had to pay £20 for giving meat to her St Bernard. A farmer from Lincolnshire was punished for wasting food: he had bought seven cheap cakes in an army canteen and fed these to his pigs; when two police officers discovered the cakes in the swill tub, he was given a fine of £10. Another farmer from Yorkshire fared even worse: he was jailed for three months for feeding bread to his cows.

The shortage of food not only led to high prices, but also to unrest amongst workers' organisations. In August 1917, 50,000 mine workers in Lanarkshire walked out for one day. In a meeting of miners and railway workers in Nottingham a month later, it was decided to call on the Food Controller to 'gather all the food in the country and distribute this fairly and according to need amongst the people, as communists would do.' In Coventry, strike action against food shortages was organised in November.

At the end of 1917, British import of goods and food was calculated to be 40 per cent less than the previous year. The consequences were manifold. Under the heading 'Workers demand rations,' *The Times* wrote on 17 December 1917 that the food queues were growing constantly. Newspaper reports mentioned that women were queueing from 5 a.m. in parts of London for margarine, some with babies in their arms, others with children in tow. More than 1,000 people waited outside a shop on New Broad

Street in the centre of the city for butter. And on the Walworth Road, in south-east London, around 3,000 people stood in a queue. Later, 1,000 of them were sent away without their having been able to buy anything.

Shopkeepers and traders also suffered. Butchers had to shut their shops for days on end because there was a shortage of meat. Fish and chip shops were closed due to a lack of fat. 'Meat, butter and margarine are practically unobtainable,' Lee wrote that month. 'The meat shortage has taken us all by surprise. My butcher has been closed for 4 days. Were it not for some pheasants and rabbits Muz sent me from the country, we should have had no meat of any sort.'

Food shortages in the United Kingdom meant prices kept rising. During the war, most products had become 50 per cent more expensive; potatoes even cost 100 per cent and eggs more than 400 per cent more.

This also led to increasing social unrest. In January 1918, ammunition workers in Leytonstone looted shops because their wives were unable to buy food. Soldiers were called in to stop the men. On 13 January 1918 there was a riot in Hemel Hempstead. The police made a shopkeeper bring out his margarine and sell it.

On the last Saturday of that month, the police in London counted more than half a million people queuing for food; this led to rationing of staples a month later.

The unrestricted U-boat campaign continued apace, meanwhile. General Ludendorff had noted triumphantly in an earlier memorandum that, according to the latest news, the U-boat war was effective: 'There is a serious food problem in France and in England and the government is having to deal with big social problems.'

POOR PEOPLE SAUCE

Even a poor quality piece of meat is delicious when the following sauce is poured over it.

Ingredients
one cup of milk
salt
pepper
shallots
parsley

Preparation
Put the milk in a saucepan with some pepper and salt. Finely chop a handful of shallots and part of the parsley which has been washed thoroughly. Put this in the milk, bring to the boil and once the shallots are soft the sauce is ready. When there is no milk, use water but season it with vinegar.

The Belgian Cook Book

BAKED COD TAIL WITH SAUCE

Ingredients
cod tail
bread crumbs
salt
pepper
meat extract
lemon
flour

Preparation
Bake the cod (almost an hour for a 2–3 pound fish) with a little butter, sprinkled with bread crumbs, pepper and salt, dousing regularly with the liquid that is produced.

Before serving it, make the following sauce: take a little meat extract, lengthened to taste with water, season with lemon, pepper and salt and stir in a little flour to thicken it. Pour this over the fish when you take it out of the oven.

The Belgian Cook Book

RAVIOLI MAIGRE

Ingredients
½ lbs Italian paste
1 lb spinach
one tablespoon of chopped onion
margarine
one tablespoon of grated cheese

Method
Prepare half a pound of Italian paste, roll it out as thin as possible, and dry it for one hour. Boil one pound of spinach in a little water, and after draining thoroughly chop it finely. In a little hot butter or margarine lightly brown a teaspoonful of very finely chopped onion, sprinkle in a heaped teaspoon of flour, and when it has cooked for a few minutes stir in the spinach. Season to taste, and when cool stir in a small tablespoonful of cheese and put all through a sieve. Cut the paste into rounds one and a half inch diameter; wet the edges of one half with water, place in the centre a little of the spinach, and cover the remaining rounds of paste. Seal the edges by pressing them together, and drop the raviolis into boiling salted water. Boil them gently for about half an hour and drain them well. Serve in a fireproof dish with a little white sauce mixed with cheese, or with tomato sauce poured over.

This homemade macaroni is delicious just tossed in butter, seasoned with pepper and salt, and served with poached eggs or as a centre to cutlets of fillets, or with boiled chicken or rabbit, or for that matter plain, and it is infinitely superior to the hard, tasteless, stale macaroni so often bought in England.

The Eat-Less-Meat Book

STAFFED [*SIC*] ONIONS

Ingredients
6 large onions (Spanish)
3 oz bread-crumbs
one teaspoon of chopped parsley
1 oz of margarine
salt
pepper

Method
Peel the onions, put them into cold water, bring to the boil and boil five minutes. Drain, and take out the centres, make a stuffing of the bread-crumbs, parsley, herbs, and mix with the margarine melted, and the beaten-up yolk of an egg, season well and fill each onion with the mixture. Put side by side in a saucepan, pour in about one pint of brown gravy or stock, cover and simmer gently for about four hours. Baste occasionally with the sauce. When tender, take them up carefully, thicken the gravy with a little flour or cornflour blended with cold water or stock and poured into the hot stock; boil up again, season, pour over the onions and serve.

The onions can be stuffed with some minced meat mixed with a little gravy, parsley, and herbs, and cooked as above, or with any remains of cold ham or tongue or chicken. Or they can be stuffed with savoury rice and stewed in white sauce.

The Eat-Less-Meat Book

WAR PUDDING

Ingredients
½ lb margarine, lard or suet
1 lb flour
4 teaspoons OXO
6 ozs onions
6 ozs carrots
6 ozs celery
6 ozs tomatoes
6 ozs potatoes
4 ozs pearl barley, parboiled
Or equal quantities of seasonal vegetables

Preparation
Cut all the vegetables into moderately sized cubes, season well. Make the pastry in the usual manner, namely mix well the chopped suet, lard or margarine with flour, make into a paste in exactly the same way as for a meat pudding. Line the basin and fill with the ingredients well mixed together.

Dissolve four teaspoonfuls of OXO in half a pint of water, pour into the pudding, cover and steam for three hours.

In this recipe one OXO cube is equivalent to a teaspoonful of OXO.

OXO helps to compensate for the shortage of meat when used in cooking vegetable dishes. It increases their food value considerably and supplies that appetising and nourishing meat basis which would otherwise be lacking.

OXO advertisement

'WE DO NOT ASK YOU TO DIE...'
FOOD SUPPLIES IN FRANCE

The only news French newspapers reported on the morning of 26 July 1914 was that Austria-Hungary had declared war on Serbia. A few days later, the French government itself signed war declarations against the Central European nations. But only when the guns were positioned in long lines in the Tuileries gardens and mobilisation posters were appearing in the city at the beginning of August 1914 did Parisians actually realise that the country was at war.

Men were seen marching towards the train stations or army depots, bundles slung over their shoulders. Groups of crying women were standing everywhere. 'At night unwonted searchlights pried into the clouds and the funny ovals of their smudged light were gazed upon in silence by thousands with upturned faces,' H. Pearl Adam, a British woman living in the French capital, noted in her diary:

> The order of mobilisation practically meant the collapse of all public and domestic service. The underground railways maintained a fluttering service for an hour or so and then it became absolutely necessary to walk, if you wanted to get about the city. The whole town was on foot, lined up in front of grocers' shops, outside banks, or escorting departing conscripts to the eastern railway station. On the Sunday evening, the first day of mobilisation, the hooligan element got to work and started smashing up German and Austrian shops and enjoying itself in a number of other illegal manners. Paris became like a big provincial city; the streets were deserted at night [...]. Almost the only sound heard was the curious note of claxons of the Red Cross cars bearing the wounded from the distributing stations in the

suburbs. The big shops were empty. As a rule, they are filled with a seething mob of grasping buyers and indifferent sales-people. The counters were deserted, and behind them the shop-girls sat sewing shirts and bandages for the soldiers.

But it was not just the shop counters that were deserted; the fields and meadows were silent too. The hundreds of thousands of men who were responsible for the harvest had reported for duty at the front. At the beginning of the war, just under 4 million men had been mobilised, including 1.5 million agricultural workers. At the end of the war, this number had grown to almost 8 million, over a third of whom had worked on the land.

Just as in the United Kingdom, no plans had been drawn up in France to re-organise agriculture around war circumstances. No scenarios existed that could be implemented straight away to maintain the number of farm workers and to be able to harvest at least as much as before the war. The troops had been supplied food from normal reserves; everyone agreed the war would be short-lived. But now that this war had broken out in August, and the corn and cereals were standing tall, ready to be harvested in the drying summer heat, getting the crops in was a matter of urgency.

On 6 August 1914, the day on which Parisians stocked up on food in massive quantities as they were afraid of big shortages, the government called on the women of France 'to continue the work in the farming regions, bring in the harvest and prepare for the harvest for the next year.' But not only women; children and elderly people also went to work in the fields to harvest and sow new crops.

A teacher from Lalley, a rural village in the south of France near Montélimar, observed on 13 August 1914:

Out of a population of less than 400 souls, 53 men disappeared. They were the men who shouldered the most and the heaviest work. Haymaking had not been completed. And so people went and helped each other. There was extraordinary dedication. Young lads took up scythes, as did young girls who took off their aprons and put aside needle and thread. It was war, people said.

Mémé Santerre recalled after the war that her husband Auguste was exempt from military service due to ill health, and in August 1914 had to bring in the harvest on a farm in northern France with the help of women, young men who had not yet been mobilised, and men who were too old to be called up. 'He worked the miracle,' Mémé Santerre said. 'At the beginning of September, the wheat was stored in the barns.'

Once the harvests had been brought in, new crops had to be sown. Out of sheer necessity, troops came to assist. Soldiers, often older ones, were granted two weeks' leave to go back home in order to work the fields alongside the women and children. Because of this collective effort, agriculture did not in fact suffer much during this first year.

The government did more to maintain social harmony. Women and families whose breadwinner was at the front received money. A law of 5 August 1914 entitled them to an allowance of 1.25 francs. For every child below the age of sixteen, fifty centimes was paid out. This sum was enough to compensate for the loss in income from a skilled worker. For families of unskilled workers, this represented a serious amount of money, and this was certainly the case for the families of farm workers. For some, the allowance was so generous that there were women who wished for the war to continue a long time.

Headteachers in rural villages, who kept diaries about the life in their communities at the request of the government, considered the benefits too high. They wrote that the measures would lead to depravity, laziness, drunkenness and too much *patisserie*. As a teacher in the Haute Savoy noted: 'Never before has the wife of a worker, the mother of three children, received so much money. She is now able to buy items she has craved all her life.'

In the big cities, life was considerably more difficult for women in the poorer sections of the population. They did not have a garden where they could grow a few vegetables. What's more, food prices were higher in the city than in the countryside. In order to ensure that unemployed women in Paris would get food, charities were set up, including the Society for the Protection of Widows and Orphans of the 1914 War, spearheaded by the Duchesse d'Uzès. Another institution was named For the Women and called on well-to-do women to lend a helping hand: 'Oh, French sister, be sweet to one another, be tender, be generous, be humane! Bend over these sad lives and listen to the songs that arise, the songs and the sobs. Be fraternal to the forsaken, the abandoned, the isolated! Oh French sisters! Let's be regenerated by love while we wait to be regenerated by victory!'

Unemployed women found work in the *ouvroir*, a kind of sheltered workshop. In August and September 1914, women from the higher classes opened hundreds of these kinds of institutions, usually in the form of sewing workshops. Poor women worked there for a pittance or just a midday meal. In the end, most of them were used as cheap labour to manufacture uniforms, sheets and other items for the troops.

The 2 million French people who lived in the ten French *departements* occupied wholly or in part by the Germans since October 1914 encountered other problems. They had no access to the government's subsidies. Moreover, it was more difficult to bring in the harvest or sow new crops because the fields had been destroyed by combat. Five-sixths of what the farmers did manage to harvest in 1914 was requisitioned by the Germans, who used this to supply their armies. They also seized pigs, horses and wine.

The ensuing shortages led to prices sky-rocketing. As in Lille, where teacher Maria Degrutère recorded in her diary that butter, lard and meat were no longer available after the city had been taken by the Germans. And it was only October 1914.

Degrutère and her fellow citizens suffered greatly. The occupied north-eastern part of France was also the region of coal mines and heavy industry. Before the war, these accounted for more than 50 per cent of French production of coal, iron and steel. But in 1914, the Germans destroyed major steelworks and closed coal mines. Parts of the textile industries in and around the city were dismantled and the machines sent to Germany. Large groups of workers ended up on the street without means of support. Fuel became increasingly scarce. Metal for repairing agricultural machinery was barely available.

A year later, the Germans banned the sale of potatoes in Lille. There was not a pound to be had. The inhabitants of the city had the good fortune that a relief committee sent an emergency supply of rice, beans, corn on the cob and pork fat to the northern French city every two weeks. 'Otherwise we're sure to go hungry, because the bread rations we're getting are far from enough,' Degrutère wrote.

Because the border with Belgium was closed and supplies could no longer be provided from that country, the shops in the north of France were empty. The little horse meat that was still on sale cost ten francs per kilo. Mature cheese commanded a price of eight francs. Vegetables had run out. Having already requisitioned cows, sheep, pigs and chickens, the Germans now demanded hares and rabbits. There were no longer any shoes, nor any fabric with which to make clothes.

French people who had stockpiled for when the need would be greatest were forced to hand over these supplies under duress. The Germans also searched their houses for metal, copper, mattresses, bed linen, pots and pans. They took food, wine, liquor and other alcoholic beverages. Gardens were commandeered to allow the chickens they had seized to roam.

The situation deteriorated even more when the occupying forces raided houses and picked up hundreds of men, who were then set to work in Germany. Now it was up to the women, children and elderly to provide for themselves. In addition to this, they were compelled, by force or otherwise, to work the fields and bring in the harvest for the Germans.

By the beginning of 1915, Paris had lost the gaiety that characterised the city in the first months of the war. In the words of Pearl Adam:

> The first heroic enthusiasm was over, self-sacrifice had changed her iridescent rags for a sober fustian gown, and we felt and said that the war was 'long.' We looked back with longing upon the days of the battle of the Marne, when a month of anguish was paid for by five days of joy: the German took to his heels and scampered and *piou-piou* [French soldiers], in dark blue and bright red, went joyously after him. Paris stood miraculously inviolate and took her *Tauben* [German aeroplanes] with light-hearted indifference. Then came the talk of the 'strong-positions behind the Aisne,' and then the days when the two armies

Everywhere in Europe the population suffered as well.
(In Flanders Fields Museum)

Preparing food in primitive conditions. (In Flanders Fields Museum)

dug themselves in and settled down to the deadlock of winter. 'The battle of the Aisne' became the 'trench warfare on the Aisne.' Winter came on, the situation never changed, the days were dark, and Paris was nearly dead. Entertaining was unheard of, and if anyone played the piano protests were certain to be made by passers-by against such frivolity.

In Paris, too, food became more expensive. Big restaurants, on the other hand, had lowered their prices, a measure they were perfectly able to afford, Pearl Adam believed, 'considering the ample margin of profit they had always kept.' Yet the establishments attracted fewer customers and the atmosphere was not as before. Adam wrote:

> But it was melancholy for the guests to see them struggling along, screens shutting off half the space, no bands, Spanish or Italian waiters who hardly knew mutton from cauliflower and had never read a wine list in their lives, and half of the occupied tables in the possession of people who were profiting by the lowered prices – which brought food to not more than four times what it would cost at home – to make acquaintance with famous establishments they had never before entered.

Everybody wore black, or the darkest blue, Adam noted:

> Tailor-made or rigid cut were *de rigeur* all day long, and small dark hats were almost a uniform. If a woman took off her coat at dinner, and was seen to be wearing a white or blue or pink blouse, she was gazed at with wonder and resentment. Laughter in a restaurant had to be discreet, or the laughter was stared into silence. The days were gone when the thorns which crackled the most loudly under the pot were considered the liveliest company. If one went to a restaurant to celebrate some pleasant occasion, and did it in the traditional fashion, it was a wonderful sight to see the waiter smuggling the tell-tale pail to the table, and opening the bottle in a great muffling of napkins that would deaden the sound of the cork.

In 1915 it was also becoming clear that the war would last longer than had been thought initially. More and more men were sent to the front, while the countryside, where much-needed cereals and crops were ripening in order to feed civilians and troops, was getting ever emptier.

The French Prime Minister René Viviani issued an appeal to French women in 1915:

> Rise up, then, French women, young children, daughters and sons of the fatherland! Replace in the work of the fields those who are on the fields of the battle. Prepare to show them, tomorrow, the soil cultivated, the crops harvested, the fields sown. In these grave times, there is no lowly labour. Everything is great that serves the country. Rise up! To action! To work! Tomorrow there will be glory for everyone. Long live the Republic! Long live France!

Once again, the women, children and the elderly went to work on the land, but were too few in numbers to be able to harvest the crops satisfactorily. Labour had to be brought in from surrounding countries to ensure that the land would produce enough. Yet Belgian seasonal workers, who used to go to northern France for a few weeks every year before the war to help with the harvest, were now cut off from the country by a strip of trenches. The same applied to Polish workers who had been put to work temporarily before the war.

Switzerland, too, by tradition, used to send a contingent of men to work in the French fields. But in light of their possible mobilisation, the Swiss farm workers were now prohibited from leaving their country. Because Italy was taking part in the war on the Allied side, the men who would normally have the chance to work in Provence were now at the front.

It was still possible to bring farm workers over from Spain and Portugal. Formalities were simplified to make it as easy as possible. Instead of the French government asking for passports, it issued simple identity cards. Train tickets were offered at a discount. Thus tens of thousands of Spanish and Portuguese set to work in the French countryside. However, this was still insufficient, so the government also recruited men from Greece and China, and workers from the colonies. In total, more than 600,000 foreign men worked in France.

But more was needed to ensure that food reserves were kept up. The regions of France occupied by the Germans were amongst the most fertile in the country, extending to well over 6 per cent of the total agricultural area. The loss was much greater than this figure suggests. In 1913, the occupied north-east produced more than 20 per cent of all wheat, more than 25 per cent of oats, more than 11 per cent of potatoes, almost 50 per cent in sugar beet and around 70 per cent of the beets that were used for distilling alcohol. Because these regions were now cut off from the rest of France, hundreds of thousands of tonnes of food were lost to the population.

In order for the agricultural areas that the country still had at its disposal to produce enough, French Army Command was ordered to deploy troops to bring in the harvest in case there was an emergency. As in the United Kingdom, farriers and mechanics serving at the front were allowed to return for short periods to their home regions. There they repaired threshing machines and reshod horses. Fathers with five children or more or widowers with four children were entitled to work in the war industries or on the land, and no longer needed to be active at the front. In 1916 and 1917, thanks to a large influx of young men into the army, farm workers between the ages of forty-six and forty-nine were exempt from service at the front. These men went to work in the fields or in the factories as well.

But the army came first. If there was an offensive during harvest or sowing time and more men were needed at the front, all agricultural leave was cancelled. This meant that, once again, the work fell on women's shoulders. The Marquise de Foucault wrote in her diary on 28 June 1916: 'There is no way of obtaining manual labour, either civil or military [...]. [A]ll agricultural permits are withdrawn as a result of a movement taking shape towards the north [...]. My head keeper Voisennet begins, with very ill grace, to turn the hay with feminine help.'

In *L'Echo de Paris*, the writer René Bazin praised those country women:

> [They] brought in the harvest of 1914, then sowed and
> brought in the harvest of 1915, then again sowed and
> brought in the harvest of 1916; many are discouraged;
> other have been vanquished by the extent of the effort; but
> most have held out, like the men in the trenches. The war
> supported as much by the daughters of France as her sons!
> What a magnificent gift offered to the absent ones and to
> the country!

Despite all their efforts and government measures, crop yields in France fell as they did in the United Kingdom and Germany: by more than 60 per cent for wheat and almost 40 per cent for barley. The potato yield was 50 per cent lower and the harvest of sugar beet less than 20 per cent of the pre-war total.

From April 1915 onwards, the 2 million French people in the occupied north-east of their country received food aid from the Commission for Relief (C.R.B.) in Belgium. This international organisation, headed by Herbert Hoover, later American President, had previously begun to ship relief supplies to Belgium with the support of several other authorities. The C.R.B. was responsible for fundraising, along with procuring and transporting food to the occupied areas. The *Comité d'Alimentation du Nord de la France Food* (Food Committee of Northern France) took care of its local distribution.

The population in the big cities, such as Lille, Roubaix and Tourcoing in particular, became increasingly dependent on this kind of charity. In these cities, people barely had any opportunity to grow their own vegetables. To make matters worse in Lille, there were hardly any vegetables or milk on sale from January 1916, and potatoes, butter and eggs were no longer available. The effects of this were considerable: halfway through that year, mortality rates in Lille rose by 100 per cent as a result of undernourishment.

Although the situation in non-occupied parts of France was not too bad, from the beginning of 1917 there was cause for increasing concern, namely about the winter, which that year was extremely cold, and about the shortage of fuel with which to heat the homes and cook. The Germans were still occupying a large part of the region on which the French were dependent for coal. There were also concerns over the small agricultural yields and over the import of food from abroad. The unrestricted submarine war declared by Germany in February 1917 meant that it became increasingly difficult to import food into France.

This was also the case for the food that the C.R.B. tried to transport to the occupied regions. Their ships carrying relief supplies were also torpedoed at sea. Moreover, as a result of the harsh winter, with all the canals frozen over, transports barely reached their destinations. Virtually everyone in the big cities in the occupied north-east of France starved. The population had no more than a little bread and jam. In the most densely populated districts of Lille, Valenciennes and Saint-Quentin, soup kitchens provided half a litre of soup per person.

France had just one goal: to keep going. That year, the government called on its people to hold back. Throughout Paris, posters appeared with the text: 'We do not ask you to die, we do ask you to live as economically as possible.'

It did not bear much fruit. The harvest of 1917 was around 3 million tonnes – 50 per cent less than before the war. At the end of November, this led the government to regulate the production and sale of bread. Bread was rationed and had to be sold by weight. Men above the age of sixteen who did physical labour were entitled to 600 grams of bread a day. Women had to do with 100 grams less. In addition, the Allied countries began to buy grain jointly from Australia, Canada, Argentina, the United States, Russia and India. The French government also decided to buy and lease merchant vessels.

Yet the prices of meat continued to rocket. Milk and butter were hardly available. Sugar was so scarce that on 1 January 1917 the government decided to close patisseries two days a week. Maximum prices were set for bread and potatoes.

As a result of the ongoing food shortages, shops in Paris had to close at 6 p.m. from November 1916. Cafés and restaurants shut at 9:30 p.m. Further restrictions were imposed. From 1917, customers could only be served two courses, and servings per plate were also restricted. Whether people adhered to these guidelines was almost never checked. And if any transgressions came to light, no or hardly any penalties were imposed.

In March 1917, the government rationed sugar; in April, meatless days were introduced. Butchers and restaurants were prohibited from selling meat on Thursday and Friday. Because everyone bought more meat than normal on the other days, the effect of this ration was marginal.

Pearl Adam was able to live perfectly well in Paris with the measures the government was taking, although she had an easier time of it because she belonged to the well-to-do. Adam also made sure she bought extra supplies outside the meatless days: 'Food Minister succeeded Food Minister, system followed upon system, and still there remained the fact that on meatless days you could always, if you were base enough, obtain meat.'

At the end of 1917, new steps were taken in an attempt to achieve bigger crops. The government set up a Department for Agricultural Machinery in October of that year, for instance, the objective of which was to provide farmers with machines and storage depots. More institutions followed, such as the General Forage Department, the Agricultural Pesticides Service, the Cereal and Climbers Commission and a Potato, Artichoke and Dried Vegetable Commission. But food costs continued to rise. Compared with the situation before the war, prices of dried vegetables, rice, fat and wine were 200 per cent higher than in 1917. The price increase for fresh vegetables and coal was even bigger. The allotments created in Paris, more than 2,500 in 1917, hardly made any difference.

That year, the people of France, like those in the United Kingdom and Germany, rose up. Strikes broke out due to dissatisfaction with rising prices and the reduction in spending power. The January strikes began in the garment industry. In May and June that year, 10,000 workers in the textile industry were again the first to walk out. Strike action by bank employees, civil servants and staff from companies that worked in the service of the war industry followed. This meant that the number of activists in the Paris region grew to 100,000. In the entire country, more than 300,000 people laid down their tools.

In 1917, the government called 'On all rural French men and women' to make the miracle of 1914 (when the harvest was brought in with might and main) happen again: 'You are working for French Victory and Peace. The country has faith in you. The country counts on you.'

But people were tired of the war and could no longer go the extra mile to answer that call. Journalist Emmanuel Labat noted: 'Sometimes a woman, overcome with fatigue, sat at the side of the road, calling to her neighbour who was passing by, bent under the same burden, saying: "We are worse than beast of burden. Why are we working like this? Let's stop working. Famine will come and the war will be over at once."'

MAYONNAISE (for ten people)

To be used with fried fish, cold meats, boiled eggs and various vegetable salads.

Ingredients
15 g mustard
5 g salt
1 g pepper
2 egg yolks
2 to 3 cl vinegar
50 cl oil

Preparation
Put 15 g mustard, 5 g salt, 1 g pepper and 2 egg yolks in a small bowl. Beat thoroughly with a whisk and add 2 to 3 cl vinegar and gentle [sic] pour 50 cl oil until the sauce has thickened. Finish off with a 2 or 3 cl splash of vinegar.

Manuel de Cuisine (*Kitchen Manual*)

CAMEL STOMACH STEW

This dish can only be made during a long stay in a camp.

Ingredients
camel stomach
camel heart and large intestine
onions
carrot
garlic
salt
pepper

Preparation
After having carefully cleaned the majority of the intestines, blanche it in water, cut into pieces, like the heart and large intestine. Place all of this in a large pan, cover with onions, carrots cut into thin slices and a few cloves of garlic. Add salt and pepper and enough water to ensure it covers everything, if desired a splash of white wine and tomatoes. Leave to simmer, but for a very long time, 6 to 7 hours.

It can be refined by adding rice 30 minutes for the end. This cooking method can also be used for preparing beef stomach, called *Tripes à la mode de Caen*.

Manuel de Cuisine (*Kitchen Manual*)

POISSON À LA MEUNIÈRE (for ten people)

Ingredients
2 kg fish
40 g flour
120 g butter, lard, oil or a mixture thereof
25 g salt
vinegar or lemon juice

Preparation
Descale the fish, wash and allow to drip-dry, dredge through flour and turn onto each side. Fry in the butter, lard, oil, vegetable oil, or a mixture thereof. Heat thoroughly and place the fish in it side by side. Add salt and fry on a low heat, turn and salt again a little later. Do the same with the other side. Add a splash of vinegar or lemon juice before serving.

Manuel de Cuisine (Kitchen Manual)

BOUILLABAISSE (for ten people)

Ingredients
2 kg sea fish
15 cl edible oil
100 g onions
20 g shallots
3 leeks
25 g salt
2 g pepper
2 g saffron
30 g tomatoes
lemon or vinegar
bouquet garni

Preparation
Descale a 2 kg mixture of sea fish (any variety), wash, cut into pieces. Fry for 5 minutes in a pan in 15 cl edible oil: 100 g onions, 20 g shallots and the heart of the leeks, chopped finely. Then add the fish, 25 g fine salt, 2 g pepper, 2 g saffron, 30 g tomatoes or 2 or 3 fresh tomatoes cut up, the juice of one lemon or a splash of vinegar and a bouquet garni. Pour 1.5 litre of preferably boiling water over this and allow to reduce for 20 minutes on high heat to less than a third. Finally, add 5 cl of oil. Remove the pan from the heat while bouillabaisse is bubbling and season.

Put grilled bread in a frying pan, place the pieces of fish onto this and pour the soup on top. Discard the bouquet garni.

Comment. Instead of the slices of bread potatoes can be used. Put these in the bouillabaisse after having cut them into four to six pieces, depending on their size, alongside the fish as they need 20 minutes to cook. Quantity: around 2 kg.

Manuel de Cuisine (Kitchen Manual)

COUSCOUS

Ingredients
meat
carrots
root
onion
500 g wheat or maize granules
stock
sea salt

Preparation
This dish is made with wheat or maize granules.

Add meat – beef, mutton or chicken, as desired – in a cooking pot and bring to boil. Add various vegetables such as carrots, roots and an onion and simmer for 15 minutes.

Wash 500 g couscous, i.e. wheat of maize granules, place in a sieve and hung [sic] above the cooking pot. Close with a lid, so that the couscous steams until cooked. The bottom of the sieve should not touch the stock. Allow to boil for 45 minutes and then spoon the couscous onto a dish. Cut the meat into pieces and put this around the dish, pour the stock over the meat, if necessary lengthened and seasoned with gravy. In northern Africa, where this is a favourite dish bar none, people add small chopped peppers and tomatoes fried in a little oil.

Manuel de Cuisine (*Kitchen Manual*)

THE WEDDING CAKE

GENEROUS GIFTS FROM THE HOME FRONT

One day in April 1917, German NCO Carl Heller came around more dead than alive in a trench. He and his comrades had been driven back by the British near Cambrai. The division they belonged to suffered great losses. Heller had no idea how he ended up in this trench. He was bleeding everywhere and was tormented by immense thirst. And he was not the only one. The NCO saw soldiers crawling around stealing their dead mates' water bottles. Practically no one could find anything drinkable. They searched the bread bags hoping for something to eat. 'The dead were turned over by their many hungry and parched comrades,' Heller recorded in his diary.

During the war, different laws applied than in peacetime. When field kitchens were far away or under fire, and the food carriers were not able to get to the front, it came down to ingenuity, the generosity of others and survival instinct.

There was great excitement when a hare or partridge was shot and caught in no man's land and could be roasted. Hunting cartridges were brought from home or ordered through the post. The men also had fishing rods in order to catch fish in the ponds. There are stories of Australians who coolly fished with hand grenades they threw into the water.

Casks of wine and champagne stored in the cellars of *châteaux* were hacked to pieces with bayonets. Dead horses were dissected and the cut-out chunks were fried like steaks. Cows that were not being milked because their farmers had fled the fighting underwent the same fate. Occasionally, the animal was allowed to live and was kept by the men in their trench so that they had fresh milk every day. The cow was given its own shelter and went out each night to graze.

Elsewhere, soldiers found beehives with honey. Some of the

houses in deserted villages had pantries full of food. Fruit trees in northern French or Belgian villages offered extra victuals. Fields were dug up by soldiers, pig sties and chicken coops emptied, and shops plundered.

'One afternoon,' German gunner Gerhard Siegert recalled in his war diary, 'an officer called out: "How are things with those roasts there?" Gunners, armed with small spades, soon rushed towards the pigs. The creatures ran away squealing when they saw us, but it was to no avail. We had soon overtaken them. With a few spade blows the possibility to reflect on their situation was knocked on the head.'

That crime doesn't always pay, especially not in stomachs weakened by days of starvation and unable to digest the large pieces of meat, was manifested a few hours later. Siegert: 'That night I began to feel very sick. I generously returned the unsalted pork I had eaten in the evening back to the French earth. With an even emptier stomach than before I got up again at dawn.'

Then there was, in addition to all the hunting and fishing catch, the iron ration. Expressly intended for emergencies, it was hardly enough food for one day and only to be used after the explicit authorisation of an officer: a meagre portion of meat, an ounce of cheese, tea, sugar, a little salt, meat extract and biscuits. 'Dog biscuits,' scoffed Harry Patch, 'they were that hard; you couldn't even bite into them.'

Harry Patch (1898–2009) has been alive for more than a century when I visit him in Fletcher House, the nursing home that he lives in. Fletcher House is located on the outskirts of Wells in Somerset. Trains do not go there, but a bus does. It is an hour's drive from Bristol through the rolling Gloucestershire and Somerset countryside. Wells is a charming town, with its cathedral dominating the centre in grand and impressive style. It is raining. Built in brown brick with small windows, the nursing home looks cheerless.

Harry Patch is sitting in the coffee lounge. Next to him, hunched on the sofa, between piles of paper handkerchiefs and blister packs with pills, his 93-year-old girlfriend, Doris Whitaker. Parked against the sofa is Patch's walking frame, suspended from which are two walking sticks. At other tables, bent figures, hunched over the tabletops, wait in silence for their lunch. Some have dropped off to sleep. In the kitchen next to the coffee lounge, two cooks are busy preparing lunch.

Patch has short-cut grey hair with a neat parting, clear blue eyes and a hearing aid in each ear. Two medals adorn the lapels of his jacket. He is the last living British veteran to have served in the trenches: Passchendaele, the Flemish land of heavy rain and clay. From June until September 1917 he fought in the Third Battle of Ypres, one of a group of four friends who operated a Lewis gun, a light British machine gun. Patch was responsible for carrying spare parts for the weapon, enough, if needs be, to construct an entirely new one.

The veteran does not know, or has forgotten, that I am due to meet him this Thursday. It appears the appointment I made via Dennis Goodwin and the nursing home's director did not get through. Patch's voice is soft, fragile. I have to sit very close to him to be able to hear him.

'Is it okay if I speak to you?' I ask him.

Patch, whispering: 'Not really…'

And then: 'Brings it all back…brings it all back…'

The first eighty years after the war, it turns out, Patch did not speak a word about his experiences at the front. Only after his hundredth birthday and his move to Fletcher House did it start: the questions, the requests for autographs, the unannounced visits. The director of the nursing home had placed an article in the local newspaper proclaiming that a 100-year-old First World War veteran was now living in her home. The next day, they had a journalist on their doorstep. For eighty years, Patch had been trying to forget this war, push away the memories. This one piece in the paper brought everything back. How he tried to avoid all these people, how he told the director of the home not to give his address to complete strangers, to no avail. And now I am sitting here.

The four months at the front were hell for Patch. A pointless, crazy enterprise whereby, in his words, only innocent people were killed. British *and* Germans. Amongst these his friends, the Lewis gunners. They met their deaths in German shellfire on the evening of 22 September 1917. Three men. Only Patch emerged alive.

His shaking hand points to his groin. A piece of shrapnel had worked its way into his body and put an end to his war. Patch says that all he remembers is a light flash.

He stops speaking. Stares ahead for a few seconds, his clenched right hand twisting in the palm of his left hand.

Then he continues. About the time that he came around after the attack and found himself on a stretcher in a dressing station somewhere behind the lines. A few weeks later he was in England, never to go back to the war again. That one light flash still dominates his life. In the morning, when he dozes in bed and a carer switches on the light, it is there again: the flash.

I find it hard to talk with Patch. His soft voice, his whispering: it intensifies everything he says. But it is his silence above all that is affecting. The way in which he stares into space; sits on the sofa without moving, to turn his head towards me to say one single word, half a sentence.

Patch begins to talk about a book which is coming out later that year and is about his life, from his boyhood up to now. Everything will be in there, including the answers to all the questions. Mine too, he says. Patch will get £2,500 for his contribution to the book. Some of the money will go to Fletcher House. But the largest sum Patch has set aside for something else.

With a trembling hand he gestures towards a bookcase. Slim fingers, those of a gunner. On one of the shelves stands a money box with a sketch of a lifeboat. Most of the money Patch receives for his book will go to an organisation that devotes itself to rescuing people from drowning off the coast. Patch wants to save lives. Perhaps that explains why he wants to talk to me after all.

Patch's companion has got up meanwhile, and without saying a word has sat down at another table with her hankies and blister packs of pills. She leaves Patch and me fraternally alongside each other in silence. I see a tear trickle down from his right eye past his nostril. It disheartens me. Do I have the right to harp on at Patch about something he clearly finds difficult? When he stares into the distance, I also see the shelling. And that one, the one with the flash. I suggest we stop here, but Patch won't hear of it. He can live with people asking questions about the war now, he says. It is the memory of the war itself that still makes him feel wretched ninety years later. It will never wear off.

Near the village of Passchendaele, Patch spent four months in the firing line. Four months of German shelling, including the supply lines. When that happened, there was nothing to eat. With an empty stomach and up to his knees in water (because the trenches had been dug to well below groundwater level), Patch was stuck. The longest time Patch was without food was three days. Three lonely days, surviving on inedible biscuits and a morsel of tinned meat. A godsend for Patch was that his mother frequently sent him parcels. 'She was on friendly terms with a shopkeeper,' Patch recalls. 'If I was in luck, every two weeks a cardboard box with food was delivered: some tobacco, packets of cigarettes, some chocolate and cakes.'

The British Army Postal Service, which employed some 4,000 people, processed thousands of postbags and around 60,000 parcels a day during the war. Although the only form of address allowed was the name of the addressee and his regiment, generally speaking it would take no longer than four days for a letter or parcel to arrive at the front. On the German side, some 28.7 billion letters, notes, small and large parcels, and telegrams were sent from home to the front and vice versa, around 16 million postbags a day. *Liebesgaben* (love gifts) the Germans called the parcels from home, sometimes sent by complete strangers. The French, too, collected goods and sent them in bulk to the front line, thus saving the men from wartime famine.

The French and Belgian soldiers and officers were also able to rely on the help of *marraines de guerre* (soldiers' wartime female penfriends) who, taking pity on the men at the front, wrote letters and sent them small gifts. The French soldiers came into contact with the women by placing advertisements in the illustrated weekly *La Vie Parisienne*. Some of them were clever enough to take up with more than one *marraine*. That meant receiving more letters and presents. One sergeant, who was in contact with more than forty-four women, deserted in the end because he could not keep up with the correspondence.

The list of products that were sent to the front was as long as it was diverse: jars of jam, socks, tins of Vaseline, cocoa powder, cooked chicken, sugar loaf, Scottish haggis, shoelaces, milk powder, eggs, nuts, handkerchiefs, tinned fish, smoked sausage, rum, pipe

Sharing soup. (In Flanders Fields Museum)

tobacco, chocolate bars, pens, oysters, bottles of wine by the box-load, crates with oranges from California for the Americans, stock cubes, peppermints, home-knitted woollen scarves and fresh flowers 'for the table.' Bavarian units were supplied with supreme-quality beer by breweries from their region, reason enough for other troops to fight for access to the Bavarian field canteens, which they were often refused because they were not entitled to their beer, in the eyes of the Bavarians.

All manner of things were organised in the various countries to send as many parcels to the front as possible. In August 1915, for instance, the British held a Million Egg Week, whereby households were urged to send fresh eggs to the troops. There was more: the big London department stores Fortnum & Mason and Harrods specialised in hampers, varying in luxury. Fortnum's fruit cake was especially popular because it would keep for a long time.

Frederic Manning, the author of *Her Privates We*, described receiving such a parcel: 'It was [...] securely packed in a box of that thin wood known as three-ply.' A great deal of space in this box was taken up by 'a long loaf of bread, called by some a sandwich loaf because it cuts into square slices and is intended to be made into sandwiches.' To his delight, Manning also found in the hamper a tin of chicken, a small but solid plum cake, a small jar of scarlet strawberry jam and a tin containing one hundred Russian cigarettes.

Once the men had taken delivery of a parcel, they would usually share out its contents. Harry Patch had a similar agreement with his friends. First, all the items from the parcel he received went to the Lewis gunner who would distribute everything. Until the day that Harry's three brothers in arms were blown to pieces by one and the same shell. No parts of them were ever found.

It was also agreed that the parcels, delivered for soldiers and officers who were active in combat at the front and not able to take delivery of the post, could be opened by others. Articles of food were eaten, and any gifts and money was shared out. The troops did not want to risk the contents rotting away in anticipation of any possible return by the person for whom the parcel was intended.

During the holidays especially, all kinds of things were organised to support the troops. Not only at the home front, but also by the armies themselves. The soldiers and officers celebrated the birthday of the German Emperor on 27 January with wine and *sekt*. During the German slaughter festivals, fattened company pigs were put on the spit. On St Patrick's Day, a special dinner was served for Irish divisions at the front. The French were given an extra ration of *pinard* and slightly better food on Bastille Day (14 July). Even a religious ceremony at the end of October 1915, to celebrate 500 years of Hohenzollern rule, occasioned an extra portion of sausage and a litre of apple sauce for every German soldier.

A brown envelope in the Liddle Collection in Leeds contains a pencilled menu for yet another celebration: the second anniversary of the departure from Britain on 16 January 1915 of the 85th Field Ambulance.

The front of the menu card features a drawing of a soldier carrying a kind of sandwich board with the text: 'Kind friends, I left England two years ago.' Diagonally below, a charming lady is depicted with a glass and two empty wine bottles at her feet. The inside of the card lists the actual meals. The food was quite something, even if the desire to get all these courses on the table may have been greater than the reality that they would actually be eaten.

Hors-d'oeuvres
> The Good Sardine
> or if preferring
> The Kippered Herring

Soup
> Potage D'Ilôt

Fish
> Rissoles D'Iventorie
> Saumon Salonique

Removes
> Lapin au petit Chat
> Steak & Pudding Kidney
> Supreme de Savoissons
> Sutepout...
> Paté Percy Pimlico

Vegetables
> Asperges des Années Terrible
> Haricots DawJack

Sweets

      Bombe Bugshire

      Patisserie Patois

Savouries

      Wray au gratin rôti

      Saddle Paste (Officers Only)

Dessert

      Bakshi Johnnie Figge

      Lauripops

      Cigar

      or

      Nuts

Wines

      Port (Kittée Frazois 1895)

      Bière: beaucoup

      Cocoa pour Kenchington

      Rhum: peut-être

The most important event was Christmas. German cooks made gingerbread and hot chocolate on Christmas Eve. For the Americans, stuffed turkey was on the menu for Christmas 1917. The birds had been dispatched in large crates from the United States. The British ate their traditional Christmas pudding.

For Christmas celebrations, especially those of 1914, when the home front had not yet tired of the war, the governments urged the general population to shower troops with presents. The French were asked to donate under the motto 'Noël aux Soldats.' In Germany, the churches called upon their congregations to give the men at the front extra clothes and food. Calls to send supplies also appeared in German newspapers and magazines. Not only food, but medication for colds and rheumatism were high on the list as well, because it was cold and wet in the trenches.

Soldiers and officers sent wish lists back home. 'Cold, cold and hungry!' German NCO Gustav Sack wrote to his wife in November 1914:

See if you can send me a tin of sardines, a sausage, chocolate, and some alcohol please, when you have the money! […] I'm starving! I can't stand the food here – at night, a little disgusting soup. I've got diarrhoea and am mainly living on some bread and a tiny bit of water. The only thing that will help is if you can send me something immediately. A parcel every day! Bacon, sausages, mustard, milk, anchovies, butter, sardines, chocolate, cigarettes and cumin!!

The British media also stressed the importance of helping the men in the trenches, especially at Christmas time. Companies, women's clubs, kindergartens: everyone saved money and goods to give the troops in France an unforgettable Christmas. Volunteers from the Women's Emergency Corps made thousands of puddings which had been ordered by officers' wives for dispatch to the front. Whiteleys made giant Christmas puddings weighing almost 300 kilograms each.

In addition, a few weeks before Christmas 1914, a fund was set up in Britain supported by the royal family. The purpose of the fund was to finance a national present for all troops. In charge of The Sailors & Soldiers Christmas Fund was Princess Mary, King George V's seventeen-year-old daughter. A collection amongst the general population raised so much money that the fund was able to buy 335,000 brass tins with gifts: tobacco, a lighter and cigarettes. For non-smokers, there were pens and sweets. Troops from India received spicy treats.

During those same weeks, Harrods came up with a special offer: the Our Soldiers Half Guinea Box. Sending such a box to the front 'obviously' did not cost the sender any postage. It contained biscuits, jam, marmalade, sardines, Nestlé Café au Lait, Biovac cocoa and milk, stock cubes, matches, tinned meat, a packet of candles, raisins and almonds, soap and a Christmas pudding. Harrods' competitor Fortnum & Mason also sold Christmas hampers. The tin with turtle soup, roast turkey, a tin of sausages, Christmas pudding, Scottish tea biscuits, fruit cake, chocolate and prunes cost 15 shillings, including postage.

The Christmas collections were a great success. During the week of 6 December 1914, 250,000 parcels were sent to the troops. The following week, another 200,000. During those same days, 2.5 million letters also reached the front.

Coningsby Dawson, a British officer with the Canadian Army, wrote in a letter home:

> This morning I was wakened by the arrival of the most wonderful parcel of mail. My servant had lit a fire in a punctured petrol can and the place looked very cheery. Then there was a sand-bag containing all your gifts. You may bet that I made for that first, and as each knot was undone remembered the loving hands that had done it up. I am now going up to a 24 hour shift of observing, and shall take the malted milk and some blocks of chocolate for a hot drink.

'The Christmas mails are getting enormous,' Captain Armstrong, who was working in Flanders as an officer with a division's transport unit, wrote in a letter home. 'We have three extra lorries temporarily attached for potential work and they make the work easier. Today we had 290 mail bags for the division.'

Not everyone was happy with the flow of goods that had to be sent to the front. According to the Railway Transport Office Major General R.H.D. Tompson, the Christmas gifts sent to the troops became a bit of a problem. Everyone would rather that people at home did not send them, Tompson claimed, as consignments of plum pudding obstructed transit and the extremely limited space on the tracks was not able to facilitate the flow of gifts. The Major General asked himself if people would send these parcels if they knew how much strain they put on the supply of ammunition and the difficulty they created on the railways behind the lines. Of course Tompson understood the other side of the story. He recalls once receiving a small box of wooden dominoes: 'kindly intended.'

In some places at the front, such large quantities of food arrived that many soldiers and officers no longer bothered to go to the field kitchen in the evening, but tucked into the treats that had been delivered. There was food, there was calm and, for a moment, it seemed as if there was peace on earth. At least as important was the fact that it gave the men the feeling that people at home were thinking about them. That this war was being waged together.

With every letter or parcel, the troops held a piece of their homeland in their hands. Or, as the French General Joffre wrote in a thank-you letter to the nation on 23 December 1914: 'Thanks to you, our brave soldiers received some refreshments and can feel once again that the hearts of those who stayed behind are beating warmly for them.'

Civilians from Germany also sent parcels to their troops at the front. German soldier Hans Hirschborn wrote during the Christmas celebrations of 1914 in the French city of Saint-Quentin:

> The gifts are distributed, gifts sent with love from the fatherland, from home. The doctors themselves distribute the gifts from the fatherland. My God, I could hardly believe my eyes. I was so grateful for everything that was placed in my *pickelhaube* [spiked helmet]: sugar, confectionery, a pipe, cake, biscuits, tobacco, cigarettes, postcards, a large bottle of beer, chocolates, wrist mufflers, etcetera [*sic*]. What love from people I have never known!

Arthur Kutscher was also excited about the beer, the rum, nuts, oranges and apples he was given. Kutscher wrote:

> The soldier's heart is happy. […] People know, or should know, how closely a soldier's heart and stomach are linked. This Christmas shows how the entire German nation is waging war together. The soldier needs to have the sense that, back home, people are thinking about him. This sense must be tangible and something you can taste, because your loved ones are so far away. Oh! How a man can cry over a lump of butter that has been packed by his sweetheart or his mother. For the officers there are all kinds of gifts as well. Countless delicacies are awaiting us every time at lunch or dinner. And, finally, even something we had long thought impossible:

> *Da erschien am Tisch des Hauses* [*On the table of this house appeared*]
> *Als das Wunder dieser Zeit* [*At this time as if by genius*]
> *Eine Gans in knupfrig-brauner* [*A goose in crispy-golden*]
> *Apfeldustger Wirklichkeit* [*Apple-cloudy realness*].

In the end, so much had to be transported for the Christmas celebrations of 1914 that both the British and the Germans postponed regular supplies for a day to enable the despatch of the innumerable Christmas hampers. Everything arrived on time. Chocolate form Cadbury's and Callard & Bowser butterscotch for the British. Brandy-filled chocolates for the French and pipes for the Germans. The latter, a national present from High Command to the troops, were swapped for tins of meat or plum pudding during a short Christmas truce with the British enemy, whilst 'Alle Menschen werden Brüder' and 'God Save the Queen' was sung. Similarly, the British acquired further souvenirs in exchange for food: a German spiked helmet was swapped for bully beef, cigars for tins of corned beef, cigarettes for Maconochie's stew, schnapps for biscuits, and pipe tobacco for Tickler's plum and apple jam.

Because of the combat in their sector, the officers of the British Battalion 13th Rifle Brigade, who were stationed in Flanders, did not celebrate Christmas Eve until 2 January. It was worth the wait. They had been back and forth three times from the mess to the French town of Bailleul, where business was still in full flow. Three consignments of delicatessen had already been transported. The officers' menu would have happily made the grade for the dinner in the Bosna Hotel, held some six months earlier on 27 June 1914 in honour of the Austro-Hungarian Crown Prince Franz Ferdinand. That evening in Bailleul, the British officers were served dishes named after well-known places associated with the war:

Hors d'Oeuvres Varie's Hannescamps
Bouillon d'Ovilers
Truites á l'encre
Ris de Porc Hulluch
Dindon Roti Monchy-le-Preux
Pommes de Terre et Petits Pois Verts
Plum Pudding au Rhum Gavrelle
Champignons Route de Menin
Glace Basseville Beek
Dessert Coffee

On a wall opposite hang two aerial photos of Passchendaele and the neighbouring village of Zonnebeke. On the photo from 1917, taken before the Third Battle of Ypres, I clearly see buildings, road junctions and fields. On a photo taken after the battle, everything has been wiped. Not one single orientation point in the landscape is still there to be recognised.

The Third Battle of Ypres lasted a hundred days and cost the Allied troops 245,000 men. On the German side, the losses amounted to 215,000. The territorial gain for the Allies: no more than 8 kilometres.

Elsewhere in the information centre, photos of dignitaries are displayed: the British King George V inspecting wooden crosses at the cemetery just after the war; Queen Elizabeth II laying a wreath; the Belgian Prince Filip walking past the graves. And in the last photo: Harry Patch seated in a chair in front of a wall on which the names of victims are carved. Date: 22 September 2004. Patch had gone back, although I wonder if he did so gladly. Patch does not harbour good memories of that war.

Or maybe one. During our chat two months ago, he had told me about his brother William, who joined up and served with the Royal Engineers. Patch, with a cautious grin: 'William told me about life at the front in such a way that I no longer wanted to fight. But I went, and when I was in the trenches myself, my brother got married in England. A week later I received a parcel.'

The parcel contained a piece of cake which Patch gave to the leader of the group of Lewis gunners. He cut it into four equal pieces and gave it to the men. I saw Patch's eye light up when he revisited that memory. That piece of William's wedding cake, it was a gift from heaven.

STOCK RICE

Ingredients
rice
salt
meat extract
butter or lard

Preparation
Boil blanched rice (4 tablespoons per person) in a generous amount of salted water (1/5 rice and 4/5 water) with meat extract. Boil for approximately 30 minutes. Finally, add butter (or lard) and meat extract and simmer so that the moisture evaporates. Pieces of tomato or tomato purée can be added as well.

Die Gulaschkanone (*The Goulash Cannon*)

POTATOES, FRENCH FRIED (for one hundred men)

Ingredients
35 lbs peeled potatoes
lard
salt

Preparation
Cut lengthwise into one half inch slices and fry in deep lard until nicely browned: after frying, dust slightly with salt and serve hot with any kind of meat. On account of the quantity of the potatoes to be prepared for an organisation mess it is not advisable to cut in thin slices, as is usually done. This is a dish much relished by the men and on account of its comparative cheapness it is recommended for frequent use.

Extracts from Manual for Army Cooks

STEWED RABBIT (for one hundred men)

Ingredients
70 lbs rabbit meat
6 lbs bacon
6 lbs flour
3 lbs onions
50 lbs potatoes
stock
salt
pepper

Preparation
Carefully skin the rabbit and leave in salted water for 30 minutes. Cut into small joints and well wash in a fresh supply of water. Cut the bacon into slices. Clean and cut up the onions into small pieces. Place a little stock into a steaming dish, add the onions. Place 3 lbs flour, ½ oz pepper and 2 ozs salt into a bowl and mix well, add the rabbit and the bacon into the dish with the onions, barely cover with stock, stir well together, replace the lid and steam for 2 hours. If this is cooked in a camp cauldron the flour, pepper and salt should be added as a thickening about 30 mins before required.

Cooking in the Field

POTATOES WITH LETTUCE AND SPINACH

Ingredients
potatoes
lettuce
spinach
lard
pepper
salt

Preparation
Braise 2 francs worth of lettuce and spinach in 1 or 2 kg lard. The potatoes you have boiled as you would normally do are added to the braised vegetables and covered with the necessary water. Add pepper and salt and stew for approximately 1 hour.

NB – The spinach can substituted by dandelion flowers. This vegetable, which are plentiful in the field, offers the advantage that it costs nothing.

Handboek van den kok te Velde (*Handbook for the Field Cook*)

POTATOES WITH PARSLEY

Ingredients
potatoes
2 to 3 medium onions
parsley
butter or lard
milk
nutmeg

Preparation
Peel the potatoes, dice and boil in salted water and drain.

Meanwhile, brown 2 to 3 medium-sized onions and add to the boiled potatoes. Add a generous spoon of flour with butter or lard and stir in the milk. Cook this into a thickened sauce, add salt, pepper and nutmeg to taste. Mix all this with the potatoes and allow to cook until done. To finish off, add a knob of butter and some finely chopped parsley.

For two men, use a little less than half a litre of milk or meat stock, a generous tablespoon of flour and 6 to 8 potatoes.

Brattische Kochvorschriften für Feldküchen (*Brattische Cooking Instructions for Field Kitchens*)

BAYERNWALD
LIFE IN THE TRENCHES

On a Sunday afternoon at half past five, I park my car in the Reningelststraat in Kemmel, in front of De Bergen, the Heuvelland tourist office and visitor centre. I haul a canvas rucksack from the trunk of my car which once belonged to the Swiss Army and which I bought in Amsterdam in an army surplus store.

Tied onto it is a sleeping bag I have borrowed from my brother-in-law, who works for NATO on behalf of the US Army. A great deal more luxurious than the bags of ticking fastened with safety pins that some of the men had in the war.

Additionally, I have a *feldgrau* haversack, which I hang around my neck. A small metal-coloured oil lamp dangles from it. Altogether, my luggage weighs more than 20 kilograms, a little less than the 27 kilograms the British soldiers lugged around, while the Germans carried more than 30 kilograms on their backs.

From the tourist information centre I continue down the road and turn left into the Kemmelstraat. A car joins the roundabout at that point and catches me in its headlights. I can see the driver and passenger gaze at my get-up with some suspicion. I raise my hand hesitantly and walk on.

I've always hated camping. The palaver with a tent where you find that the poles and pegs do not fit; the fiddling with a gas ring; the burrowing in and out of a sleeping bag – none of this is my thing. And now, at the end of November, with exceptional permission from the Heuvelland tourist office, I am subjecting myself to the ultimate camping test: three nights bivouac in Bayernwald, a reconstructed German trench, located on a hilltop somewhere between Ypres and Kemmel.

What were the circumstances like there, one hundred years

ago? The cold, the lack of sleep, the meagre rations, the day-to-day monotony: life in the trenches. Questions to which I hope to receive some sort of an answer over the coming days.

It's not even a ten-minute drive by car, but on foot the 5 kilometres route to Bayernwald suddenly seems a lot longer. The evening is fresh, the sky clear. I feel a little tense, but also full of adrenaline. I hold on to the strap of my rucksack with my left hand, and steady the oil lamp with my right hand to stop it from swinging annoyingly in front of my waist. I feel the iron rim of the canvas rucksack slowly digging into the flesh of my back.

My right boot seems a bit too big. Treading along the concrete cycle path next to the Kemmelstraat, I rub my heel up and down against the inside of the boot. I fear that my preparation has been too slack on this point. Three days ago, when I bought the second-hand combat boots I am wearing now, I only tried on the left-hand one.

Apart from the boots, a scarf, a hat and woollen gloves, I am wearing long johns, knee-high woollen socks, a vest, a shirt, old army trousers, a woollen jersey and an old army coat.

I hump my body more and more under the weight of the ballast on my back and around my neck, and sway from side to side with each step. In the process, I feel the oil from the little lamp running down my right hand. A generous 20 kilograms is beginning to feel to me like 25–30 kilograms.

At the time, the troops often marched more than 15 kilometres from the hinterland to the front. Sometimes wading up to their hips in mud. Amongst them the Canadians and Australians who are buried at La Laiterie, a war cemetery I pass to my left. A little further along on the right is an American monument to the men who fought in this region in 1918. The presence of these memorials shores me up. Why am I moaning about the welts on my back and my heel scraping against the back of my boot? Men have given their lives here.

Finally, after a march lasting a good forty minutes, the big Goudezeune concrete factories loom up. It is a right turn there, into the Vierstraat, towards the village of Wijtschate. Darkness has fully set in now. Stars twinkle above my head; to my left and right are arable fields and the odd farm. The road starts to climb here. I fight off the pain in my back and heel and start singing softly: 'It's a long way to Tipperary' and 'Die Wacht am Rhein.' I am imagining that I am not walking alone here, but amidst hundreds of comrades. Our singing breaks the silence and wafts loudly over the ploughed fields. It helps, even though I am almost creaking when I climb the steep section, before taking a left turn into the Voormezelestraat. Here, on both sides of the road, lies a strip of woodland.

Not much further, I think. I hear an eagle-owl or other kind of owl (my knowledge of flora and fauna is not that great). Sweat gushes down my back. On the move, I remove my hat, scarf and gloves.

After 500 metres along the Voormezelestraat there is a right turn for me to take and then I am finally standing outside the Bayernwald enclosure. I fumble in my trouser pocket for the piece of paper on which I have written down the code that should open the gate to give me access to this historic location. I am delighted when, a moment later, after walking for an hour and twenty minutes, I've entered the site and I can take off my rucksack and haversack: running a finger along the cuts in my back, I feel blood.

The moon has not risen yet. I have to light the oil lamp to find my way in the entrenchment. When I hold a match to the lamp's wick, nothing happens. I shake the object back and forth but hear no sloshing: it has emptied out completely as I made my way here. Cursing and swearing, I search in my rucksack for the bottle of lamp oil I have taken with me, twist the top of the lamp's reservoir and fill it with fuel. Top on, strike a match and there is light.

I heave the rucksack on to my back again, swing the haversack around my neck and, holding up the oil lamp, I feel my way around the site. Because I have been here before, I know exactly where I need to be. Last set of steps on the right into the trench, left around the corner past the old pillbox, and then, after 15 metres along the wooden duckboards, there are the remains of an old shelter. The dug-out is around 90cm high, 80cm wide and 1.5m deep. Above it lie two colossal weathered concrete slabs. Because the sandy ground is on a slight incline, it is the only sheltered spot on the site that is not under water.

I take off my rucksack and haversack once again and put them in the shelter. The contents of my kit:

Mess tin
Primus gas stove
Oil lamp
Beaker
Cutlery
Pocketknife
Groundsheet and tarpaulin
Entrenching tool
75g tobacco
Cigarette papers
Matches
One bottle of lamp oil
Ten tea lights (4cm wide)
Towel
Face mitt
Toothpaste
Toothbrush
Four pairs of long woollen socks
Thermometer
Notebook and biro
Two books
3 litres of water
1 tin of pea soup (300ml)
Three tins of vegetables (red cabbage, French beans and spinach)
   (200g each)
Two tins of tuna in oil (185g each)
Twelve slices of brown bread
Two potatoes
Two sachets of dried sausage (117g each)
Three packets of army biscuits (125g each)
One jar of chicory coffee substitute
Four teabags
Twenty sugar cubes
0.2 litres of rum

And now? I'm thinking. Here I am, pretending to be a soldier. Exactly twenty-five years ago I was a conscientious objector in the Royal Netherlands Army; now I am clad in khaki green. Alone, in a trench stretching 320 metres. It is cold; weather to wear a winter coat in. I wrap my scarf around my neck, put my hat on my head and button up my jacket to its collar. Then I roll a cigarette, light it and look around me. The site is fringed by dozens of trees. A visitor's hut, a kind of car port showing a model of the former trenches around Wijtschate, is facing me, jet black and menacing in the light of the moon. A fence runs around the site, some 40 metres removed from me. In the war it was a bustling ants' nest here. Thousands of troops were lying on both sides of the front line. The British positions were no more than 50 metres apart from the Germans.'

Now it is quiet. There is only the sound of the wind rustling through the trees. I wonder how low the temperatures can fall here at night. I place the dark green groundsheet at the bottom of the shelter. Using an old German pocketknife, the only original part of my kit, I cut two holes in the tarpaulin and pull it over two protruding posts in the trench wall. I'll be better protected from rain that way. Then I pace all the passages, swinging the oil lamp 20cm above the ground to look for stones to hold the sheet in place better. When I have settled into my quarters, I eat two slices of dry brown bread.

Attacks are not something I need to be afraid of. Here, there is no enemy facing me. What do give me a fright every so often are the shadows I catch with my oil lamp. In addition, Peter Gombeir, the Heuvelland tourist office director and manager of this site, told me that a few weeks before my arrival some vandals had climbed over the fence and kicked sections of the wooden boards in the trenches to pieces. At least that's the suspicion. On another occasion, the lock to Bayernwald's entrance gate was ground open with an angle grinder. Just to be on the safe side, I take the entrenching tool that I bought in an army surplus store out of my rucksack and lean it against the trench side. That way I have something to defend myself with should the need arise.

Although the trenches were never far apart over the entire front, the enemy kept a low profile both day and night. The joke went around that, amongst the Germans, there were so many men who had worked in the service of hotel restaurants in London and Paris that, in order to coax them to stick their heads above the trench wall to shoot them, you only needed to call out: 'Waiter!'

There were sounds in the trenches: of digging, repairs to the walls, coughing and hacking of the men on the other side, a brief order. You could feel that there was life on the enemy side, but it was more than anything the not being able to see that made the situation so threatening. The idea that you did not quite know what was going on kept the men in constant tension. Every rustle, every murmur gave them a start. Crouched with their heads below the trench wall, they listened, ears pricked, for whether there was something on the enemy side that could constitute immediate danger. Looking with your head above the trench during the day, or at night with a cigarette dangling from your mouth, could be deadly. Snipers were lying in position on the other side or camouflaged in no man's land. There was fear every minute of the day. Eating, a sip of rum or hot tea alone gave the men a sense of security, of fellowship.

Before my march to Bayernwald I ate four sandwiches at home and then a piece of chocolate en route. At 9 p.m. I feel my stomach rumbling, but I decide I am not allowed another two slices of bread until midnight. Together with the tea I will be brewing then. During the war, the men standing guard or working were given some food around midnight and – because of the cold – a cup of tea. Or, as the British Trench Standing Orders stated, the men should be given soup or another hot drink between midnight and 4 a.m.

At 10 p.m. the oil lamp gives up the ghost. After a great deal of fumbling in the half-dark, I manage to extract a faint glow. Half an hour later, it is definitely curtains for the lamp. Fortunately, it is a full moon and the general area fairly well lit. In the far distance I can see the illuminated tower of the Cloth Hall and a church in Ypres. In order to feel a little less alone here, I light two tea lights and put these in the shelter. The earthen walls light up in a reddish-brown colour, making everything seem bleak.

Around midnight I place four large tea lights on a flat protrusion of one of the concrete shelters in the trench. Inside, it's no higher than 1m 20cm. Good enough to shelter in during shelling, but not for habitation. More generous constructions than these would affect the troops' offensive mindset, the German Army commanders believed. The men had to be outside, not inside around a fire. Everything had to be focused on capturing British positions.

To the left and right of the tea lights I place two flat stones. On top of that, my mess tin with a small lining of water, enough for a cup of tea. According to British Army regulations from the war, the heat from the tea lights would make the water come to the boil in around fifteen to twenty minutes. Tea could also be brewed on a small cooker made from a cylindrical cigarette tin with strips of cloth soaked in methyl alcohol before departure to the front. But most British soldiers had a professional Primus stove.

After fifteen minutes, small air bubbles float up to the top of the mess tin. Every three minutes, I look to see if the water is boiling, but not much is happening. After forty minutes I call it a day; the water is warm enough for making tea. Even though it has not come to the boil, it tastes delicious.

After 3 a.m. I crawl into my sleeping bag. It's clammy and damp in the shelter. Every now and then a bead of condensation drops down from the large concrete blocks covering the spot. As well as an 80cm-wide entrance, there are holes in the left and right corners. So far, I've been lucky: it's not raining. But it is freezing. It feels as though there is a ground frost, even if my thermometer shows a temperature of just above zero. The chill permeates my bones through the groundsheet. I thrash about in my sleeping bag and pull my legs towards my chin to make myself as small as possible. This provides most heat, or rather, the least cold.

Finding the right position to sleep in requires precision. The shelter's base is like a mirror that's been smashed. Thick fragments with sharp corners and edges. One tiny movement, one dry cough, is enough to feel a pointy edge pierce my back, legs or shoulders. Besides, I am petrified that the large concrete slabs will break loose and fall on top of me. I would not be the first person to have been crushed to death in a dug-out by falling rubble and buried alive.

When, on Monday morning, after a few hours' sleep, I crawl out of the shelter, it's still pitch-black. I take two swigs of rum to warm myself up. The farmers in the field on the other side, where the British front line was, have started to harvest sugar beet at the crack of dawn. A crane loads the tubers onto a truck. The thundering din with which they drop into the loading bins sounds like the noise of guns in the distance; in a reflex, I duck my head to far below the trench side. At 8 a.m. I make tea, drink this with some sugar and shovel down two slices of dry brown bread.

Because this area is situated 40 metres above sea level, it had great military-strategic value one hundred years ago. That's why, in November 1914, France and Bavaria were engaged in heavy combat for its possession. After the German capture, the woodland was called Bayernwald. From 1914 until the summer of 1917, the Germans developed this site into an almost unassailable stronghold.

Adolf Hitler also served in this position. As a *Gefreiter* (a kind of lance corporal) of the 16th Bavarian Reserve Infantry Regiment, he was slightly injured when, together with a comrade, he carried a wounded lieutenant from no man's land back into their own lines during a gunfight. In December 1914, Hitler was awarded the Iron Cross (2nd Class) for this. Here, he also made a painting of Bayernwald.

The restored section, which was opened to the public in 2004, covers only 10 per cent of the original trench system. During the war, this sector at the front was relatively quiet. On warm summer evenings, regimental orchestras played in the local areas until nightfall. They went swimming in the large enclosure of a farm not far from here. At times, football matches were scheduled.

Both armies were in total deadlock in their trench war. To break this, they tried to undermine each other's position below ground. In 1916, the British worked on a large offensive. They literally wanted to blow the Germans out of their positions on higher ground. To achieve this, they dug mine shafts in fourteen locations along the entire front line, with tunnels reaching to beneath the German trenches. The tunnel end was a large chamber packed with explosives.

In Bayernwald that year, the Germans did not feel confident that they were safe. They believed that the blue clay they saw further along at Bois-Carré, Sint-Elooi and also at Hollandse Schuur was a sign that the British were digging deep and laying thousands of kilos of explosives.

In response, the Germans built six metre-deep listening shafts, Berta 1 to Berta 6, in order to be able to follow the British operations better. Deep underground, they hoped to hear where the British were digging in order to destroy their work. They also launched dozens of offensives on enemy territory to see what the British were planning.

Bayernwald was spared because the British only worked on a 400-metre-long infantry communication trench for their second line at Bois-Carré to the front line in the Voormezelestraat. On 7 June 1917, no less than three explosive charges detonated underneath the nearby Hollandse Schuur and one underneath Sint-Elooi, where there were German troops as well. The evening before, despite their unease, the Germans had held big beer fests in the town of Menen.

In addition, a further sixteen deep mines exploded in the area that day. One tunnel end had been intercepted by the Germans and defused, and the four southernmost mines were not set off, out of strategic considerations. Thousands of tonnes of earth, concrete, trenches, weaponry and German forces were blown up by the British mines. The detonation of a total of half a million kilograms of explosives could be felt far across the Channel; the chaos was indescribable.

Edward Lyons, who served as Company Quartermaster Sergeant with the Royal Army Service Corps, was one of the first to view the damage caused by the mines and the bombardment that followed. When he arrived at the mine crater, Lyons, who served the entire First World War at the Western Front, saw that an enormous hole had been created. It looked to him like a small valley, albeit stripped of all vegetation. Nothing more than large piles of earth. Down in the crater, small creatures, souvenir hunters, were rummaging in the earth. Lyons then walked on to the village that had once been Wijtschate and passed the remains of a small woodland. Every leaf and every branch had been shot off and most trunks were split. Shortly afterwards, they got to the edge of a former village. Not one stone was on top of another. Everything had been razed to the ground. It was something Lyons would never forget, and he believed that there would be no examples more terrible of the destructive force of concentrated gunfire for the rest of the war.

Following the mine battle and the subsequent attack on the German positions, the British took so much ground that Bayernwald ended up far behind their front line. The British later stated that Bayernwald had been the best defended underground sector in

Flanders. In the spring of 1918, during the Fourth Battle of Ypres at the Kemmel mountain, the Germans recaptured their position. Their presence was short-lived. In the end, the woodland was recaptured on 28 September 1918 by British units of the 34th Division.

Monday at noon, I boil my water on my gas burner and make a cup of chicory, a kind of substitute coffee. The stuff has a strangely bitter taste that is almost impossible to get rid of. I try to neutralise my mouth with two slices of dry brown bread and two small dry sausages. My back is still aching from the march the day before, and my legs are stiff with cold, despite my constantly stamping my feet in an attempt to stay warm.

That afternoon, a pick-up truck makes its way onto the site. Behind the wheel is a man who later introduces himself as Kim Reekmans. He tells me that he looks after the Bayernwald grounds with his company, Arbor Vitae. He calls in every week to do repairs to the entrenchment.

I suggest I join him today as, during the war, the men were also continually repairing the trenches. Reekmans gives me a spade and together we shovel out the collapsed walls, making a number of duckboards accessible again as a result. It is good to have some company and at the same time to do some useful work. It kills time.

The present trenches have been fully restored based on archaeological research. The substructure of the trench consists of inverted A-frames with duckboards on top and is based on a British model. The water is carried away below it. Just as during the war, the trench walls are made of alder wood and this turns out not to be the best material.

'This timber rots after three or four years,' Reekmans explains. 'The intention during the war was not to be here for a particularly long time. A few weeks, months perhaps. But because we wanted to restore the site here as far as possible to its original condition, the same wood was used during reconstruction.'

Part of the entrenchment is indeed looking sorry. Timber has decayed. Wattle to support the earthen walls has collapsed. The repairs cost 1,000 euros per metre, Reekmans says, and the responsible local authority does not have any money for this. Thus, slowly but surely, a sizeable part of the only recently restored trench is being lost.

After two hours of digging, we call it a day and Reekmans drives out of the gate. It is quiet again in Bayernwald after his departure. During the war, the work we did this afternoon was mostly done after nightfall. I wonder how the men were able to do that one hundred years ago. Even though there is plentiful moonlight, there is virtually no visibility at night. Making tea or coffee, preparing and clearing away food, and also repairs took an eternity in the depths of the night.

That night, I decide to eat the two potatoes I brought from home. I peel them, place them in the mess tin filled with water and bring it to the boil on my gas stove. When the steam rises above the boiling water I hold my hands above the tin to try and warm them up. It takes an awfully long time before my potatoes are anywhere near done. I keep prodding the tubers in the hope they will become softer. After forty-five minutes, when the tin has as much as boiled dry and the potatoes have almost burnt, they are still rock hard. I add some extra water and let them boil for another thirty minutes. During my twenty-four hours at Bayernwald I have used more than a litre of water, I notice. That's going too fast. I need to be more frugal, like the men in the war. Clean water was barely available at the time. What was brought in from the hinterland was never enough to quench everybody's thirst, and so the troops had to turn to rain or groundwater that was sieved through a handkerchief or sackcloth. Not that this was particularly advisable.

Take the story that Reekmans told me earlier that afternoon about the officer who ordered his men to brew a cup of tea. Water from a nearby pool was painstakingly brought to the boil. Delicious, the officer thought. Nice and sweet especially. Until, the following day, when he passed the pool from which the water for the tea had been taken and saw that it was full of dead bodies.

When my potatoes are still not done after the extra thirty minutes of cooking time, I sprinkle salt on one, and chew on it until I manage to get it down with some difficulty. For want of anything better, I throw the other one over the fence that shields this spot from the outside world: uncooked it is barely edible. Ducks gaggling, a noise that seems to come from somewhere on the other side of Bayernwald, sounds as if I am being laughed at straight to my face.

Waiting in line for a little food. (In Flanders Fields Museum)

Serving hot food to American soldiers from rolling kitchens in France.
(US National Archives)

The civilised world is not far away from where I am. I hear dogs barking on nearby farms and the drone of cars. Occasionally, I see the lights of trucks thundering along the road from Armentières to Ypres. During the war, real life was not far removed from here either. Poperinge is only 15 kilometres further along. This was where there was alcohol, food, women, a bath and a bed; everything a serviceman needed to feel human again. Now there is silence, cold and darkness. I'm rubbing my cheeks with the wool of my hat. I suddenly realise that I have been doing this all day to keep myself warm.

Peering in the dark, I see shadows move in a strip of woodland on the edge of Bayernwald, like Javanese shadow puppets dancing. When I focus, it turns out to be no more than a tree, or the branches of a shrub. Not used to nature, I hear all kinds of rustlings and flutterings I cannot identify. That night, lying in my shelter, I hear a drone as if a tank wants to plough through Bayernwald's fence with roaring force. I turn my head with a start. Silence. I continue to listen tensely for a little longer, but there does not seem to be anything. You can drive yourself crazy like this. It was no different during the war years. At night, many a nervous shot was fired which hit no more than foliage or a heap of earth.

At sunrise on Tuesday, a murder of crows fly over Bayernwald. I eat two slices of dry brown bread and warm up the tin of red cabbage, which I devour outside my shelter. I am finally beginning to warm up and it starts to feel good to be here. A whiteish-grey cat slinks along the trenches, casts me a curious look, but is not interested in a piece of bread and quickly takes to its heels.

After breakfast, in order to keep moving and to have something to do, I scoop up the rotting autumn leaves from the trench with my entrenching tool. From the corner of my eye I see a polecat darting across the grass towards the woodland edge. I have not caught sight of a rat yet. There were millions at the time, drawn to the thousands of food tin remains which were thrown out of the trenches into no man's land. Brown and black rats. Some as big as adult cats and with hairless heads. Both types not only polished off the contents of the tins, but also gnawed at the dead bodies of the servicemen who had perished and on the cadavers of the horses found right across the front. The eyes and liver especially were delicacies for the rodents. The creatures spread diseases such as typhoid, Weil's disease and trench fever, an illness that usually began with acute shooting pain in the shins and would then switch to high fever.

The men tried to control the vermin using all possible means. By shooting them, by clubbing them to death or by stabbing them with a bayonet. The men manufactured hefty snap traps for catching rats. But the animals tended to be so strong that they tried to get away, iron bars and all, creating a lot of noise in the process.

'One night, with a big moon rising behind Jerry's line, I put a piece of cheese on the parapet, a black mountain against the moon's face,' recalled George Coppard, a British machine-gunner, after the war. 'I cocked a revolver close to the bait and stood motionless. Rat after rat came in quick succession, took one sniff and died.'

Every killed rat could yield a bonus: cigarettes, a piece of bread, sausage. There was not much point to it. Lack of food did not chase away the creatures. What's more, a healthy couple of rats can produce hundreds of offspring a year.

Nothing was safe from these rodents. Knapsacks and bread bags were gnawed apart. When the men slept, the critters would simply walk across their bodies and faces to get to the food, which had been hung from a thin rope from the dug-out ceilings as a precaution. If they could not reach it, they made such an almighty racket that sleeping was impossible. Coppard:

> At one time a sandbag full of peas hung from the vaulted roof in Vermelles brewery, a safe enough place we thought. When all were asleep, a rat stood on a man's head and tore at the bag. Suddenly a cascade of peas showered on the sleeper's face, and he woke up shouting and striking out in his alarm. Pandemonium and foul language spread through the vaults.

During the cold winter months, even the rats suffered from hunger and escaped from their nests by the thousand. They demolished everything: chocolate, bread, soap. In an officers' mess, they once ate a table cloth, paper combat plans and a large cat that should have exterminated the rodents.

Around noon, a weak autumn sun is out. I still have not felt a spot of rain. On the contrary, it suddenly seems springlike. My thermometer tells me it is 18 degrees in the sun and I am dozing on my feet, tin of tuna in my hand. I am tired, my body aches and the wooden boards in the trench are slippery with mud. But at least I am not standing up to my knees or hips in it, as was sometimes the case one hundred years ago.

Peter Gombeir, the director of Heuvelland tourist office, called in this morning. Like an officer inspecting the troops on the front line and inspiring them with courage before a big push. Gombeir, a tall, sympathetic guy, offered me cigarettes, asked if I was okay and promised me a cup of hot coffee upon my return to the civilised world.

Later that day, the site's warden appeared: a 64-year-old man and, like me, clad all in green, although he was wearing more of a hunting outfit. He took off his coat to show me the title 'Special Forest Ranger' on the epaulettes of his jersey. I should know I was dealing with proper authority. He was suspicious and worried: about the locks on the gate, the fencing around Bayernwald, the alleged local vandals and the British schoolchildren who visit the trenches like hooligans. Not that the Germans were such angels at the time, he said. 'But then again, they had good soup, eh?'

Soup is something I have as well: the 300ml tin of pea soup that I have brought along and will warm up in my mess tin this evening. Much of the other food I leave for what it is. The tins of spinach and one of the tins of tuna. Lack of food means I have too little energy to heat and choke these down as well. The same goes for two of the three packets of army biscuits, which have to do for the hard, dry biscuits the forces had at the time. All in all, the bread I have eaten, the one packet of army biscuits, the tins of tuna and pea soup make up an average of 950 calories a day. According to a nutritionist friend whom I asked later, this means I was 'below the required daily energy level of 1,000 to 1,500 calories necessary to keep basic metabolism on track.'

'You can imagine how this would affect your bodily functions in the long term,' she writes later. 'Especially considering the fact that physical and mental exertion also played a part then, the nutritional situation could be called deplorable. The effects of a below-required energy level in the long term are: a feeling of listlessness, reduced resistance, poor concentration and the breakdown of muscle tissue.'

During the night of Tuesday into Wednesday, the moon is up again, even though it is cloudier than on previous nights. The circumstances under which food was ingested were far from ideal one hundred years ago. There was mud, damp, cold. The stench of sweat, faeces and rotting meat permeated everywhere, although attempts were made to combat the smell of dead bodies by sprinkling calcium chloride. Dead horses and dead troops were sometimes not buried for months. And the corpses that were buried would come to the surface again as a result of bombs and shells landing close by.

I can imagine that people thought at the time: bring it on. Here, with this enemy, because it would mean an end to the grind. An end to routine actions such as cleaning and repairing the trenches. Forgetting the hunger and cold for a moment; the mud, rats, lice, fleas and other vermin. Not to mention the fear. Bring on whatever will make me forget the hardships and misery, and which means I can feel all the fibres in my body again and say I am alive.

I for one have still not got used to the silence, the loneliness, the contours of the trees in the sallow-hued light or the cold. Leaning against the concrete wall of a shelter, I scrape my mess tin with pea soup until it is completely empty. I feel the warmth of the food reach down to my toes. My whole body is tingling.

That night, I break up the time into half-hour slots. At eight o'clock, a cigarette. Half past eight: a sip of water. Nine o'clock: a nip of tea to keep the cold at bay. Half past nine: another cigarette. This is the only way to make the time seem to pass faster. I am constantly pacing the wooden duckboards, without idea, without plan. I have to do something to keep myself warm. I light a few more tealights and carefully feel the concrete slabs covering my shelter. These must surely be secured in some way, I hope, but in the dark I can see no evidence of this. Ten metres to my left there is a post in the trench wall; the top of it has the shape of a face. The head of an old German is how I picture it, and once in while I speak to him in passing: '*Wie geht's, du Alte?*' He is the only one who has kept me company all this time.

I feel miserable and depressed when I crawl out of my sleeping bag early on Wednesday morning, because sleep has eluded me again. It is dark and cold. It smells of autumn. With some difficulty I pull on my soldier's boots. I take two swigs of rum to wake up my stomach and to feel something warm. Jersey on, coat. I do up the buttons with numb fingers. Then I crawl out and wait for the morning light.

After three days of a bivouac in the trenches I am hungry and tired, but at least I have felt what it is like to live in a trench on meagre rations. I have experienced how important a few bites of warm food can be. Only that can give warmth and solace and will keep you going in the cold and during the long hours. But it's easy enough for me to talk, because I have not experienced anything like what the men went through all those years ago.

When the sun has come up and the farmers have begun working in the fields, I gather my things, open the gate in the fence enclosing Bayernwald and pace into the Voormezelestraat. On the way back to the civilised world I feel an outcast, with the mud on my boots and the sludge on my tunic. The damage is not too bad, it turns out: a few scratches, weals on my back, blisters on my right heel, a splash of mud on my face, skin as dry as parchment, my lips full of cracks. Later that day, when I stand on the bathroom scales in my hotel room, I observe that after three days of frugal rations, I weigh exactly 2 kilograms less than when I set out.

The sun rises late and lights up the woods on the Kemmelberg, which lies ahead like the promised land in a copper-red hue. There, hot coffee, a bed, a juicy piece of meat and a glass of beer await me.

Marching along the fields on the Vierstraat, I start to sing softly:

> Pack up your troubles in your old kit-bag,
> And smile, smile, smile.
> While you've a lucifer to light your fag,
> Smile, boys, that's the style.
> What's the use or worrying?
> It never was worthwhile, so
> Pack up your troubles in your old kit-bag,
> And smile, smile, smile.

TINNED VEGETABLES

Ingredients
tinned vegetables

Preparation
Drain the vegetables, as the water often tastes of tin. It is a good idea to mix the vegetables with hot salted water, which is also drained. Warm some flour and butter in a pan, add salt and cook it with the water and meat extract and then add the vegetables, which is ready in minutes.

Asparagus, beans and green peas can also be eaten if heated by pouring boiling salted water over them and then warm butter. For the beans, add a splash of citric acid or vinegar.

Die Gulaschkanone (*The Goulash Cannon*)

SEMOLINA DUMPLINGS

Ingredients
semolina
lard
potato flour

Preparation
Cook the semolina in salted water and some lard into a thick porridge. Allow to cool and knead into a mixture with potato flour. Place in boiling water. Dumplings that rise to the surface are done.

Anweisungen für Truppenküchen (*Instructions for Soldiers' Kitchens*)

RISOTTO

Ingredients
rice
lard
meat stock
grated cheese, tomato purée, meat leftovers or poultry liver

Preparation
Put the lard in a pan and add the dry rice. Pour in the meat stock and allow to cook while stirring constantly. Once the rice is cooked, add a great deal of grated cheese, or tomato purée, meat leftovers or poultry liver.

Kochbuch für den Schutzengraben (*Cookbook for the Trenches*)

STEWED APPLES

Ingredients
apples
sugar

Preparation
Soak the apple rings for about eight hours in water corresponding in quantity to the fruit. Place the apple rings with the liquor in which they were soaked, cloves and sugar into a boiler and simmer gently for one and a half hours. Stir regularly.

Manual of Military Cooking and Dietary

À LA MODE BEEF

Ingredients
2 kg lard
2 kg onions
pepper
salt
2 kg prunes
sugar

Preparation
Melt 2 kg lard in a pot and brown 2 kg onions. Half or the entire quantity of fresh or preserved meat will be cut in the number of portions as there are people eating. Place your meat in the lard, season with pepper and salt. Add 2 kg prunes, a few lumps of sugar and enough warm water so that your sauce will not appear too fatty. Simmer for 1 to 2 hours on low heat.

Handboek van den kok te Velde (Handbook for the Field Cook)

DANTE'S INFERNO

FAMINE IN GERMANY

Potsdamer Platz is an icon of capitalism in the world of international business, of progress, perhaps. Sony, PricewaterhouseCoopers, Deutsche Bahn; modern high-rise offices glisten in the sunshine.

It is also home to the Ritz Carlton and Hyatt five-star hotels, and a grand shopping centre in which all the global brands are represented. Day and night, Berliners and tourists spend millions of euros a year here. Which probably was exactly what Daimler Chrysler had in mind when, in 1989, it decided to build its new headquarters on this particular spot in Berlin. When, a year after the reunification of the two Germanies, Potsdamer Platz turned out to be the very centre of the city, it needed an imposing presence. As though the Kaiser Wilhelm II's Reich had risen triumphantly from the ashes.

There, on that square, in the shadow of these buildings, stands a small and grubby lump of stone to commemorate the socialist Karl Liebknecht. On that spot, on 1 May 1916, he called for a revolution against what he regarded an imperialist war.

Berlin was a grey, sombre city in those days. A city that lived on war. In every district, warehouses, buildings, factories and depots had been set up as ammunition workshops. A sizeable part of the population earned a living in arms manufacturing. That's where the jobs still were. But, over and above that, Berlin was a city that had suffered under the war.

'The town seemed to have been enveloped in an impenetrable veil of sadness, grey on grey, which no golden ray of sunlight ever seems able to pierce,' Evelyn Blücher wrote in her war diary about Berlin. Blücher was a British woman who had married a German, and for that reason had been deported from Britain at the outbreak of the war. From sheer necessity, she lived in a city that during the war was an increasingly miserable place, 'and which forms a fit setting for the white-faced, black-robed women who glide so sadly through the streets. Some bearing their sorrow proudly as a crown to their lives, others bent and broken under a burden too heavy to be borne.'

The sadness lay in the long lists of names of the dead and missing which were published every day. And in the number of unemployed, which grew steadily. The war ever more began to affect the economy. People were losing their jobs in all kinds of industries. Even in the arms factories there were insufficient places to give work to jobseekers. And those places were by and large filled by women; most men were at the front.

The living conditions deteriorated. The lack of food, price rises, the poor quality of what was still available, hard labour for a pittance – they were the talk of the day.

Blücher wrote:

> Women are realising the enormous burden imposed upon them. They have to do the men's work as well as their own, and when they have earned their pay it all goes into the pockets of others who sell them food at enormous prices. Naturally they begin more than ever to say: 'Why should we work, starve, send our men out to fight? What is it all going to bring us? More work, more poverty, our men cripples, our homes ruined. What is it all for? What do we care whether we have a bit more land added on to our big Germany? We had enough land. We'd rather fight for a more just division of the goods of this earth. For whether we obtain land or money for the "Fatherland" after this war, *we* shall not see any change in our lives; the wealth will not come our way. The State which called upon us to fight cannot even give us decent food, does not treat our men as human beings, but as so many screws in the great machine of the German army.'

From the outset, Germany was locked in a battle on two fronts. On one side was hostile France; on the other, opposing Russia. The other neighbouring countries – the Netherlands, Belgium,

Luxembourg, Switzerland and Denmark – were neutral. Only the Austro-Hungarian Empire sided with the country. Fairly soon after the outbreak of the war, the neutral countries signed an agreement to cease trading with the Germans. Germany thus became increasingly isolated.

The noose around the country's neck was tightened when the Royal Navy blocked the ports of Bremen and Hamburg. After that, the German Reich was no longer able to conduct any trade of significance. No ship was allowed to enter the seaports to supply Germany with arms, machinery or basic materials, and no German ship went offshore. Not a single parcel went in or out.

There was a flour shortage in Germany as early as the end of October 1914, which forced the bakers in Berlin to add potato flour to their bread. Stocks of fat, coffee, tea, sugar, milk, eggs and potatoes dwindled one by one. Time and again, in an attempt to guarantee equal distribution of increasingly scarce foodstuffs, the German government had to introduce measures to ration products.

Big cities signed contracts with food suppliers, arranged warehouses for food and organised distribution from them. Soup kitchens were set up where the poorest sections of the population could find a meal: a motley crew of war invalids, widows and unemployed that grew ever larger. In exchange for food coupons, these people received monotonous, cheap, but nutritious food. Maximum prices were levied on all kinds of scarce products to ensure that everyone – rich or poor – was able to buy barley or rye. Traders capitalised on this by forming cartels. Collectively, they transported stocks to locations where the maximum price for products had not yet been introduced. This meant they could demand big sums for their goods.

All the shortages meant that life became more and more expensive. On 16 October 1915, the newspaper *Vorwärts* printed a chart of the price of nineteen different products. The price of potatoes had increased by 133 per cent. Butter cost 66 per cent more and beans 172 per cent.

Just like in the United Kingdom and France, agriculture yielded dwindling crops. Compared with the previous year, the 1914 crop was poor. In the case of potatoes, for instance, the soil had produced almost 10 per cent more the previous year. In 1915, too, the harvest fell short of expectations because of a shortage of artificial fertiliser, amongst other things. The majority of this came from abroad, but was no longer obtainable as a result of the wartime trade blockades. The chemicals still available to Germany, moreover, were needed for the manufacture of explosives. This meant the amount of artificial fertiliser at the farmers' disposal was halved.

Likewise, the volume of natural fertiliser plummeted, largely as a result of the depletion of livestock. In 1915, it was decided to slaughter millions of pigs, one third of the total. It was thought that the animals ate too much of the food that the general population needed.

The only presents Australian musician Caroline Ethel Cooper, who lived in Leipzig during the war, received for Christmas 1915 was food: 'You would laugh if you saw my table of presents,' she wrote her sister in Australia. 'A tin of sardines, a large sausage, two pots of jam, cakes, a pound of tea, fruit and, which touched me most, ¼ of butter [...]. When one knows the time and trouble that it costs to get any butter, that becomes very valuable indeed.'

The following year, all Cooper was able to give herself for Christmas was a cleaning cloth and a piece of soap. She did receive some food, however: soup, mustard, curry powder, baby food, coffee, jam, tinned fish, stock cubes, dried mushrooms and a packet of biscuits. 'Invaluable things which will make life easier for weeks and weeks to come,' she wrote to her sister. She apologised that her letters were so much about food: 'But we only have two topics of thought or conversation – first, the paper – then food! There is nothing else.'

It was almost impossible to distribute the little food that was still being grown. A lack of appropriate warehouses meant that reliable transport was crucial, especially for perishables such as potatoes. But the railways struggled with shortages of coal, locomotives, railway carriages, parts and manpower to load and operate the trains.

There was also a shortage of labour in the fields, which, coupled with the lack of fertilisers and poor distribution, rendered the farming industry increasingly unable to produce enough. Farm workers were relinquished in favour of the army or work in the arms industry. These tended to be boys and men whose absence in the fields was keenly felt during sowing and harvest times.

Wilhelm Niedermeyer's father was one of them. His parents had a small farm in the village of Stockhausen near Bielefeld: two cows and a plot for growing potatoes and cereals. The garden produced vegetables and fruit.

Father Niedermeyer was a bricklayer. Before the war, he had worked partly on the land and in construction during the summer months. From the end of 1915, he was deployed in the arms factories in the Ruhr area. Two or three times a year he came home on leave. That was the only time available. The government did all it could to meet the growing shortage of labour. Some 430,000 farm workers from outside Germany were set to work in the fields, as were almost 900,000 prisoners of war. During harvest time, some soldiers were given longer leave to help out at home.

In wartime Stockhausen, it came down to women and children. Wilhelm Niedermeyer was four years old when the war broke out, and was one of the German schoolboys who helped out in the fields from a very young age, as did his brothers and sisters.

'Tending the cows, helping to sow, making hay,' Niedermeyer tells me in his modest home in Bremen, where he has been living on his own for a number of years:

> With our two cows and plot of land, we could survive. Half of the land we cultivated was for our use, the other half belonged to the Obernfelde country estate. To use it, we had to pay more than 400 Reichsmark in rent. That was a lot of money. On the other hand it did make us self-sufficient. The only things we needed to buy were herbs, salt and sugar.

During the war, people regularly came from cities in the Ruhr area to Stockhausen to beg for food, Niedermeyer recalls. 'My father brought colleagues from the arms factory home with him. These people had nothing to swap, no money, no goods. They begged for food. We always helped these people. We gave them bread and potatoes.'

The situation was a lot worse in the cities, he came to realise:

> People really starved. I experienced this in the Second World War, but people had a much worse time during the First World War. Even in a small town like Lübbecke, near

Stockhausen, the food situation was deplorable. People had built sties in their gardens to keep a pig. Ninety per cent of the town's inhabitants did this. Having a pig was crucial to survival.

A proportion of what the land yielded had to be surrendered by the farmers to the authorities. Everything that they grew or tended was registered. This included the pigs. They were allowed to keep one pig for slaughter, the other had to be handed over for the production of meat. This was inspected. Niedermeyer: 'Everyone in the village knew that two pigs were slaughtered sometimes. One was hung to be checked and the other hidden for personal use, because it was not as if there was all that much food.'

Much agricultural machinery was out of action because the horses had been requisitioned by High Command. This included Stockhausen. 'Our neighbour across the road had two of them,' Niedermeyer recalls. 'He had to hand one over to the army. From that day onwards he tilled the land with a horse and cow in front of the plough. What did we eat? Turnip, potatoes, bread. It was all very frugal.'

The villagers did not really speak about the war and food shortages, Niedermeyer says. 'The only topic of conversation were the dead. That was the main concern. In the village, bills were posted with the names of the fallen and missing. I can still see how the women wailed and cried.'

These days Niedermeyer is a keen amateur cook. 'After my wife died I bought a recipe book. I cook meals with rice or pasta, sometimes a small piece of meat. I only eat things I enjoy eating.'

During the war years, numerous recipe books appeared which taught German housewives how to put a nutritious and tasty meal on the table with limited means. The books had titles such as *Wer spart, hilft Siegen* (*Saving Leads to Victory*), *Wie baue ich mir selbst eine Kochkist?* (*How Do I Make Myself a Haybox?*), *Sächsisches Kriegskochbuch* (*Saxon War Cookery Book*) and *Kriegsküche für Jedermann* (*Everyone's War Kitchen*).

The first fully German war cookbook to appear was *Die Deutsche Hausfrau im Weltkrieg, ausführliches Kriegs-Kochbuch aller Ernährungsarten – nebst Ratschlägen in gesunden und kranken Tagen und praktische Winke im Haushalt* (*The German Housewife During a World War: A Detailed War Cookbook Including All Styles of Feeding – Together with Advice for Healthy and Sick Days and Practical Tips for Housekeeping*). The German Kaiserin received the first copy. As with all cookery books that came on to the market, its author urged the housewife not to throw anything away, to prepare balanced meals, not to eat unnecessary meals in order not to overload her body and produce germs, and to eat only when genuinely hungry. It contained recipes for dishes such as white flour soup, bread soup and potato soup. The book also gave tips for how food might benefit health: green lettuce and asparagus that purify the blood and are good for the kidneys; raw carrots for children with worms; and Lepidium for cancer patients.

German companies, such as the Rex Preserving Glass Company from Bad Homburg, also did their bit to help the nation get through the lean times. In 1916, this company issued a recipe book extending to more than 200 pages which explained how food such as fruit, vegetables, meat and fish could be preserved at home with the 'world famous Rex Sterilising appliance' and preserving jars which could hold up to 4 litres. The cookbook contained dozens of recipes for the preparation and preservation of various kinds of food, including boiled fish, calf's tongue, pot-roast pheasant, goose liver pâté and potato pudding.

Another cookbook, the *Hessisches Kriegskochbuch, Ein Ratgeber für Zeitgemässes Kochen* (*Hesser War Cookery Book: Advice for Up-to-Date Cooking*) gave tips for using a haybox. This was labour- and fuel-saving, and was convenient for women who had to work away from home during the day or who had small children. The haybox, or fireless cooker, served to complete the cooking process of food items that were cooked briefly in a box insulated with wool, newspaper, sawdust, wood, wool or straw. A box of this kind kept food warm in times in which wood, coal and other fuels were becoming increasingly scarce.

Necessity is the mother of invention. At the weekend, people went into the woods to forage for berries, nuts, herbs, mushrooms and seeds. Recycling became sacred and chemical industries came up with new preservatives. Farmers used kitchen waste as animal feed. And when there was almost nothing left to recycle because products became more scarce, 'ersatz' became the buzzword. Bread was made up partly from sawdust and powdered potato and turnip, and was sprinkled with chalk instead of flour. Coffee was made from dried acorns, chicory, or dried and roasted turnip. Powdered chalk and bricks substituted for cocoa. Tea consisted of dried raspberry leaves. No wonder people fell ill, lost pounds in weight and sometimes wasted away.

'I have been in bed with what some people say is influenza, but I feel inclined to call it "Ersatz" illness,' Evelyn Blücher wrote in March 1916. 'Everyone is feeling ill from too many chemicals in the food. I don't believe Germany will ever be starved out, but she will be poisoned out first with these substitutes!'

Early 1916. The shortage was so great that in the shops it was a case of 'first come, first served.' In the middle of the night, thousands of housewives, clutching a shopping bag in one hand and a kitchen chair in the other, stepped out of their houses and trudged to the baker or the butcher. There they waited in a shabby queue outside the shops' doors until opening time, exhausted and embittered. If the women had work, then the children took over their place in the queue until the shops opened. This would allow them, if they were not too late, to pick up their miserly rations: the weekly egg, some bread and maybe half a herring. In the words of the Berlin doctor Alfred Grotjahn: 'I bumped into an ex-patient today, who had lost 66 pounds in a short time. True starvation has begun.'

In April that year, the situation was dire. People looked anxiously for all kinds of ways to lay their hands on food. In Cologne, the mayor was twice dragged out of bed in the dead of night to open the market, so desperate was the population. One night, a cat with its eyes pierced was suspended from his door; the same fate would befall him if he did not look after his townspeople better. In other cities, women robbed shops and knocked over market stalls. That month, strikes erupted in 300 workplaces, including Krupp's arms factories and the coal mines, all businesses that made an important contribution to the war industry.

On 1 May 1916, Labour Day, there were gatherings throughout Berlin. Men and women with furious faces stood together in agitation. The tension was palpable. Revolution was in the air. On Potsdamer Platz, more than 10,000 people assembled in the early hours of the morning. The typed flyers which had been distributed the day before called on the population to demonstrate with the words 'Bread! Freedom! Peace!' Every day, Karl Liebknecht handed out a pamphlet titled: 'The main enemy is in your own country.' That morning, his voice resounded across the square: 'Down with the war!' and 'Down with the government!' Eight words. Immediately afterwards, the socialist was pulled from the crowds, arrested and jailed for two and a half years.

Fearful of looting, butchers closed their shops for two, sometimes three weeks. Vegetables were pretty much unobtainable. Milk and butter were a rarity. In June that year, the socialist Spartacus League, led by Liebknecht and Rosa Luxemburg, published a pamphlet:

> The inevitable has happened: Hunger! Hunger! In Leipzig and Berlin, in Braunschweig, Magdeburg, Munich and Kiel and in many other towns and cities, starving masses are rioting in front of food shops. In both Kiel and Braunschweig the workers of the Germania shipyards have gone on strike in protest against the deplorable national food policy. The government has just one reply to the people's cry of hunger: reinforcing martial law, police swords and military patrols.

This was right: the men and women rebelling were forcibly driven back into the factories and put to work. Strikers and protesters appeared to have gained nothing. Not one single demand that had been advanced for the struggle was met.

The days became greyer and more miserable than previously. Meat, potatoes and eggs were rationed, and at the end of May the government found itself having to set up the *Kriegsernährungsamt* (War Office of Food) to take care of the equal distribution of food. One of the measures the office had carried out was the killing of around 2 million dogs. The food that these animals ate could be given to the German people.

During the autumn of 1916, the harvest failed. Again. Instead of potatoes, turnips became the most important food staple. Once used as cattle fodder, it now filled the stomachs of Germans.

'Turnips!' Ida Wundtke, born in 1899, exclaims in her room in a Berlin care home. She shakes her head. 'Nothing but turnip. We

Wine and music. Even in the trenches at times. (In Flanders Fields Museum)

Food en route. (In Flanders Fields Museum)

did the craziest things with it to try and put something tasty on the table, including turnip pies. It didn't taste good, but we did eat it.'

Turnips were incorporated into all kinds of comestibles, from marmalade to beer. A brochure about healthy eating featured turnip recipes for four people, in an endless sequence of variations on a theme: turnip with potatoes, turnip soup, brown turnip, turnip pudding, turnip mince sausages, turnip chops, green cabbage with turnip, red cabbage with turnip, turnip salad, sour turnip, turnip with apples, stuffed turnip and turnip sauce.

At the time, Ida Wundtke lived in Stettin, a German city which these days is known as Szczecin in Poland. She now spends most of her time in her small room in the Barbara-von-Renthe-Fink-Haus on the Bundesallee in Berlin, the city she has lived in since 1921. She shares this room with another lady of very advanced age. It contains not much more than two anonymous beds, a table and a sideboard, all of the cheapest quality.

A photograph close to her bed features her sitting sprightly in a wheelchair belonging to the Berlin Zoo: a visit to polar bear cub Knut, a present for her birthday from the city authorities. In the photo, she is neatly coiffured and made-up, and is wearing her best dress. You'd think she was twenty-five years younger.

Now, on a wintry day shortly after noon, she is not smartly dressed and made-up, but her face nevertheless shows remarkably few wrinkles. Wundtke wears a navy jersey and worn green corduroy trousers, and her hair has not been combed. She has just had lunch; her dessert of chocolate custard remains untouched on her table.

Today, she is not as cheerful as she looks in the photo taken at the zoo. The device that was once put in her body to keep her heart going just keeps on going, she says. And that makes her a little downcast. She would have preferred to have died a long time ago. Who wants to get this old in a lonely state, with all those long days to get through?

Even though she has to dig deep in her memory, Wundtke has plenty to say about the Great War. People were not happy when it broke out, she tells me, and they did not become happy: 'There was so much starvation.'

Wundtke was fifteen when the war broke out. In Stettin, her

father worked as a shepherd. Shortly after mobilisation, he went to the Eastern Front as a gunner, as did both of her brothers. 'People talked about food constantly, but what could they do? Everything that was imported, and this included food, went to the army. My mother worked at home, she made men's trousers. She earned some money which allowed her to buy a few things.'

Wundtke had the good fortune to get a job as a domestic servant for the family of a businessman and his Austrian wife:

> They had money and decent food. I benefitted from this. In the evening I went home, because we lived around the corner. I often kept back small portions, took them home and gave them to my mother. She was ill, had stomach complaints. All that turnip did not go down well. With the food I brought home, she managed to get something nutritious inside. She was always really glad of that.

The *Kriegsernährungsamt* kept statistics. At the end of 1916, the nutrients the population were getting were found to be far from sufficient: only 59 per cent of the required carbohydrates, 25 per cent of necessary proteins and 19 per cent of fat needed. Even less than in France and the United Kingdom, where there were also food problems.

The inadequate quantities and poor quality of food led to malnutrition. The mortality rates amongst women increased by 11.5 per cent in 1916; by 30.4 per cent in 1917. Other groups also died of starvation, namely the very weakest – the elderly, the sick. Child mortality was up by 30 per cent. As a result of the starvation blockade, a total of more than 1 million people died during the war.

The harsh winter that year was extremely detrimental. In Berlin, temperatures of minus 20 degrees were recorded. The frost lasted from 4 January to 10 February 1917. Railways became unserviceable and canals froze over. The supply of fuel came to a halt. Theatres, cinemas and museums closed their doors. Schoolchildren were given time off school for weeks. Warm clothes and shoes had become more or less impossible to get hold of.

Throughout Berlin, there was a veritable epidemic of burst water mains. 'And as there are no plumbers to repair the damage, people are beginning to think that the torments of Dante's inferno are capped by the hardships of this deadly winter of 1916–1917,' Evelyn Blücher noted in her diary.

> There are practically no motors to be had, and the few antediluvian *droshkies* [a low, four-wheeled carriage] are being dragged wearily along by half-starved beasts who, if they happen to stumble and fall don't attempt to rise, but lie still, humbly thankful for the respite from work, on the cold frozen ground. As for the mood of the people, the heroic attitude has entirely disappeared. Now one sees faces like masks, blue with cold and drawn by hunger, with the harassed expression common to all those who are continually speculating as to the possibility of another meal.

By the beginning of 1917, the weekly ration for adults in Berlin was one 800g loaf of bread, made with potato flour or turnip, 80g of butter, 250g of meat (including bones), 180g of sugar and half an egg. In reality, the amounts were never attained and many people had to turn to the city's soup kitchens. There, some 170,000 helpings of badly tasting, watery soup was doled out every day. The shortage of food was sometimes supplemented by vegetables grown on any bit of waste land. People even ate cats, dogs, sparrows, crows, ravens or jackdaws. These would be soaked in camomile tea first in order to neutralise their strong taste.

The writer Richard Huelsenbeck returned home in January 1917 after spending some time in Zurich and described Berlin as 'a city of tightened stomachers [a type of waistcoat], of mounting, thundering hunger, where hidden rage was transformed into boundless money lust, and men's minds were concentrating more and more on the questions of naked existence.'

Not everywhere did people resign themselves to their fate of meagre rations. In March 1917, hundreds of housewives demonstrated outside the town hall of Charlottenburg in Berlin. Shouting the slogan 'Hunger, hunger, we want turnips!' they called on the authorities to give them food. Research had shown that the population's daily calorie intake was 40 per cent lower than before the war. But more food was not forthcoming. In April that year, the government came up with a plan to restrict the bread ration even further.

A day later, strikes broke out in the big industrial cities. In Berlin alone, 217,000 workers downed tools. There were large demonstrations throughout the city. The rations per household were minimal and, because of their low wages and the high prices on the black market, the workers were no longer able to supplement their limited quantities of food. Work in ammunition workshops, engineering factories, the aviation industry and in electricity companies came to a stop. In the big cities, shops were ransacked. The workers set up anti-imperialist workers' councils. High on their list of demands was better distribution of food.

This time, too, the strikers were back at work within days. Armed forces occupied the weapons and munitions factories. Dozens of arrests followed. Labourers were told that they would be put on a train to the front if they did not turn up at work. Because the production of ammunition and weapons had to continue, concessions were made. The men and women who did heavy work in the factories were entitled to extra food.

In the army, there were also signs of war fatigue and exhaustion. Troops that came for reinforcement at the front and soldiers on furlough from Germany brought with them a mood that was not conducive to the men's morale. Soldier Johannes Haas wrote:

Reinhold, a boy from my group, had a letter from his wife saying that she taken all their furniture, apart from the beds, to the pawnbroker's. Then officers on the ground wonder that the men have had enough. These Champagne-and-Wine types party while we are dying in the mud and get twelve spoonfuls of rubbish marmalade and fourteen sugar cubes for Christmas. That bigmouth Liebknecht is the only man the soldiers still feel some sympathy for and whom they trust.

According to General Ludendorff, morale amongst the men was sinking. Not only because of the lack of food and coal, money worries, the length of the war and the loss of family members, but also, he believed, because of 'agitation by seditious elements.'

The scarcity of food amongst many troop units and the unfaltering differences between the amount of food the officers and the soldiers were allocated engendered a rift exploited by revolutionary elements, Ludendorff thought. After the Russian Revolution and the deposition of the Tsar, and at the conclusion of the war in that country, Bolsheviks began to gain some influence as well.

When the social democrat Adolf Linke came home from the Eastern Front on leave for Christmas 1917, he could easily see that his wife and children were undernourished. The opinion amongst his friends, family and acquaintances was the same everywhere: 'Do as the Russians do! End this stupid war, we are starving to death!'

That winter, the Berliners were only getting 30g of butter and 50g of margarine a week with their ration coupons. The average ration dropped from 3,400 to less than 1,000 calories. Hunger oedema became normal. No wonder that large strikes once again broke out in Germany on 28 January 1918.

The streets of Berlin were shrouded in a thick fog that day, which distorted the buildings into strange shapes in the eye of the beholder. Towards 9 a.m., the rolling and stamping of the machines stopped and silence fell. A reporter of the newspaper *Vorwärts* saw the gate outside one factory opening and three workers walking out, one clutching a mug of coffee. They grabbed a cigarette and gave each other a light. Then the next group of workers came out. And so it went on. Men and women walked out of the gate with grave faces and stopped outside in anticipation of what might come. One them said: 'They're all coming.'

In groups, the workers walked into the fog in order to regroup in the garden of a beer hall. One of the men got up to speak: 'I don't need to tell anyone why we laid down our tools. Everyone knows why.'

Amongst the strikers was one Elsbeth Schmidt. She worked at the Loewe factory in Berlin. Barely twenty years of age, she had no grasp of politics or socialism. That is until the day that a fellow worker gave her a stack of pamphlets with the request that she distribute them unnoticed amongst the other workers. The title was: 'Outside to demonstrate against the war.' Like so many other workers, the young Elsbeth cooperated. The decision to take part was easy for her: 'I'm so hungry all the time, the war must stop!'

Shortly after the strike and the assembly in the beer garden, the mounted police appeared and began to attack the strikers with their sabres. Yelling: 'Down with the war! Hunger! Hunger!' the workers dispersed.

A day after the outbreak of the mass strikes, more than half a million workers had downed tools in Berlin. They all worked in the munitions and steel factories. Number three on their list of demands: more food to be obtained by opening up the food stocks in the production companies and trade depots in order to guarantee more equal distribution amongst all sections of the population.

The strike soon spread. Hamburg followed, Leipzig, Cologne, Breslau, Munich and other cities. Once again, workers' council were set up. The leaders of the social democratic party, which throughout the previous years had supported the war in all respects, declared its solidarity.

Two days later, large red placards appeared in Berlin on which the authorities proclaimed martial law. Any disturbance of the peace would be quashed using all possible means. The police force, meanwhile, would be reinforced by 5,000 soldiers.

The following day, police officers opened fire on the assembled crowds in the Berlin district of Charlottenburg. The soldiers who appeared in the city were jeered at and called 'bloodhounds.' Workers put up roadblocks by overturning trams and lorries. The war that had been raging solely on the front was now being waged in the homeland as well.

On 1 February 1918, the authorities placed the most important war industries in Berlin under military command: the German arms and munitions industries, the Schwartzkopff and Borsig factories, AEG in Hennigsdorf, the Argus engine and Daimler factories, and the aircraft factory in Johannisthal. Countless rounded-up strikers were forced onto trains headed for the front. Five days after the outbreak of the strike, the uprising ended, again without any of the demands having been met.

People were getting thinner and thinner. 'The rounded contours of the German nation have become a legend of the past,' Blücher wrote. 'We are all gaunt and bony now, and have dark shadows round our eyes, and our thoughts are chiefly taken up with wondering what our next meal will be, and dreaming of the good things that once existed.'

'The truth is, the soul of the people is sick unto death of the useless carnage and hateful sinfulness of it all,' Blücher continued:

> In the Reichstag the same old bombastic phrases still bring down a volley of applause, so that the quiet observer is astonished at the childishness of these representatives of the nation [...]. One intrepid Socialist, goaded to despair at the artificiality of the speeches, shouted out the truth in the face of the whole assembly: 'The people don't want war; what they want is peace and bread and work' – but he was only snubbed by contemptuous derision in reply.

WHITE FLOUR SOUP

Ingredients
white flour
water
oil or butter
salt
parsley

Preparation
Bring salted water to the boil and add some oil or butter. Whilst stirring constantly add two tablespoons of white flour. Parsley salt gives a powerful flavour.

Die Deutsche Hausfrau im Weltkrieg (*The German Housewife During the World War*)

OATMEAL SOUP

Ingredients
90 g oatmeal
20 g lard
soup greens
salt
1.5 litre water

Preparation
Boil the soup greens in the water and drain the liquid through a sieve. Add the oatmeal which has been made into a soft paste in a little water to the liquid while stirring constantly. The soup should cook for 30 minutes.

Kriegskochbuch, Anweisungen zur einfachen und billigen Ernährung (War Cookery Book: Instructions for Simple and Cheap Nourishment)

MEAT PANCAKES

Ingredients
250 g flour
250 g meat leftovers or bacon
chives
1 small onion
1 tablespoon lard
salt
pepper
8 to 10 tablespoons lard for frying

Preparation
Make a smooth batter. Flatten the meat and bacon and add this to the batter together with the onion and lard. Fry thin pancakes with these.

Kriegskochbuch, Anweisungen zur einfachen und billigen Ernährung (War Cookery Book: Instructions for Simple and Cheap Nourishment)

PRESERVED BEANS (for four people)

Ingredients
2 lbs preserved beans
water
1 tablespoon lard
2 to 3 eggs
flour
1 onion
pepper
parsley

Preparation
Wash the beans the night before. Put in with hot water and bring to the boil. Drain, add fresh warm water and boil for 30 minutes. Place the pan with beans in the haybox. The next morning, drain the beans through a sieve. Make a brown flour sauce with the lard, flour and finely chopped onion, add water, pepper and salt to the beans. Bring the vegetables to the boil again and put in the haybox until use. Before serving, add a little finely chopped parsley.

Kriegskochregeln für Benutzung der Kochkiste (*War Cookery Guidelines for Use of the Haybox*)

RICE PUDDING WITH CHERRIES

Ingredients
250 g rice
0.75 litre milk
cinnamon stick
120 g butter
150 g sugar
8 eggs
750 g sweet or sour cherries

Preparation
Allow the thoroughly washed rice to swell in water until half-cooked. Drain and cook the rice in the milk with sugar and cinnamon until very soft. Once the rice has cooled down, stir in the egg yolks, the butter beaten into cream and the egg whites beaten till they are snow white. Fill a buttered Rex preserving jar alternately with the rice mixture and the cherries in such a way that the topmost layer comprises the rice mixture. The cherries can be used with or without stones. Sterilise everything for 2.5 hours at a 100°C.

The pudding can be enjoyed cold or can be warmed up in a bain-marie for 30 minutes.

Rex-Kochbuch (Rex Cookery Book)

KARTOFFELSUPPE, KARTOFFEL-SUPPE...UND KEIN FLEISCH

THE FINAL BATTLE, 1918

In 1917, Germany had defeated Serbia and Romania. Even more significantly, the ceasefire signed with the Bolsheviks following the Russian Revolution at the end of that year meant that Germany had brought Russia almost to its knees. For the Germans, the war on two fronts was effectively at its end, and thus they could concentrate more or less fully on the fighting in Belgium and France.

And yet the future looked sombre in the autumn of 1917. In view of the food situation in Germany and at the front, it remained to be seen how much longer the Reich would be able to keep going. Sky-high prices had to be paid for the simplest articles of food. A carrot cost half a week's wages. Eggs were only for sale in twos or threes and only on doctor's orders. There was no fuel for hot water, no soap with which to wash, no tobacco and no medicines.

Rye and potato yields were falling. Few or no electric trams were running. There was no coal. Public buildings were no longer heated. Clothes were threadbare.

People were constantly looking for food. If not in the city, then they took themselves off into the countryside to forage for something edible. Only the wealthy were able to buy a few things on the black market, but they too were hungry. The middle classes were as badly off as the workers.

Trains transporting food were ambushed and raided daily, even by railway workers. Transport by boat was no longer safe either. Dispatches were ground to a halt. Goods were transferred under duress into smaller boats and carts. Civil servants sold books, furniture and other objects from government buildings in exchange for food. Youths broke into farm barns at night looking for food. To survive, the law had to be broken.

This was the situation in Germany itself. As far as the armies were concerned, the German staff was soon aware there would be a shortage of men. Every month, 79,000 reservists were called up for military service, but this influx was only just enough to retain troop levels. From January 1918, the army was due to shrink in size. But that was not all. The reservists who might be sent to the front tended to be young, inexperienced, barely trained and, to some extent, undernourished. After January 1918, the only draft available would be those born in 1900. Soldiers aged 18; boys.

For the Allies, the reverse was the case, partly due to the fact that the United States had joined them. On 1 February 1917, the German government had declared an unrestricted submarine war, which meant a decision to attack all boats, Allied or neutral, warship or trading vessel. As a result, America, which had been neutral up until then, became more and more entangled in the war. Whereas before the country had been primarily a supplier of war provisions to the French and British, now there were American casualties. On 6 April 1917, the United States accordingly declared war on Germany. Hundreds of thousands of well-armed American troops were ready to go to the front.

German propaganda, which had been initially disseminated in the United States to keep the country out of the war, had had no effect. In the 1916 pamphlet *The Archive of Reason*, Americans were advised to enact the war rather than to experience it personally by digging a shoulder-height trench in their gardens, half-filling this with water and standing in it. They were encouraged to stay there for two or three days on an empty stomach and to hire madmen with guns and revolvers to shoot them at close range. This would give them a complete picture of the war and would cost the country must less.

Reality had overtaken propaganda: now that American merchant vessels were sent to the bottom of the sea by German torpedoes, the United States had practically no other choice but to partake in the war. Thus, Germany would have to face an overwhelmingly superior strength in troop numbers. It was judged that, for that reason alone, the Germans would lose the war in due course.

In a last attempt to win the war, Germany focused all its attention on the Western Front, hoping to defeat the British and French before the Americans were able to bring over their troops to France in large numbers. The aim was to deal the Allies such a heavy blow that, in the ensuing peace negotiations, Germany would be able to put stringent demands on the table. It wanted to keep its navy and army intact. Moreover, it was not prepared to cede its African colonies. The same applied to Alsace-Lorraine and Belgium, which were mostly German occupied.

In Mons, in Hainaut Province, German High Command considered the various offensive strategies. It was decided to implement Operation Michael, also called *Kaiserslacht* (Kaiser's Battle) or Spring Offensive. The date: 21 March 1918. The architect behind the operation: General Erich Ludendorff. The German commander was optimistic. He believed that, for Germany, the situation had become favourable after the disappearance of Russia as an enemy: 'As in 1914 and 1915 we could consider deciding the war through a territorial offensive.' The trenches had to be abandoned. Movement became the motto.

Ludendorff did not want to lose any time. Not only because he did not suspect the Americans to come into action until the spring of 1918; any sooner would not be organisationally feasible for the United States. The matter was urgent because Germany's ally Austria-Hungary was about to reach the end of its military power through sheer exhaustion. Now the armies could still be usefully deployed. Ludendorff was convinced that only an offensive on the Western Front would lead to victory. All that needed to be done was to amass sufficient troops.

The latter objective was one of the reasons for signing a peace treaty with Russia on 3 March 1918. This would be the only way in which the German armies which were still stationed at the Eastern Front could be deployed in the west. Many soldiers in the east were keen to go to Belgium and France. They did not want to live through another Russian winter. Moreover, the food there was atrocious.

Operation Michael was the last card the German General Staff was able to play. Preparations were exhaustive, and the training of the infantry and artillery more intensive than ever. One by one, the soldiers were trained. Extensive areas of Belgium and behind the front in the west of Germany were in effect one large training camp. The men were given new and more powerful weapons. Large quantities of artillery were transported in. The air force's strike power was enhanced. Aeroplanes were equipped with special radios and cameras with telelenses in order to perform reconnaissance flights and report enemy positions. The Germans, meanwhile, conducted gunnery bombardments to keep the enemy occupied. They executed small, scattered attacks on British and French positions to disguise their true intentions. Radio reports were also broadcast to mislead the Allies.

And yet the plan did not really succeed. The British and French gathered information from which they could deduce that the Germans were planning to open a new offensive. In their attempts to get their hands on more detailed plans, the Allies conducted attacks on the German positions. In the process, they hoped to take prisoners of war who might be able to provide interesting intelligence whilst assessing the strength of these positions.

As it was not clear when the Germans were going to attack, everyone stood guard for a few nights before 21 March, recalled Private Edward Lyons. Every night, all combat posts were occupied, and each morning at 8 a.m. the order was given to stand down. Around 19 March, a number of Germans had been captured who then revealed that their offensive would begin on the morning of 21 March, preceded by a bombardment lasting ten hours, two of which involving gas shells. During the night of 20 March, the combat posts were manned again and Lyons and his comrades took part in a forty-five-minute exercise for a gas attack. They went to sleep as usual with the idea that, as on the previous nights, nothing would be happening.

In Germany, the population had faith in the impending offensive, despite the January and February strikes. There simply was no other option: the Germans hoped that a victory would finally solve the many problems in their country. People were back at work and almost 7 million of them subscribed to the eighth government war bond. This loan generated a record sum of 15 billion Deutschmark for the German state. The vast majority of the Germans were resolute: Operation Michael *had* to succeed.

One of the German soldiers wrote in his diary on New Year's

Day 1918: 'Everyone's talking about Calais, Amiens and Paris, like they did in the first months of the war, and at the same time they are talking about peace which will definitely be agreed towards the spring.' The German soldiers and officers recharged themselves in the hope that a last offensive would finally bring an end to the horrors of war.

Another motive was the shortage of food in the German armies. 'Maybe 20 to 30% of our unit were keen because they hoped to find plenty of food and alcohol; they were mostly young ones,' Lieutenant Rudolf Hartmann noted. 'But the rest of us weren't all that enthusiastic; we just wanted to get the war over and done with and go home.'

Soldier Hans Spiess was happy with all the preparations for the offensive, and noted in a letter to his sister that, with a bit of luck, the German Army's success in Russia could be followed by victory on the Western Front. Only the supply of food was not succeeding as planned, he noted, which meant there was a shortage of food. And Sergeant Paul Knoch wrote to his parents that 'the rations are hampering the offensive. We have nothing to put in our sandwiches! The stocks of ham and bacon have gone off.'

The Germans did not have the necessary resources to equip all divisions in the same way. That's why High Command formed fifty-six special attack and raid divisions. Soldiers between the ages of twenty-five and thirty-five were selected for this and were equipped with the best weapons. The others – older soldiers and newcomers – were less well-armed and formed part of the trench divisions. The specialised infantrymen, also called *Stosstruppen* (stormtroopers), formed the advance guard. They had to force their way through the enemy positions, disrupt communications, create chaos and then get to the artillery and disable it. These stormtroopers were armed with light machine guns, light trench mortars and flamethrowers.

The emphasis was on infiltration methods. Ludendorff did not want to let his stormtroopers march steadily 'in tirailleur' (spread out), as had been the custom until then. Not one of those advances in which every man kept a close eye on his comrades to his left and right and the slowest man set the pace. The troops had to grab the enemy by the throat and advance, because there was one important condition for the success of the offensive: the advance was not allowed to stop. Not as a result of tiredness, nor because heavy equipment could only be moved forward slowly. Only then would the German offensive succeed, Ludendorff believed.

After the stormtroopers came the other fighting troops. These comprised infantry, engineers, machine gunners, trench mortar groups, field artillery and ammunition-carrying sections. These troops had to attack the heavily defended positions which the stormtroopers had passed through in their attempts to eliminate the enemy's artillery as quickly as possible. The purpose of these fighting groups was furthermore to fend off counter-attacks with bayonets or guns. The adage for these troops, too, was never to be held back by any obstacle. If a specific unit was too lightly armed to be able to secure an enemy position, then this position had to be left for another, more heavily armed unit to deal with. Onwards it had to go.

Operation Michael was executed in three phases. The aim of the offensive was to break through the Allied front from Ham to Péronne, the area held by the British. In March 1918, 1.3 million Germans were at the front. Amongst them were 123,000 men who had been dragged from the German factories to the front by Ludendorff. The troops were spread over 192 (understaffed) divisions. Likewise, the 178 (some sources speak of 169) Allied divisions were not at full strength. Although the Germans had more men, they had less weaponry at their disposal. They had 3,670 aeroplanes, 14,000 guns, ten tanks and 23,000 trucks. The Allies possessed 4,500 planes, 18,500 guns, 800 tanks and 100,000 vehicles.

General Ludendorff was nonetheless convinced of the success of his plan of attack and he was proud of his troops, amongst whom his stepson also served. Shortly before the attack, he told the Kaiser: 'The army was assembled and well-prepared to undertake the "biggest task" in its history.'

It was cold and there was a grim, thick fog on the morning of 21 March 1918. The previous evening, the German infantrymen had been fed a meal. Some were given hot food, but most received theirs cold. In addition, they received two flasks with tea or coffee mixed with rum. The men were told that they had to make their fluids last as long as possible, and the officers warned their troops: watch out for fake mines, snipers *and* poisoned food and water.

Operation Michael began with an artillery bombardment whereby 6,473 guns over a front some 70 kilometres wide opened fire on the Allied positions. At 4:40 a.m., 'to the second, a flare went up and as if automatically, the thousands of guns began to thunder,' German NCO Carl Heller recorded:

> A horrible whining and whistling went over our heads only to explode over there with enormous bangs. For a few seconds it was quiet again. Then a deafening, terrible crashing. An artillery hurricane of unprecedented intensity had suddenly broken out. The ground was shaking and trembling, and, because of the constant flaring of guns, it almost seemed as if dawn had broken.

At that same time exactly, Company Quartermaster Sergeant Edward Lyons was woken by the booming violence. He lit a candle, took a puff from a cigarette and at first was not aware of what was happening. Then he realised that grenades were landing all around him. He leapt out of bed and quickly got dressed. One of his men put his head around the door and asked him what to do. Lyons told him to send everyone outside and take the horses somewhere safe. He himself was soon outside and it was like purgatory. It was pitch-black, with a thick fog. The noise was deafening. Shells seemed to hit by the thousands with a screaming thundering din.

Not only were the British trench positions shelled, but also junctions, headquarters, troop assembly points and artillery positions. Telephone lines that might be buried up to 2 metres underground were rendered unserviceable as a result of the shelling. The strikes caused shock waves, resulting in farm roofs and walls collapsing. The gun barrels became too hot touch with bare hands, which meant they could not be fired with much effectiveness. The gunners wrapped the barrels in wet bags and constantly poured water over them.

Railways and airfields became heavily damaged; the majority of British barbed wire entanglements were blown away as well. Shell bursts caused entire sections of their furthest forward trenches to collapse; the ones at the rear were partly destroyed as well. The Germans even managed to neutralise most of the British artillery.

At 9 a.m. the German artillery changed tactics and launched a barrage. As part of this tactical change, the enemy positions 100 metres further ahead were bombarded every three or four minutes. The infantry advanced concurrently. This meant that the men should be able to advance quietly, in the knowledge that that the artillery had laid waste to the terrain to be captured. At this point, there were almost 8,000 British casualties.

In order to ensure that each independent company would stay as closely together as possible, the Germans used buglers, even in the thick fog and the chaos of those first hours of battle. All of the players had learned twenty-four different tunes, each of which represented a particular command. In order to remember the tunes, the troops composed simple rhymes to the music. That morning, the notes of 'attack' were sounded the most frequently. The German infantrymen's jingle had been adapted to suit:

Kartoffelsuppe, Kartoffelsuppe [Potato soup, potato soup]
Den ganzen Tag, Kartoffelsuppe [All day potato soup]
Kartoffelsuppe [Potato soup].

And to vary the last line it could go:

Und kein Fleisch [And no meat].

When the offensive burst out that morning, few Germans were thinking of the British enemy. They were after loot: the stocks in the shops and dug-outs, the cigarettes, biscuits, tinned meat. They knew these treats from earlier battles, when they had plundered British hideouts. Then, they had gaped in wonderment at the British food in its large quantities. Chocolate, coffee, corned beef, wine, Maconochie's stew, spirits: they had hungrily wolfed down everything. Now, the Germans were even worse off. Their day began with a warm brew that had to pass for coffee, but which tasted of turnip. In the afternoon they were fed thin soup, made from turnips or dried vegetables. Sometimes they were given a sausage so bad it was named 'rubber sausage.'

The British defence was negligible. Even before they could take action, their guns had been destroyed or crews killed. The German soldiers advanced without much resistance, all the while relieving the dead of their cakes and tins of meat. The men in the second wave of attack were actually jealous of those in the first wave because they were able to snatch the best food from under their noses. The odd soldier crept towards the front line in order to be able to join the forward troops.

The general orders the German troops had received were short and snappy: 'Keep moving forward and keep up with the rolling barrage.' Yet entire companies suspended their offensive to tuck into food and drink in the deserted British supply depots or into the enemy's personal supplies.

Officers had great difficulty in getting the men to keep moving. If they did succeed, everyone hastily crammed food into their mouths. One person would empty a tin of preserved meat, another would stuff their pockets with a Briton's cake. The German soldiers were even forced to throw food away, as they simply could not take everything with them. The scraps were picked up by the men in the second wave of attack.

The Germans' morale improved greatly now that food was there for the picking. After all, in the words of a German officer: 'Four long years, in tattered coats and fed worse than Chinese coolies, we hurried from one battlefield to the next.'

The Germans routed the British. It was no longer an attack, but a chase. Not for the sake of Kaiser Wilhelm, General Ludendorff's plan of attack or out of patriotism, but driven by hunger. The craving for food was so great that chunks of meat were even cut from dead horses.

The troops were careless of the warning not to touch food and drink in case it was poisoned. Carl Heller:

> The bounty could be large: cigarettes, bread, meat, yes, they even found a jug of brandy. Everything was dispatched with relish. In the communication trenches too, men were searching everywhere. They were using shovel and pickaxe because a lot of the food had been buried. The enemy had thrown into the water a huge number of tins containing cakes, which went off because the tins had been spiked with bayonets beforehand, so that water could seep in. When we

came across all these delicious things which had been left to the mercy of decay on purpose, we were furious of course.

Even the wounded were left to fend for themselves. Nothing could stop the Germans. Ernst Jünger:

Ignoring the growing din of firing, we settled into the dugout, and helped ourselves to the provisions left behind, since our stomachs reminded us that we hadn't eaten anything since the beginning of the offensive. We found ham, white bread, jam and an earthenware jar of ginger beer. […] The space next door housed the kitchen, with supplies we stared at in wonder. There was a whole crate of eggs, which we sucked on the spot, as eggs were little more than a word to us at this stage. On shelves along the walls were, piled high, canned meat, tins of delicious English jam, and bottles of Camp coffee, tomatoes and onions; everything to delight an epicure's heart. It was a scene I often came back to later, when we lay for weeks in trenches on miserable rations, watery soup and thin nondescript jam.

NCO Max Strobel and his men did the same. Strobel wrote:

We took as much as we could carry, even champagne. When later that evening we had to spring into action and use our machine gun, I was forced to fill the cooling reservoir with champagne, because we had run out of water. Unfortunately I had forgotten that for cooling, only clean water could be used. When we resumed shelling, the stench of warm champagne soon became unbearable. One of my gunners had arranged everything down to a fine art; he put chunk after chunk of Gruyere in his mouth.

Others' first action would be plundering a British hideout, and only later would concern themselves with the British men they had captured in the process. 'When we saw the enemy retreating, we put our machine guns on the top of the embankment and fire at them streaming across a large field between Flavy-le-Martel and

Failloul,' recalled Lance Corporal Georg Maier, 3rd Machine-Gun Co, 1st Bavarian Division:

> Myself and a friend were the first to go over to the other side of the embankment and began looking for souvenirs. There were many dead Englishmen. We found hundreds of cigarettes in the dead soldiers' knapsacks, along with chocolate, fine biscuits and lots of good things we didn't know any more. I didn't smoke, but I took all the cigarettes I found and gave them to my comrades. [...] When we were finally relieved, we looked over the English prisoners, especially the ones who had harassed us so much from the rear. I guess they were glad to still be alive.

On the first day of Operation Michael, 40,000 soldiers were killed, injured or missing on the German side. The British lost more or less the same number of men. The German wounded who were still able to walk were 'overjoyed.' They retreated to behind their own lines; they no longer had to take part in the battle and some were confident of a one-way ticket home to be patched up. 'They had thrown away their entire kit and, at least those who were able to do this to some extent were instead carrying bags with all kinds of looted foodstuffs,' Carl Heller recorded. 'With a "good luck, all the best comrade," they passed us blissfully happy, watched by us with envy.'

Many British cut their losses and ran away ahead of the Germans. Soldiers and officers who remained at the front line hoped for reinforcements, ammunition and food. Their hope was in vain, it appeared. The Germans were more successful, because they had kept back troops in reserve behind the front who could replace their casualties and fatalities. These were not always reinforcements. 'New reserves came forward continuously,' Heller recorded. 'Instead of hand grenades, the men had British tins in their pockets. They were worth much more!'

When night fell and the fighting abated, the Germans tried to prepare for the next day. They wanted to eat and sleep. In those places where the cooks and their field kitchens had been able to keep up with the advance, a few souls obtained a hot meal. The majority ate seized British rations. Lance Corporal Willy Adams:

After we had dug some kind of trench, we went into the cabin. What we found was a goldmine for hungry soldiers. I think it was a pantry. There were tins of corned beef, tins of food that only needed to be heated up, various kinds of jam, marmalade and other food supplies: all things we had not seen in years. What a difference from our food! We stuffed ourselves. I came across a tin with a hundred cigarettes: the best cigarettes I've ever smoked in my life. We opened every tin to see what was in it, because none of us could read English. What has stayed with me more than anything else is a tin of baked beans and pork. I thought it was delicious.

During the first days, the Germans pushed the British back by several kilometres at times. After three long years, there was finally some movement in the war. The advance progressed so well that supplying the men soon became impossible. They hoped to find enemy supplies in order to be assured of food, like the men of the 1st Bavarian Infantry Regiment, who after having had to live off paltry rations for three days and nights, found a French provision depot in the town of Guivry. Lieutenant Reinhold Spengler recalled:

It was not as assorted as the English one we left in Montescourt, but it was a hungry man's paradise. The depot was stocked with all kinds of meat, sausages, mountains of white bread, real coffee, cocoa, canned milk, tea, cheese, chocolate and candied fruit. We stayed here the rest of the day, and had plenty of time to feel like guests of the French. One man of my light-machine-gun platoon delighted us with a juicy roast. He loved to cook, and an hour after settling down in Guivry he served us a delicious baked chicken. That night we had pork roast and bread dumplings – a feast so well loved in Bavaria. All this proved too much for my stomach, which was not used to such treats (not by my own choice). Soon I was sick, and the next morning I looked like a living corpse, barely able to stand on my legs.

Other German troops had set up systems of a kind to clear and store enemy food supplies. This meant they were assured of food every day. Lieutenant Fritz Nagel and his men, members of an infantry company, had commandeered a British truck. At night it gave them protection against the cold; during the day they used it as a moving store for the food they had captured. During the march to the town of Albert, they plundered all the provision depots they came across. It did not take long for the truck to be loaded up with crates of condensed milk, tea, cocoa, corned beef, sugar, bacon, butter, tinned biscuits and countless packages of Woodbine cigarettes.

The British armies, meanwhile, retreated, kilometre upon kilometre. So rapidly that their commander Field Marshal Haig noted with amazement that his troops had been pushed back to behind the River Somme after only two days. By no means all the British got away safely. The Germans captured tens of thousands of men, who were taken too far behind their lines. There, the Germans left them to fend for themselves. They were barely given any food. British rifleman Fred White was fed what he described as 'a bit of rotten cabbage leaf floating in dishwater most of the time.' Some prisoners of war even died of starvation. Corporal Ted Gale, who had also been captured, recounted:

> We had nothing to eat for three days, and we was all worn out. Marching, marching, marching. God knows where. They kept us on the go all the time. Several times a French farmer who saw us going along would throw us a carrot or turnip. The women would leave pails of water along the side of the road and if the Jerry was agreeable – and they weren't always! – they'd let us scoop it up with our hands. After three days they gave us a basin of soup. It was that thin, that if you'd have a newspaper you could have read it through the stuff. Vegetable soup it was supposed to be. The vegetables were missing!

Delighted with the initial results of Operation Michael, the Kaiser gave German schoolchildren a day off on 23 March to celebrate the victory. Two days later, Wilhelm II ordered the entire Reich to fly the flag to celebrate the German victories at Monchy, Cambrai, Saint-Quentin and La Fère. It looked as if the Germans had already won the war. A premature conclusion, it appeared. Despite the fact that the British had been beaten back, they managed to regroup and were able to offer renewed resistance.

As much as their advance progressed strongly during those first few days, the Germans began to encounter greater difficulties. The terrain on which they launched their offensive had been more or less ploughed up during the Battle of the Somme in 1916. The area that the Germans captured kilometre by kilometre consisted of mud, sludge, squelchy, squidgy soil and sticky tree stumps where there had once been woodlands. Villages had been wiped off the earth in earlier battles; roads hardly existed. Communication with field headquarters was virtually impossible because telephone and telegraph wires had been severed by the shelling.

'We are glad if ration-carts and field-kitchens can get to us at night; then men and horses feed for the next 24 hours at one sitting,' German officer Rudolf Binding recorded in his diary on 23 March, two days after the start of offensive. 'We have now reached the zone in which all the wells and streams have been wrecked, and the water for the attacking troops has to be brought up in water-carts. [...] The horses have to wait until we cross the canal at Moislains-Nurlu. The devastation is immeasurable.'

A few days later:

> We have now spent two nights in the crater-field of the old Somme battle. No desert of salt is more desolate. Last night we slept in a hole in the crumbly, chalky soil, and froze properly. Yesterday I was looking for Bouchavesnes, which used to be quite a large place. There was nothing but a board nailed to a low post with the inscription in English: 'This was Bouchavesnes.'

To make matters worse, the weather was terrible, with all that this entailed. Carl Heller:

> We had been in this trench for ten days and were constantly involved in combat with the enemy. They were retreating inch by inch, but continued to offer stubborn resistance. We had to take every pit, every trench by assault, which led to great losses. The persistent rain falling during those last days meant

that we had to suffer a great deal. It was virtually impossible to deliver food or ammunition on the bad roads behind us.

In the end, Heller and his comrades were three days without food. Once on their retreat, it took another day and a half walking on barely passable roads before they reached the village of Vis. There, an officer told them that they had to continue a further 10 kilometres to find their own battalion. Heller:

Ten kilometres in the rain, on a bad road and some even without shoes. It seemed an absolute impossibility to us. But we had no choice, the kitchen and the long-awaited rest was there. We trudged along slowly and towards the morning we reached Barrail. Worn out as we were, we lay down on a street corner in the rain. At that point our kitchen drove past and stopped in an orchard blown to bits. Now, all of a sudden, our sorrows were at an end. Food! We were going to get food. This prospect got us back on our feet and soon we were lapping up the barley soup, which had gone sour that night during the long drive.

The British who had retreated on the other side were better off. The area around Albert which had been kilometres behind the front until only the week before had been evacuated so recently that all kinds of food were to be had in the deserted villages. In the village of Ham, cow parts were still hanging on meat hooks in butchers shops, and elsewhere the troops found cocks, chickens and pigs.

Major Harrison Johnston said of his retreat through the village of La Houssoye:

During our stay in this bit of the line we had certain unusual luxuries, such as rabbits (out of hutches), pigeons (shot off roofs) and chickens – all of which might have starved or been killed by shell-fire had we not saved them! Champagne was also greatly enjoyed (the bottles would certainly have been broken). A certain amount of drinkable red wine and a good supply of vegetables of all kinds were also available.

The men enjoyed themselves, although, according to Johnston, Sergeant Alex Dunbar had a nasty moment during an attack the following day: when he opened the lid of the ammunition chest, he was expecting enough supply for a new salvo. He urgently, at that precise point in fact, needed ammunition. He was shocked to find that the chest contained a few dozen tins of condensed milk. He scraped together some ammunition for a few salvoes, but suddenly, with wicked pleasure and that bit of extra luck, he placed one of the tins of milk in front of the gun's muzzle and fired his first shell. Later, over the years, he kept wondering whether some unfortunate German soldier had died for Kaiser and fatherland as a result of the random impact of a tin of milk that had hit him at high speed.

Ludendorff's tactic was aimed at keeping the men advancing. But this soon ceased as a result of the troops' plundering. Officer Binding noted:

> Today the advance of our infantry suddenly stopped near Albert. Nobody could understand why [...]. Our way seemed entirely clear [...]. When I asked the Brigade Commander why there was no movement forward, he shrugged his shoulders and said he did not know either [...]. I turned around at once and took a sharp turn with the car into Albert. As soon as I got near the town I began to see curious sights [...]. There were men driving cows before them, others who carried a hen under one arm and box of notepaper under the other. Men carrying a bottle of wine under one arm and another one open in their hand.

Officers found it increasingly difficult to keep their men in line. Colonel Albrecht von Thaer noted that entire divisions overindulged in food and drink and failed to follow through with the crucial attack. One officer came up with a proposal to introduce the lash for soldiers who were guilty of looting.

Binding believed that the men's excesses not only cost thousands of German lives, but also halted the advance. The city of Amiens, which according to German High Command had to be captured during the first days of the offensive in order to give it a chance to succeed, was not reached. Binding's assessment:

It is practically certain that the reason why we did not reach Amiens was the looting at Albert and Moreuil [...]. The two places, which were captured fairly easily, contained so much wine that the divisions, which ought properly to have marched through them, lay about unfit to fight in the rooms and cellars. The imprudence, together with hunger, thirst, and the general sense of years of privation, were simply too great and too overpowering. The disorder of the troops at these two places, which has been fully attested by German officers, must have cost us a good fifty thousand men, apart from the lost opportunity, for the troops which moved out of Albert the next day cheered with wine and in victorious spirit were mown down straight away on the railway-embankment by a few English machine-guns, while those who escaped were laid out by French artillery in their next attack.

German Field Marshal Von Hindenburg concluded later: 'Our advance became slower and slower. We ought to have shouted into the ear of every man: "Press on to Amiens. Put in your last ounce. Perhaps Amiens means decisive victory." It was in vain; our strengths exhausted.'

Operation Michael did not last long: officially, it ended on 5 April 1918, fifteen days after its launch. The Germans had taken 90,000 prisoners of war and captured 1,300 guns. On the British side, there were 178,000 casualties. The French numbered 70,000. The official German figure amounted to 239,000 casualties, killed or injured.

Amongst the dead was General Ludendorff's stepson. Yet afterwards, in his book *My War Memories*, he spoke of a *Eine Glänzende Waffentat* (a brilliant feat), and will be ever regarded so in history, he thought. 'What the English and French had not succeeded in doing,' Ludendorff continued, referring to the fact that the war had begun to move again and many kilometres of territory had been taken, 'we had accomplished. And that in the fourth year of war!'

The general was disappointed in the attitude of his men, all the same, in 'the way in which the troops stopped round captured food supplies,' Ludendorff wrote after the war. 'Individuals [who] stayed behind to search houses and farms' had also caused a great deal of delay: 'Valuable time was lost.'

The general was bitter because none of the officers, experienced or otherwise, had been capable of controlling the troops and leading them onwards in their advance against the Allies. If the troops 'did not achieve all the success that was possible [this] was due, not only to reduced fighting value, but above all, to their not being always under the firm control of their officers.' This was not on account of the inadequate care of the men, Ludendorff believed. They were given less food than the Allies, but it was 'sufficient.' The German general blamed the anarchy on the relaxation of the penalties for insubordination.

According to Ludendorff, the looting was a sign of 'poor discipline,' which was caused primarily by the mood in Germany itself. There was increasing unhappiness about the growing shortage of food and the failure of peace to materialise, which had been hoped for so fervently.

Operation Michael was followed by a series of further German attacks under the code names of Georgette, Blücher-Yorck, Gneisenau, as well as the offensive on Marne-Reims in April, May, June and July of that year. In addition, the German armies launched an attack on Calais, Boulogne and Dunkirk. Again, they pushed the British and French troops kilometres back. At times, it looked as if the French ports would have to be evacuated. In the heart of France, the Germans penetrated so far that they were able to shell Paris with their long-range guns.

The prospect of food and drink encouraged the Germans to go for the attack during the follow-on offensives. 'One of the motivations from which our infantrymen derived their courage was their craving for looting,' noted General Karl von Einem, Commander of the German Third Army. For far too long, all kinds of things had been withheld from the troops. The capture of Albert had given them a taste of the luxury that they had dreamed of for so long. Lieutenant Binding recalled:

> Yesterday an officer sitting beside me in the car suddenly called out to the driver to stop at once, without so much as asking my leave. When I asked him in astonishment what

he meant by stopping the car when we were on an urgent mission, he answered: 'I must just pick up that English waterproof lying beside the road.' The car stopped. He jumped out, seized an English waterproof which lay on the bank, and then jumped joyfully back again, as if refreshed and waked to a new life. If this lack of restraint seized an officer like that, one can imagine what effect it must have on the private soldier to have craved and hungered and thirsted for months on end.

Just as earlier in Albert, some units indulged themselves in veritable orgies of food and drink. At the end of May, the Germans had reached the Champagne region, where the bottles were stacked high in the cellars of Soissons and surrounding villages. The streets of Soissons were overrun with drunken Germans who boozed away their misery. In the end, many men were driven back to the front line by the *Feldpolizei* (Secret Field Police).

The discipline that made the German soldier such a feared opponent had in some places completely disappeared. In May 1918, Rupprecht, Crown Prince of Bavaria reported that 20 per cent of the troops who had been moved from the Eastern to the Western Front had deserted. Deserters who were caught were given a four-month prison sentence. This was exactly what the soldiers wanted because, throughout that time, they would not be at the front. But, on 23 June, General Ludendorff issued a general order with regard to deserters: every man who went over to the enemy would be sentenced to death upon his return to Germany.

A month later, High Command appointed a so-called *Beute Offizier* (Collection Officer) and a *Beute Truppe* (Collection Unit). This *Beute Truppe* comprised an officer and a few reliable men who were responsible for the distribution of captured food, clothes, alcohol and tobacco. The items which were distributed in this way were for immediate use. The remaining loot was handed to the military police and placed under the care of a divisionary *Beute Offizier*. He had to see to it that units behind the front also received a share of the bounty. Items were also held in reserve, in order perhaps to distribute them later.

At the front, meanwhile, stood German soldiers with empty

stomachs, in a strange country, carrying old and irreplaceable weapons with a shortage of ammunition. In Germany itself, there was growing support for socialist and pacifist propaganda which advocated an end to the war. There were renewed strikes and demands for food, higher wages and shorter working times. Things were so bad in Berlin in the summer of 1918 that the prospect of the approaching winter alone unleashed a wave of suicides amongst the civilian population, which grew bigger by the day. Added to the fatalities from starvation, there were so many corpses that furniture removal vans had to be used to transport the dead to cemeteries.

Letters from home, detailing the hunger and misery at home in Germany, did not improve the situation at the front. Fresh recruits confirmed these stories. It all affected the mood on the front line. In 1914, the Germans would arrive at the front in trains saying 'Nach Paris' ('To Paris') or 'Jeder Stoss ein Franzos, jeder Schuss ein Russ' ('Everyone must stab a Frenchman, everyone must shoot a Russian'). Now, in 1918, a train with soldiers of the 2nd Bavarian Division sported the words 'Red Guard.'

The continuing attacks by the Allies slowly but surely wore out and depleted Ludendorff's elite troops, the stormtrooper divisions, and rendered them less deployable. What remained was a weakened army, and an army that was largely under the influence of a revolutionary spirit at that. Despite the threat of the death sentence, more and more people deserted. Many men did not return from leave. Those who did come back united with others who were equally rebellious and wandered through the hinterland. They took no notice of the *Feldpolizei*, but plundered supply locations and stole provisions.

Towards the middle of June, German losses were running up to 1,000 men a day. Between March and July 1918 there were 227,000 casualties, dead or missing. A further 765,000 men were injured. Almost 2 million German soldiers and officers fell ill. The majority were suffering from Spanish flu, an illness that would claim 186,000 men. 'We learned that the disease was also spreading among the enemy,' Ernst Jünger wrote. 'Even though we, with our poor rations, were more susceptible to it.'

Out of a total of 2,952,000 men who dropped out, just over 2 million were able to resume their duties after some time. However,

951,000 men were permanently incapacitated: a fifth of the German army. These were losses that could no longer be compensated for. There were simply too few men available for active duty at the front.

The Allies also suffered great losses. Just like the Germans, the French and British did not have many reserves to make up for these. American involvement meant the Allied armies were able to maintain their strength, however. In the middle of June, twelve American divisions were active on the Western Front. More doughboys came. From May 1918, on average 250,000 men a month arrived in France from the United States. In July, there were more than 1 million in total; by November 1918, more than 2 million. Their arrival could not have been delayed much longer. As Winston Churchill observed on 12 January 1919 in the *Sunday Pictorial*: 'A very little more and the submarine warfare, instead of bringing America to our aid, might have starved us all into absolute surrender.'

The German advance had ground to a halt, and the armies entrenched themselves again as though nothing had changed. Once again it appeared that after a few months of movement, a situation had come about in which the armies would fight each other from the trenches. The arrival of the Americans and the weakened position of the Germans meant this did not happen: during the night of 17 July an allied Allied counter-attack ensued. Between the River Aisne and Château-Thierry, thirteen French and three American divisions were ready and waiting to attack the German lines. Within a few days, the Allies pushed the Germans back a few kilometres.

The attack may not have been as successful as the German offensives during the previous months, but it demonstrated more than anything that the war was at a turning point. The question was how long the exhausted German troops could keep going.

On 22 July, Ludendorff decided that his troops should be withdrawn and the front be shortened. The increasing losses, exhaustion and Spanish flu meant he had no choice. In the officers' logs, the troops' living conditions were described as 'extremely hard.' Prior to the retreat, the troops emptied the farm estates in the Vesle Valley, between Soissons and Rheims. 'The masses of stores accumulated there were absolutely vital to us,' Ludendorff noted. The following day, the German Crown Prince announced that twenty-one divisions of the Seventh Army could do no more fighting and would have to be replaced.

At the beginning of August, Ludendorff observed: 'The attempt to make the nations of the Entente inclined to peace before the arrival of the American reinforcements by means of German victories had failed.' The German troops were no longer capable of anything: fighting a defensive war, let alone beginning an offensive. The Allies, on the other hand, were ready and able to do just this.

In the early morning of 8 August, at 5:20 a.m., in thick fog, the British Fourth Army opened fire along the entire length of the front where the German Second Army was stationed. Infantry and tanks went on the offensive as soon as the barrage began. En route from Amiens to Roye, the German troops were totally caught off their guard by the enemy and allowed themselves to be overrun. Divisions which only a few days previously had been moved behind the front because of exhaustion had to be mobilised post-haste. The German front collapsed and the British, aided by Canadian and Australian troops, were quickly able to gain ground.

Ludendorff later referred to 8 August as 'a black day of the German Army in the history of this war.' He received reports about the troops he 'should not have thought possible in the German Army.' Such as the story that 'retiring troops, meeting a fresh division going bravely into action, had shouted out things like "Blackleg" and "You're prolonging the war."'

German High Command concluded in August 1918 that the defensive should be held. They hoped to be able to remain on French territory in this way and to acquire a favourable negotiating position for peace talks.

The Allies launched new offensives. At the end of August, an attack on the Meuse followed, along with in the Argonne, on the Siegfried line and in Flanders in late September. The Germans were pushed back, but they were able to prevent the occupation of German territory.

'We captured thousands of Germans,' the veteran Henry Allingham told me when I met him. 'A little soup and a crust of bread is what they could have. Because there were so many of them, that's all we had, but they were delighted. It was the turning point of the war. If you are without food, as they were then, you simply cannot fight.'

The Allied advance was rapid. Just like the Germans earlier that year, the French and British troops now had difficulties with food supplies. The supply lines became too long and the field kitchens could not keep up with the pace. By 2 October there was no longer any food. Aeroplanes were used to drop food at the front.

A month later, on Sunday 3 November, the German population's patience and perseverance snapped. In the naval port of Kiel, mutinying seamen started a revolt. 'Unmanly and hysterical!' General Ludendorff reflected after the war in his memoirs. The explanation he gave for the revolt was a lack of 'albumen and fats, for the maintenance of physical and mental vigour.'

Once again, the uprising quickly spread to other parts of the country. The government feared another Bolshevist revolution, like the one that had taken place in 1917 in Russia, and closed the doors of the Russian embassy. But the rebellion grew. Red flags flew in the ports of Kiel, Lübeck and Hamburg. The abdication of the Kaiser was demanded.

A few days later, on Saturday 9 November, in Berlin, mutinying soldiers marched in large rallies, alongside thousands of workers. They carried placards saying: 'Freedom! Freedom! Bread! Brothers, don't shoot us, join us!'

Police officers who wished to stop the demonstrations were disarmed by the soldiers and sent home. Other German soldiers released political prisoners from their cells. Work had ground to a halt in more and more Berlin factories, including those of Daimler, the artillery factory of Otto Jochmann, the Silex factory, Knorr-Bremse AG, Siemens and the factories on the Weissensee. There was no stopping it: the revolution was a fact. Members of the national assembly forced the Kaiser to abdicate and then formed a new government.

Wilhelm II cut his losses, fled Germany and arrived in the Netherlands on Sunday 10 November. There, he spent his first days in Amerongen Castle, the property of the Dutch Bentinck family. In the evening, he appeared in the dining room in his finest uniform. The table had been laid for more than forty people and set, in honour of the Kaiser, with the Bentincks' best silverware, dating from 1700. There were vases with flowers picked in the castle gardens. What followed was a dinner with many courses and the very finest wines. After this, the Kaiser sat around the fireplace in the drawing room with the Bentinck family until midnight. They primarily talked about who was to blame for the war. The Kaiser said: 'My conscience is clear. The Lord knows that I never wanted this war.'

A day later, on 11 November 1918, hostilities ceased at 11 a.m. London celebrated with abandon. In Paris, too, people went onto the streets to cheer the end of the war. In Berlin, the mood was sombre. The country had suffered an enormous defeat, and now that the Kaiser had fled there was uncertainty about how it would be governed in the future. Above all, winter was imminent. Potatoes were scarce. Meat, fat or bread was nowhere to be seen. What remained was a miserable ration of tasteless vegetables and often no fuel with which to cook these. That November, thousands of people died in Berlin every day.

Two days after the armistice, German Crown Prince Wilhelm wrote to his troops that he was laying down command: 'The army has not been beaten by weapons,' he noted. 'We were forced to capitulate by hunger and want.'

Interior of a US Army subsistence warehouse in France. (US National Archive)

EASY POTATO SOUP (6–8 helpings)

Ingredients
10–12 medium-sized potatoes
½ medium-sized onion
2 leeks
celery
bacon
butter or lard
pepper
finely chopped parsley
1–2 beef cubes (optional)

Preparation
Peel the potatoes, clean them, cut into small pieces and put them in a pan with water, covering them entirely. Boil the potatoes until done and drain. Meanwhile, cook a few scraped and finely chopped carrots, ½ medium onion, 2 leeks, celery and some bacon in 2 litres water until well done. Mash the potatoes, add a generous knob of butter or decent lard, the vegetables with its boiled water, season to taste. Add pepper and finely chopped parsley, and beef cubes if necessary.

Brattische Kochvorschriften für Feldküchen (Brattische Cooking Instructions for Field Kitchens)

SOUR POTATOES

Ingredients
potatoes
bacon
onions
flour
vinegar
pepper
sugar
salt

Preparation
Peel and wash the potatoes and boil in salt water until done. Meanwhile, fry some bacon with onions, stir in some flour, bring to the boil, add some cold water and the potatoes. Add pepper, vinegar and sprinkling of sugar, the boiled potatoes and bring to the boil once more.

Die Gulaschkanone (*The Goulash Cannon*)

TOMATO PURÉE

Tomato purée that is obtainable in tins is highly recommended. To make a purée of fresh tomatoes:

Ingredients
tomatoes
butter
stock
breadcrumbs

Preparation
Fresh tomatoes can be puréed by washing them, chopping them and simmering them in a little butter or water. Sieve and bring back to the boil. This tomato purée with a little added water, stock, butter and breadcrumbs, makes an excellent tomato sauce for eggs, beef and the like.

Kochbuch für den Schutzengraben (*Cookbook for the Trenches*)

FISH

Ingredients
fish
peppercorns
bay leaf
salt

Preparation
Descale the fish and clean it, place in salted boiling water on the fire, add peppercorns and bay leaf and briefly cook.

Kochbuch für den Schutzengraben (*Cookbook for the Trenches*)

SAUERKRAUT

Ingredients
sauerkraut
lard

Preparation
Wash the sauerkraut (if very salty, drain after 30 minutes of cooking). Cook for at least 3 to 4 hours. If possible, add some leftovers of lard. Sauerkraut can be thickened by adding potatoes or flour for the final 30 minutes of cooking.

Anweisungen für Truppenküchen (*Instructions for Soldiers' Kitchens*)

BIBLIOGRAPHY

63rd (R.N.) Division (2005) *Trench Standing Orders (2nd Edition) 1917.* Uckfield, Naval & Military Press.

Andriessen, J.H.J. (2003) *De Oorlogsbrieven van Unteroffizier Carl Heller, geschreven tijdens de Eerste Wereldoorlog.* Soesterberg, Abacont.

Anon (1916) *Handboek voor den kok te velde.* Nancy, Imprimerie Berger-Levrault.

Anon (1916) *Kriegskochregeln für die Benutzung der Kochkiste.* Karlsruhe, Druck und Verlag E.F. Müllersche Hofbuchhandlung m.b.h.

Anon (1916) *Rex-Kochbuch zur Haushalt-Conservierung von Obst, Gemüse, Kompott, Marmelade, Säfte, Moste, Pilze, Suppen, Fleisch, Puddings, etc.* Bad Homburg, Rex-Conserven-Gesellschaft.

Anon (1917) *Chef des Generalstabes des Feldheeres.* Berlin, Nachrichten – Abteilung.

Anon (1917) *Cooking in the Field.* Issued by the Quartermaster-General's Branch.

Anon (1993) *Kriegskochbuch, Anweisungen zur einfachen und billigen Ernährung.* Hamburg, Gebrüder Hoesch.

Arthur, Max (2002) *When this Bloody War is Over: Soldier's Songs of the First World War.* London, Judy Piatkus.

—— (2003) *Forgotten Voices of the Great War.* London, Ebury Press.

—— (2006) *Last Post: The Final Word from Our First World War Soldiers.* London, Phoenix.

Asworth, Tony (2000) *Trench Warfare 1914–1918: The Live and Let Live System.* London, Pan Books.

Atwell, W.A. (2005) *Laurence Attwell's Letters from the Front.* Barnsley, Pen and Sword Military.

Audoin-Rouzeau, Stéphane (1986) *14–18, Les Combattants des Tranchées.* Paris, Armand Colin.

Audoin-Rouzeau, Stephane & Becker, Annette (2000) *14–18, De Grote Oorlog opnieuw bezien.* Amsterdam, Mets & Schilt.

Augé-Laribé, Michel & Pinot, Pierre (1927) *Agriculture and Food Supply in France During the War.* New Haven, CT, Yale University Press.

Barbusse, Henri (2001) *Het Vuur.* Amsterdam, De Arbeiderspers.

Becker, Jean-Jacques (1990) *The Great War and the French People.* New York, St. Martin's Press.

Beckett, Ian (2006) *Home Front 1914–1918: How Britain Survived the Great War.* Richmond, The National Archives.

Bentinck, Norah (1921) *Der Kaiser im Exil.* Berlin, Ullstein.

van Bergen, Leo (2001) *Zacht en Eervol, lijden en sterven in een Grote Oorlog.* The Hague, SDU.

Berger, P. (1915) *Manuel de Cuisine.* St. Etienne, self-published.

Bihl, Wolfdieter (ed.) (1991) *Deutsche Quellen zur Geschichte des Ersten Weltkrieges.* Darmstadt, Wissenschatftliche Buchgesellschaft.

Binder, Heinrich (1915) *Mit Dem Hauptquartier nach Westen, Aufzeichnungen eines Kriegsberichterstatters.* Stuttgart & Berlin, Deutsche Verlags Anstalt.

Binding, Rudolf (1925) *Aus dem Kriege.* Frankfurt, M. Rütten & Loenig Verlag.

Bircher, Dr Eugen (1918) *Die Schlacht an der Marne.* Bern, Akademische Buchhandlung vorm. Max Drechsel.

Blake, Robert (ed.) (1952) *The Private Papers of Douglas Haig, 1914–1919.* London, Eyre & Spottiswoode.

Bloem, Walther (1916) *Vormarsch.* Leipzig, Verlag Grethlein & Co. Gmbh.

Blond, Georges (n.d.) *De Slag bij Verdun.* Utrecht, Het Spectrum.

Blücher, Princess Evelyn (1920) *An English Wife in Berlin.* New York, E.P. Dutton & Company.

Blunden, Edmund (1936) *Undertones of War.* London, Penguin Books.

Bourne, John, Liddle, Peter & Whitehead, Ian (2001) *The Great World War 1914–45. 2: Who Won, Who Lost?* London, HarperCollins.

Brenneke, R. (1915) *Die Deutsche Hausfrau im Weltkrieg, ausführliches Kriegs-Kochbuch aller ernährungsarten – nebst ratschlägen in gesunden und kranken Tagen und praktische Winke im Haushalt.* Leipzig, Verlag des Vereins Leipziger Frauenhilfe.

Briscoe, Diane (1985) *The Diary of a World War I Cavalry Officer / Brigadier General Sir Archibald Home.* Tunbridge Wells, D.J. Costello Publishers.

Brown, Malcolm (2002) *The Imperial War Museum Book of the First World War.* London, Pan Books.

—— (2005) *Tommy Goes to War.* Stroud, Tempus.

Brown, Malcolm & Seaton, Shirley (2001) *Christmas Truce: The Western Front 1914.* London, Pan Books.

Buchan, John (n.d.) *De strijd aan de Somme, de eerste fase.* Edinburgh, Thomas Nelson & Sons. Ltd.

—— (n.d.) *De strijd aan de Somme, tweede fase.* Edinburgh, Thomas Nelson & Sons. Ltd.

Bull, Stephen (2002) *World War I Trench Warfare: 1916–1918.* Oxford, Osprey Publishing.

—— (2003) *Trench Warfare.* London, PRC Publishing.

Burrage, A.M. (2009) *War is War – Army Life.* Available from: www.firstworldwar.com/diaries/burrage.htm.

Buyse, T.C. (1917) *Les Batailles de la Marne, par un Officier D'État-Major Allemand.* Brussels & Paris, G. Van Oest et Cie, Éditeurs.

Cable, Boyd (1918) *Front Lines.* London, John Murray.

Cameron, James (1959) *1914.* London, Cassell & Co.

Casson, Stanley (1935) *Steady Drummer*. London, G. Bell & Sons.

Cazals, Rémy (ed.) (1998) *De Oorlogsdagboeken van Louis Barthas (tonnenmaker), 1914–1918*. Amsterdam, Bas Lubberhuizen.

Carrington, Charles (2006) *Soldiers Returning from the War*. Barnsley, Pen and Sword Books.

Céline, Louis-Ferdinand (1988) *Kanonnenvoer*. Amsterdam, Meulenhoff.

Chapman, Guy (1937) *Vain Glory*. London, Cassell & Co.

Chapman, Paul (2000) *Cameos of the Western Front: A Haven in Hell, Ypres Sector 1914–1918*. Barnsley, Leo Cooper.

Chapman, Stuart (2007) *Home in Time for Breakfast: A First World War Diary*. London, Athena Press.

Chevrillon, André (1917) *Lettres d'un Soldat*. Paris, Librairie Chapelot.

von Clausewitz, Carl (1915) *Vom Kriege*. Berlin & Leipzig, B. Behr's Verlag.

Clayton, Anthony (2005) *Paths of Glory: The French Army 1914–1918*. London, Cassell & Co.

Coolidge, Olivia (1961) *Winston Churchill en de twee wereldoorlogen*. Amsterdam, De Spiegel.

Coppard, George (1999) *With a Machine Gun to Cambrai*. London, Cassell Military Paperbacks.

Corday, Michel (1934) *The Paris Front: An Unpublished Diary: 1914–1918*. New York, E.P. Dutton & Co.

Corrigan, Gordon (2003) *Mud, Blood and Poppycock: Britain and the First World War*. London, Cassell & Co.

Cowley, Robert (ed.) (2004) *The Great War: Perspectives on the First World War*. London, Pimlico.

Cron, Hermann (2002) *Imperial German Army 1914–18: Organisation, Structure, Orders-of-Battle*. Solihull, Helion & Company.

Crozier, Brig. Gen. F.P. (1930) *A Brass Hat in No Man's Land*. London, Cape.

Dallas, Gregor (2000) *1918: War and Peace*. Woodstock, NY, The Overlook Press.

Daniel, Ute (1997) *The War from Within: German Working Class Women in the First World War*. Oxford, Berg.

Darrow, Margaret H. (2000) *French Women and the First World War: War Stories from the Home Front*. Oxford, Berg.

Davis, Belinda J. (2000) *Home Fires Burning: Food, Politics and Everyday Life in World War I Berlin*. Chapel Hill, NC & London, The University of North Carolina Press.

Dawson, Coningsby (1917) *Volhouden! Brieven in Oorlogstijd*. Amersfoort, Patria.

Deckers, René (1999) *Deckers Diary 1914–1919, Notities van een oorlogsvrijwilliger*. Ghent, Snoeck-Ducaju & Zoon.

Dehmel, Richard (1919) *Zwischen Volk und Menschheit, Kriegstagebuch*. Berlin, G. Fischer Verlag.

Denholm, Decie (ed.) (1982) *Behind the Lines: One Woman's War, 1914–1918: The Letters of Caroline Ethel Cooper*. Sydney, Collins.

Deunzel, Karl (1915) *Vom Kriegsschauplatz, Feldpostbriefe und andere Berichte von Mitkämpfern und Augenzeugen*. Leipzig, Erster Band, Hesse und Becker Verlag.

Dorgelès, Roland (2004) *Houten kruisen*. Amsterdam, Arbeiderspers.

Drury, Ian (1995) *German Stormtrooper 1914–1918*. Oxford, Osprey Publishing.

Duffy, Christopher (2006) *Through German Eyes: The British & the Somme 1916*. London, Wiedenfeld & Nicholson.

Duhamel, Georges (1919) *Vie des Martyrs 1914–1916*. Paris, Mercure de France.

—— (2007) *Civilisatie 1914–1917, arts aan het front van WOI*. Amsterdam, Arbeiderspers.

Duncan Morse, Katharine (1920) *The Uncensored Letters of a Canteen Girl*. New York, Henry Holt & Company.

Easton, Dr C. (1917) *Jaren van Strijd*. Amsterdam, Scheltema & Holkema's Boekhandel.

Eisenhower, John S.D. (2001) *The Epic Story of the American Army in the World War I*. New York, The Free Press.

Ellis, John (1989) *Eye-deep in Hell: Trench Warfare in World War I*. Baltimore, Johns Hopkins Press.

van Emden, Richard (2003) *The Trench: Experiencing Life on the Front Line, 1916*. London, Corgi Books.

—— (2006) *Britain's Last Tommies: Final Memories from Soldiers of the 1914–1918 War in Their Own Words*. London, Abacus.

Evans, Martin Marnix (2002) *1918: the Year of Victories*. London, Arcturus Publishing.

Farwell, Byron (2000) *Over There: The United States and the Great War, 1917–1918*. New York, W.W. Norton.

Ferguson, Niall (1999) *The Pity of War*. New York, Basic Books.

Ferro, Marc (2002) *The Great War: 1914–1918*. London & New York, Routledge Classics.

Fraser, Edward & Gibbons, John (eds.) (1925) *Soldier and Sailor Words and Phrases*. London, George Routledge & Sons.

von Freitag-Loringhoven, Baron (1918) *Deductions from the World War*. London, Constable & Company.

French, Sir John (1917) *Sir John French's Despatches, Official Records of the Great Battles of Mons, the Marne, and the Aisne, as told in his despatches by Field-Marshal John French to Field-Marshal John Kitchener, Secretary of State for War*. London, The Graphic, Tallis House, Whitefriars, E.C. No. 1.

—— (n.d.) *Sir John French's Despatches, Official Records of the Battle around Ypres, Armentières, &c. And the Defence of Antwerp; including the Roll of Honour, and Illustrated by Specially Drawn War Maps*. London, The Graphic, Tallis House, Whitefriars, E.C. No. 2.

Fridenson, Patrick (ed) (1992) *The French Home Front, 1914–1918*. Oxford, Berg.

Fromkin, David (2004) *Europe's Last Summer*. New York, Random House.

Fussel, Paul (1977) *The Great War and Modern Memory*. Oxford, Oxford University Press.

Geiss, Imanuel (1978) *Das Deutsche Reich und der Erste Weltkrieg*. Munich, Carl Hanser Verlag.

General Staff, War Office (2003) *Field Service Pocket Book 1914*. Uckfield, Naval & Military Press.

Genevoix, Maurice (1916) *Sous Verdun Août – Octobre 1914*. Paris, Libraire Hachette et Cie.

German Ministry of the Interior (1916) *Ernährung und Teuerung, Ausgabe der Ernährung im Kriege für Frühjahr 1916*. Berlin, Ministerium des Innern.

German War Office of Food (1917) *Ist die behördliche Ernährungsregelung notwendig?* Berlin, Seydel & Cie.

—— (1917) *Die Kriegsernährungswirtschaft 1917*. Berlin, Kriegs-Ernährungsamt.

Gesche, Paul (1926) *Heeresverpflegung und Zusammenbruch im grossen Kriege*, self-published.

Gleichen, Lord Edward (ed.) (2000) *Chronology of the Great War, 1914–1918*. London, Greenhill Books.

Glubb, John (1978) *Into Battle: A Soldier's Diary of the Great War*. London, Cassell & Co.

Grafteaux, Serge (1985) *Mémé Santerre: A French Woman of the People*. New York, Schocken Books.

Graves, Robert (2001) *Dat hebben we gehad*. Amsterdam, De Arbeiderspers.

Great Britain War Office (1917) *Manual of Military Cooking and Dietary*. London, His Majesty's Stationery Office.

Gudmundsson, Bruce I. (1995) *Stormtroop Tactics: Innovation in the German Army, 1914–1918*. Westport, CT, Praeger Publishers.

Hafkesbrink, Hanna (1948) *Unknown Germany: An Inner Chronicle of the First World War Based on Letters and Diaries*. New Haven, CT, Yale University Press.

Hagood, General Johnson (1927) *The Services of Supply: A Memoir of the Great War*. New York, Houghton Mifflin Company.

Hall, Michael (1993) *Sacrifice on the Somme*. Newtownabbey, Island Publications.

Hanson, Neil (2005) *The Unknown Soldier: The Story of the Missing of the Great War*. Reading, Corgi Books.

Hardach, Gerd (1987) *The First World War 1914–1918*. Harmondsworth, Penguin Books.

Hart, Liddell (1938) *Foch, der Feldherr der Entente*. Berlin, Vorhut Verlag Otto Schlegel.

von Hausen, Max Clemens Lothar Freiherr (Generaloberst) (1920) *Erinnerungen an den Marnefeldzug 1914*. Leipzig, K.F. Koehler Verlag.

Haythornthwaite, Philip J. (1996) *The World War One Source Book*. London, Arms and Armour.

Helmolt, Hans F. (ed) (1914) *Der Weltkrieg in Bildern und Dokumenten nebst einem Kriegstagebuch*. Leipzig, Johannes M. Meulenhoff Verlag.

—— (ed.) (1915) *Der Weltkrieg in Bildern und Dokumenten nebst einem Kriegstagebuch, Zweite Folge*. Leipzig, Johannes M. Meulenhoff Verlag.

—— (ed.) (1916) *Der Weltkrieg in Bildern und Dokumenten nebst einem Kriegstagebuch, Dritte Folge*. Leipzig, Johannes M. Meulenhoff Verlag.

Herbert, A.P. (2006) *De Verborgen Strijd*. Bodegraven, Vorroux.

Hergemöller, Bernd-Ulrich (ed.) (1999) *Karl Pietz (1886–1986), Kriegsnotizbuch, 5. Mai 1915 bis 21 November 1918, Aufzeichnungen aus dem Ersten Weltkrieg*. Hamburg, Verlag Dr Kovac.

Herwig, Holger H. (1997) *The First World War: Germany and Austria-Hungary 1914–1918*. London, St. Martin's Press.

Heul, Hedwig (n.d.) *Die fettarme Küche*. Berlin, Verlag der Zentral Einkaufsgesellschaft.

Higgins, Thomas James (2005) *Tommy at Gommecourt*. Leek, Churnett Valley Books.

BIBLIOGRAPHY

Hirschfeld, Gerhard, Krumeich, Gerd & Reiz, Irina (eds.) (1993) *Keiner fühlt sich hier mehr als Mensch ... Erlebnis und Wirkung des Ersten Weltkriegs*. Essen, Klartext Verlag.

Holmes, Richard (2007) *Riding the Retreat: Mons to Marne: 1914 Revisited*. London, Pimlico.

Horne, Alistair (1971) *Dood van een generatie, van Neuve Chapelle tot Verdun en de Somme*. Leiden, A.W. Sijthoff.

────── (1993) *The Price of Glory, Verdun 1916*. London, Penguin Books.

van de Hulst, Wim & Koch, Koen (2004) *Ooggetuigen van de Eerste Wereldoorlog*. Amsterdam, Anthos.

von Ilsemann, Sigurd (1967) *Der Kaiser in Holland, Aufzeichnungen des letzten Flügeladjudtanten Kaiser Wilhelm II aus Amerongen und Doorn, 1918–1923*. Munich, Biederstein.

Jackson, John (2005) *Private 12768: Memoir of a Tommy*. Stroud, Tempus.

Jahr, Christoph (1998) *Gewöhnliche Soldaten; Desertion und Deserteure im deutschen und britischen Heer 1914–1918*. Gottingen, Vandenhoek & Ruprecht.

Jones, Edwin Evan (2009) *The Diaries of Edwin Evan Jones*. Available from: www.firstworldwar.com/diaries10.

Jünger, Ernst (2002) *Oorlogsroes*. Amsterdam, De Arbeiderspers.

Jürgs, Michael (2004) *De Kleine Vrede in de Grote Oorlog*. Amsterdam, Mets & Schilt Uitgevers.

Keegan, John (2003) *De Eerste Wereldoorlog 1914–1918*. Amsterdam, Olympus.

Kilvert Jr., B. Cory (2004) *Echoes of Armageddon, 1914–1918: An American's Search into the Lives and Deaths of Eight British Soldiers in World War One*. Bloomington, IN, Authors House.

Kitchen, Martin (2001) *The German Offensives of 1918*. Stroud, Tempus.

Kittel, Walther, Schreiber, Walter & Ziegelmayer, Wilhelm (1939) *Soldatenernährung und Gemeinschaftsverpflegung*. Dresden, Theodor Steinkopff.

Köppen, Edlef (2005) *Heeresbericht*. Berlin, List Taschenbuch.

von Kuhl, H. (1921) *Der Marnefeldzug 1914*. Berlin, Verlag von F.G. Mittler & Sohn.

Kutscher, Arthur (1915) *Kriegstagebuch; Namur, St Quentin, Petit Morin, Rheims, Winterschlacht in der Champagne*. Munich, Becksche Verlagsbuchhandlung Oskar Beck.

Levere, William C. (2006) *My Hut: A Memoir of a YMCA Volunteer in World War One*. Lincoln, iUnifresh.

Lewis, Jon E. (2003) *The Mammoth Book of Eyewitness World War I. Over 180 First-hand Accounts of the 'War to End All Wars*. New York, Caroll & Graf Publishers.

Liddle, Peter (2001) *The 1916 Battle of the Somme*. Ware, Wordsworth Military Library.

Liebermann, Max & Reichsbund Jüdischer Frontsoldiers (1935) *Gefallene Deutsche Juden, frontbriefe 1914–1918*. Berlin, Vorttrupp Verlag.

Littler, Thomas Frerick (2009) *The Diaries of Thomas Frerick Littler*. Available from: www.firstworldwar.com/diaries/littlerdiary.htm.

Lomas, David (2004) *First Ypres 1914: The Birth of Trench Warfare*. Oxford, Osprey.

Loveling, Virginie (2005) *Oorlogsdagboeken, een vrouw vertelt over haar Eerste Wereldoorlog*. Antwerp, Meulenhoff/Manteau.

Luck, Mrs Brian (ed) (1915) *The Belgian Cook Book*. London, William Heinemann.

Lucy, J.F. (1993) *There's a Devil in the Drum*. Uckfield, Naval & Military Press.

Ludendorff, Erich (1919) *Meine Kriegserinnerungen*. Berlin, Ernst Friedrich Mittler und Sohn.

Ludwig, Emil (1929) *Juli '14*. Arnhem, Van Loghum Slaterus.

Lüpkes, Leutnant, Stabarzt, Dr Meixner & Feldintendantur-Sekr. Schmidt (1918) *Anweisungen für Truppenküchen, im Auftrage der Et.-Inspektion 6 bearbeitet und zusammengestellt von der Kommission für die ständige Lehrküche der Et.-Inspe. 6*. Publisher unknown.

Macdonald, Lyn (1983) *Somme*. London, Penguin Books.

—— (1999) *To The Last Man, Spring 1918*. London, Penguin Books.

—— (2005) *Passendale 1917*. Amsterdam, Anthos.

—— (2006) *1915, Het verlies van de onschuld*. Amsterdam, Anthos.

Mackay, Robert Lindsay (2009) *The Diaries of Robert Lindsay Mackay*. Available from: www.firstworldwar.com/diaries.

Maclean, Murray (2004) *Farming and Forestry on the Western Front, 1915–1919*. Ipswich, Old Bond Publishing.

Manning, Frederic (2001) *Geslacht*. Amsterdam, De Arbeiderspers.

Marc, Franz (1987) *Brieven van het front*. Zeist, Uitgeverij Vrij Geestesleven.

Marlow, Joyce (ed.) (1999) *The Virago Book of Women and the Great War*. London, Virago Press.

McNeile, H.C. (Sapper) (1932) *Sapper's War Stories*. London, Hodder & Stoughton.

McPhall, Helen (2001) *The Long Silence: Civilian Life Under the German Occupation of Northern France, 1914–1918*. London, I.B. Tauris.

Mead, Gary (2001) *The Doughboys, America and the First World War*. London, Penguin Books.

Melching, Willem & Stuivenga, Marcel (2006) *Ooggetuigen van de Eerste Wereldoorlog*. Amsterdam, Bert Bakker.

Merewether, Lt Col & Smith, Sir Frederick (n.d.) *The Indian Corps in France*. Uckfield, Naval & Military Press.

Middlebrook, Martin (1984) *The First Day on the Somme, 1 July 1916*. London, Penguin Books.

—— (2000) *The Kaiser's Battle*. London, Penguin Books.

Moran, Lord (2007) *The Anatomy of Courage*. London, Constable & Robinson.

Moyer, Laurence V. (1995) *Victory Must Be Ours: Germany in the Great War 1914–1918*. New York, Hippocrene Books.

Munson, James (ed.) (1985) *Echoes of the Great War: The Diary of Reverend Andrew Clark, 1914–1919*. Oxford, Oxford University Press.

Neillands, Robert (2007) *The Death of Glory: The Western Front 1915*. London, John Murray.

O'Connor, Mike (2005) *Airfields & Airmen of the Channel Coast*. Barnsley, Pen and Sword Books.

Offer, Avner (1991) *The First World War: An Agrarian Interpretation*. Oxford, Clarendon Press.

Owen, Thomas A. (2009) *Stand to on Givenchy Road*. Available from: www. firstworldwar.com/diaries/standto.htm.

Paterson, Alexander (2009) *Bravery in the Field?* Available from: www.firstworldwar. com/diaries/braveryinthefield.htm.

Passingham, Ian (2005) *All the Kaiser's Men*. Stroud, Sutton Publishing.

Paul Vincent, C. (1985) *The Politics of Hunger: The Allied Blockade of Germany, 1915–1919*. Athens, OH, Ohio University Press.

Patch, Harry, with Richard van Emden (2007) *The Last Fighting Tommy: The Life of Harry Patch, The Only Surviving Veteran of the Trenches*. London, Bloomsbury Publishing.

Pearl Adam, H. (1919) *Paris Sees It Through: A Diary, 1914–1919*. London, Hodder & Stoughton.

Peel, C.S. (1917) *The Eat-Less-Meat Book: War Ration Housekeeping*. London, John Lane.

Pegler, Martin (2001) *British Tommy, 1914–1918*. Oxford, Osprey Publishing.

Pitt, Barrie (1964) *1918, Het Laatste Bedrijf*. Amsterdam, Strengholt.

Plessner, Adolf (1915) *Wie es Josef Kraft in der 'feindliche Synagoge' erging und andere jüdische Feldpostbriefe aus dem grossen Weltkrieg*. Berlin, Erster Band, G.F.Z. Verlag.

—— (1915) *Roschhaschonoh in den Vogesen und andere jüdische Feldpostbriefe aus dem grossen Weltkrieg, Zweiter Band*. Berlin, G.F.Z. Verlag.

Popp, Prof Dr Max (1917) *Unsere Volksernährung auf der Grundlage unserer Landwirtschaft*. Leipzig, Verlag von Quelle & Meyer.

Prior, Robin & Wilson, Trevor (2003) *The First World War*. London, Cassell & Co.

Rabbethge, E. (1916) *Volksernährung und Tierhaltung*. Magdeburg, publisher unknown.

Remarque, Erich Maria (1929) *Van het westelijk front geen nieuws*. Utrecht, Erven J. Bijleveld.

Renn, Ludwig (1930) *Krieg*. Frankfurt, Frankfurter Societäts-Druckerei G.M.B.H. Abteilung Buchverlag.

Richards, Frank (2004) *Old Soldiers Never Die*. Baston, H.J. Krijnen & D.E. Langley.

Roerkohl, Anne (1991) *Hungerblockade und Heimatfront, Die Kommunale Lebensmittelversorgung in Westfalen während des Ersten Weltkrieges*. Stuttgart, Franz Steiner Verlag.

von Rohden, Gotthold (1917) *Feldpostbriefe und Tagebuchblätter, Erstes Bändchen*. Tübingen, J.C.B. Mohr.

von Rohden, Heinz (1917) *Feldpostbriefe und Tagebuchblätter, Zweites Bändchen*. Tübingen, J.C.B. Mohr.

Roynon, Gavin (ed) (2006) *Home Fires Burning: The Great War Diaries of Georgina Lee*. Stroud, Sutton Publishing.

Saint-Mandé, Wilfred (1933) *War, Wine and Women*. London, Cassell & Co.

Samson, I. (1917) *Brieven, indrukken en beschouwingen van het westfront der geallieerden*. Amsterdam, W. Ten Have.

Sassoon, Siegfried (2003) *Memoires van een infanterieofficier*. Utrecht, IJzer.

Schaffer, Ronald (1991) *America in the Great War: The Rise of the War Welfare State*. New York, Oxford University Press.

Schmidkunz, Walter (1915) *Die Gulaschkanone, Soldatenkochbuch für's Feld!* Munich, Verlag Walter Schmidkunz.

von Schmidt-Pauli, Edgar (1916) *Kriegsritte, Erlebnisse eines kavallerie offiziers*. Berlin, Verlag Dr Ensler & Co.

Schwarte, Max (----) *Der Weltkampf um Ehre und Recht, Die Erforschung des Krieges in seiner wahren begebenheit aus amtlichen urkunden un akten beruhend, dritter Teil vom Winter 1916–1917 biz zum Kriegsende*. Leipzig, Ernst Sinking.

Sheldon, Jack (2005) *The German Army on the Somme, 1914–1916*. Barnsley, Pen and Sword Military.

Sieg, Ulrich (2001) *Jüdische Intellektuelle im Ersten Weltkrieg: Kriegserfahrungen, weltanschauliche Debatten und kulturelle Neuentwürfe*. Berlin, Akademie Verlag.

Siegert, Gerhard (1929) *Kriegstagebuch eines Richtkanoniers*. Leipzig, Verlag von K.F. Koehler.

Simpson, Andy & Donovan, Tom (2006) *Voices from the Trenches: Life and Death on the Western Front*. Stroud, Tempus.

Solano, Captain E.J. (ed.) (1916) *Camps, Billets, Cooking, Ceremonial, written by an Officer of the Regular Army*. London, J. Murray.

Spears, Edward (2000) *Liaison 1914*. London, Cassell & Co.

Spinner, Franz (1915) *Brattische Kochvorschriften für Feldküchen*. Oppenau, publisher unknown.

Stevenson, David (2004) *1914–1918: The History of the First World War*. London, Penguin Books.

Stilgebauer, Edward (1925) *Inferno*. Amsterdam, LJ Veen.

Strachan, Hew (2004) *The First World War*. New York, Viking Penguin.

Sulzbach, Herbert (2003) *With the German Guns: Four Years on the Western Front*. Barnsley, Pen and Sword Military Classics.

Sumner, Ian (1995) *The French Army, 1914–1918*. Oxford, Osprey Publishing.

Tannenbaum, Dr Eugen (1915) *Kriegsbriefe Deutscher und Österreichischer Juden*. Berlin, Neuer Verlag.

Teilhard de Chardin, Pierre (1964) *Het Voorspel 1914/1916*. Utrecht, Het Spectrum.

Terraine, John (1970) *Impacts of War, 1914 & 1918*. London, Hutchinson.

—— (2002) *Mons: Retreat to Victory*. Ware, Wordsworth Edition.

—— (2003) *General Jack's Diary: War on the Western Front 1914–1918*. London, Cassell & Co.

Thomas, Nigel (2004) *The German Army in World War I, 1917–1918*. Oxford, Osprey Publishing.

Toland, John (1980) *No Man's Land: The Story of 1918*. London, Eyre Methuen.

Travers, Tim (1987) *The Killing Ground: The British Army, the Western Front and the Emergence of Modern Warfare 1900–1918*. London, Allen & Unwin.

Treves, Sir Frederick & Goodchild, George (eds.) (1916) *Made in the Trenches*. London, George Allen & Unwin.

US War Department (1917) *Extracts from Manual for Army Cooks, July 1917*. Washington, D.C., Washington Government Printing Office.

Verseput, Jan (1935) *Voorgeschiedenis van de Oostenrijk-Hongaarse nota aan Servië van juli 1914*. Utrecht, Kemink en Zoon.

Voigt, F.A. (1929) *Combed Out*. London, Jonathan Cape.

Warner, Philip (2000) *The Battle of Loos*. Ware, Wordsworth.

Werner, Hans (1915) *Kochbuch für den Schutzengraben*. Berlin, Verlag von Otto Janke.

Wilson, Trevor (1986) *The Myriad Faces of War: Britain and the Great War, 1914–1918*. Cambridge, Polity Press.

Winter, Denis (1979) *Death's Men: Soldiers of the Great War*. London, Penguin Books.

Winter, Jay & Robert, Jean-Louis (1999) *Capital Cities at War: Paris, London, Berlin, 1914–1919*. Cambridge, Cambridge University Press.

Witkop, Philipp (1916) *Oorlogsbrieven van Duitsche studenten*. Amsterdam, C.L. van Langenhuysen.

Wolff, Leon (2001) *In Flanders Fields: Passchendaele 1917*. London, Penguin.

Young, Geoffrey (1914) *From the Trenches: Louvain to the Aisne, the First Record of an Eye-witness*. London, T. Fisher Unwin.

Zieman, Benjamin (1997) *Front und Heimat, Ländliche Kriegserfahrungen im südlichen Bayern, 1914–1923*. Essen, Klartext Verlag.

Zweig, Arnold (1974) *Erziehung vor Verdun*. Frankfurt, Fischer Taschenbuch Verlag.

Archives

Gastronomische Bibliotheek, Amsterdam

Imperial War Museum, London

In Flanders Fields Museum, Ypres

Koninklijke Bibliotheek, The Hague

The Liddle Collection, Leeds

Staatsbibliothek zu Berlin, Berlin

Universiteitsbibliotheek Universiteit van Amsterdam, Amsterdam

Het Utrechts Archief, Utrecht

ACKNOWLEDGEMENTS

Writing a book is not something you do on your own. That's why I owe a large debt of gratitude to the following people: Henry Allingham, who allowed me to ask him questions for several hours. Jan van Biljouw, for many translations from German into Dutch. Kristof Blieck of Memorial Museum Passchendaele 1917 in Zonnebeke, who made it possible for me to take part in the re-enactment weekend in April 2008 and who gave me tips and advice. Jan and Kitty Blom, for innumerable translations from English and for their unremitting support and enthusiasm. John van den Broek, for his translations from French into Dutch. Johannes van Dam, who granted me access to his extensive gastronomical library. Richard Davies, archivist at Leeds University Library's Special Collections Department. Peter Gombeir of Heuvelland tourist office in Kemmel, who gave me permission to bivouac at Bayernwald for a few days. Dennis Goodwin, founder of the World War One Veterans Association, and his wife Brenda, for their hospitality and the trouble they took in order for me to meet Henry Allingham and Harry Patch. Arnold Gruppen and Johan Gruppen, for the time they allowed me to devote to this research. Achim Knuth, who helped me to get in touch with Wilhelm Niedermeyer. Martijn Blom, Humphrey Ludwig, Milena Mulders and Koen Koch, who read my texts and gave me useful criticism. Ronald Maas, who joined me on my visits to Henry Allingham and Harry Patch and filmed the conversations. Tatjana Mulders, who helped me work out the rations. Wilhelm Niedermeyer, who so kindly welcomed me into his home in Bremen. Harry Patch, who spoke to me so patiently and told me his story. Ester Picavet, for graphic design advice. Julyan Putkowski, who shared his knowledge with me. Brankica Radovic, who helped me to get make contact with Dr Zihad Sehic of the University of Sarajevo. This same Zihad

Sehic, who gave me additional insight into the last night of Franz Ferdinand and his wife in Bosnia. The cooks Peter Scally, Andrew Harris and John Stelling, with whom I worked during the re-enactment weekend in Zonnebeke. Brigitte Schmiemann of the *Berliner Morgenpost* and Birgit Jochens of the Heimat Museum in Berlin, who helped me to get in touch with Ida Wundtke. Annick Vandenbilcke of the In Flanders Fields Museum, for her hospitality and help in my search for sources for this story. Roger Verbeke of the In Flanders Fields Museum, who read my texts and shared his incredible knowledge of the First World War with me. Annelies Vermeulen, who showed me around Talbot House in Poperinge, and Ida Wundtke, whom I was able to visit in Berlin. Many thanks as well to Suzanne Heukensfeldt Jansen for her meticulous work on the wonderful translation into English, and to Ryan Gearing for his ceaseless efforts to get to book published in translation.

But the very largest debt of gratitude I owe is to Patricia van den Broek, who, with her sharp vision and expert commentary, prevented me from making all kinds of foolish mishaps in this book, and above all else, I thank her for her love and support.

Rick Blom

Amsterdam, 2019